The Complete Idiot's Reference Card

Great Piano Composers

Bach	Preludes, Fugues, Partitas, Suites
Clementi	Sonatas
Scarlatti	Sonatas
Haydn	Sonatas, Suites
Mozart	Sonatas, Fantasias, Concertos
Beethoven	Sonatas, Concertos, Pieces
Schubert	Sonatas, Pieces
Schumann	Concertos, Fantasies, Suites
Chopin	Nocturnes, Etudes, Preludes, Ballades
Liszt	Etudes, Concertos, Pieces
Brahms	Concertos, Sonatas, Pieces
Debussy	Preludes, Etudes, Pieces
Ravel	Concertos, Pieces
Rachmaninoff	Concertos, Etudes, Pieces

Great Classical Pianists of the Recording Era

Artur Rubinstein	Chopin, 19th century
Vladimir Horowitz	Liszt, Scriabin, Scarlatti
Rudolf Serkin	Beethoven, Schubert
Glenn Gould	Bach
Van Cliburn	Chopin, 19th century
Vladimir Ashkenazy	Beethoven, Chopin
Andre Watts	Entire repertoire
Philippe Entremont	French composers
Maurizio Pollini	Chopin, Liszt, 19th century
Jorge Bolet	19th century
Garrick Ohlssen	Chopin, everything else

alpha
books

Great Jazz Pianists of the 20th Century

Steve Allen	Songwriter, TV personality
Kenny Baron	Modern soloist
Count Basie	Swing-era bandleader
Carla Bley	Modern soloist
Joanne Brackeen	Modern soloist
Dave Brubeck	Swing-to-modern ensemble leader
Hoagy Carmichael	Songwriter
Buddy Cole	1950s Hollywood pianist
Nat "King" Cole	Balladeer, songwriter, soloist
Chick Corea	Modern soloist and composer
Duke Ellington	Swing-era bandleader
Bill Evans	Father of modern jazz harmonies
Erroll Garner	Pre-modern soloist
Dave Grusin	Modern soloist and film composer
Vince Guaraldi	"Peanuts" composer
Herbie Hancock	Modern soloist
Keith Jarrett	Modern improvisational master
Scott Joplin	Seminal ragtime composer
Jelly Roll Morton	Pre-jazz Dixieland, Boogie-Woogie
Oscar Peterson	Swing and blues legend
Bud Powell	Modern soloist
Art Tatum	Early swing virtuoso
Fats Waller	Pre-jazz to swing-era composer

Some Modern Piano Brands

Steinway	Legendary name, tone, craftsmanship, and price tag
Baldwin	Bright, clear tone
Yamaha	Consistent, even touch, high reliability
Kawai	Rich tone, competitive quality
Kimball	Wide choice of styles, good tradition
Bosendorfer	High-end concert instruments
Young Chang	Attractive prices, worthy instruments
Wurlitzer	Popular uprights, long tradition

Some Digital Keyboard Brands

Yamaha	Digital pianos, synthesizers, home keyboards
Kurzweil	Digital pianos, synthesizers
Korg	Digital pianos, synthesizers, home keyboards
Roland	Synthesizers, home keyboards
Ensoniq	Synthesizers

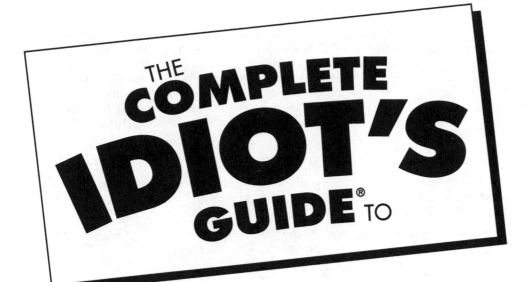

THE
COMPLETE
IDIOT'S
GUIDE® TO

Playing the Piano and Electronic Keyboards

by Brad Hill

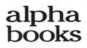

alpha books

A Division of Macmillan General Reference
1633 Broadway
New York NY 10019

Macmillan Publishing books may be purchased for business or sales promotional use. For information please write: Special Markets Department, Macmillan Publishing USA, 1633 Broadway, New York, NY 10019.

International Standard Book Number: 0-02-864925-7
Library of Congress Catalog Card Number: 98-41183

00 99 98   8 7 6 5 4 3 2 1

Interpretation of the printing code: the rightmost number of the first series of numbers is the year of the book's printing; the rightmost number of the second series of numbers is the number of the book's printing. For example, a printing code of 98-1 shows that the first printing occurred in 1998.

Printed in the United States of America

Library of Congress Cataloging-in-Publication Data
Hill, Brad, 1953-
   The complete idiot's guide to playing the piano and electronic keyboards / by Brad Hill.
      p. cm.
Includes bibliographical references (p.   ) and index.
ISBN 0-02-864925-7
1. Piano--Methods--Self-instruction. 2. Electronic keyboard (Synthesizer)--Methods--Self instruction. I. Title
MT248.H537 1998
786.2' 193--dc21

                                                           98-41183
                                                              CIP
                                                               MN

Alpha Development Team

Publisher
Kathy Nebenhaus

Editorial Director
Gary M. Krebs

Managing Editor
Bob Shurman

Marketing Brand Manager
Felice Primeau

Senior Editor
Nancy Mikhail

Development Editors
Phil Kitchel
Amy Zavatto

Assistant Editor
Maureen Horn

Schirmer Development Team

Publisher
Paul Boger

Development Editor
Richard Carlin

Production Editors
Jane Andrassi
James Hatch

Copy Editor
Laura Morelli

Production Team

Cover Designer
Mike Freeland

Music Autography
Scores International

Illustrator
Jody P. Schaeffer

Designer
Ruth Lewis

Indexer
Riofrancos & Co. Indexes

Layout
Michelle R. Lee

Contents at a Glance

Contents

Introduction

They say the first time is the best. I vividly remember my first childhood explorations of the piano: pressing the keys, combining notes, and on the second day, playing the complete piano sonatas of Beethoven. (Maybe it was the third day.)

My first piano experiments were unsupervised, and without instruction. I can still recall the excitement of creating those pure piano tones by pressing the keys, and the thrill of putting notes together by playing two keys at once. But a time came when free experiments had to give way to organized learning, or I would still be pressing keys at random today. I gradually learned how music works in general, and how the piano works in particular. This book leads you along the same path, and gives you a few gratuitous laughs along the way.

How to Use This Book

Learning any instrument requires a combination of *knowledge* and *practice*. Music knowledge is called *theory*, which sounds scientific, but in fact it's just notes, keys, scales, sharps, flats, and all the other elements that make music work. Music knowledge is all the technical stuff of music, just as grammar is the technical stuff of language. Practice, on the other hand, is the hands-on aspect of learning music. Music theory gives you something to practice, and the more you practice the more theory you're ready to learn.

This book is for beginners, and I don't assume that you know the first thing about the piano, keyboards, or reading music. Its parts and chapters feed you theory bit by bit, and give you plenty of exercises and easy pieces to practice. With a little effort, you can learn to:

➤ Understand and play written music notes

➤ Perform simple pieces smoothly and evenly

➤ Play a song from a lead sheet, music chart, or "fake book"

➤ Understand time signatures, key signatures, and scales

➤ Bungee jump off the Eiffel Tower (actually, I'll cover that in the second edition)

I've organized this book into big parts that, ingeniously, are called "parts." Here's what they cover:

Part 1, Overture: So You Want to Play the Piano, gets you started with some good reasons for choosing the piano (or electronic keyboard) as your instrument, plus some very basic knowledge about how pianos and keyboards work. This part teaches you a bit about the history of the grand old instrument, and if you've ever wondered what in the world a "harpsichord" is, this is where you find the answer. (If you have remained blissfully unencumbered by such weighty questions, all the more power to you.)

Part 2, Give Yourself a Hand, shows you the notes played by the right hand. Along the way you learn how those notes appear in sheet music. While you're learning these notes, I also fill you in on certain *types* of notes, and how to count while playing music. (I assume you already know how to count when not playing music.)

Part 3, Give Yourself Another Hand, broadens your musical horizons by adding the left hand notes to the big picture. This is exciting stuff, but also challenging, and I give you several ways of practicing the coordination of two-handed playing. Furthermore, chords enter the picture in this part, as you begin to learn all kinds of ways for your left hand to make the right-hand melody sound good.

Part 4, Master Class, deepens your understanding of how music is written, performed, and practiced. The chapters include more advanced details of music notation, how to use the piano pedals, tips for power practicing, how to "fake" a song arrangement, and advice about what piano music is worth learning and listening to. Part 4 even has a chapter on electronic home music studios.

Part 5, Bringing It Home: Buying an Instrument, runs down the ins and outs, crucial questions, prices, and options when purchasing a piano or digital keyboard. An extra chapter explains how to maintain and repair a piano in your home.

Extras

A quick riffle through these pages reveals many shaded boxes containing assorted facts, anecdotes, quotes, and word definitions. I love these little boxes, and stuffed in as many as I could. Then I assigned clever (that's a matter of opinion) names to them so you could identify each box at a glance. This is what the shaded boxes boil down to:

Grace Notes
In music, a grace note is a brief, ornamental note played immediately before a main note. These ornamental bits of text comprise sideline facts and anecdotes related to the main text.

Music Speak
These handy boxes define musical terms introduced in the surrounding text. (You can also look up words alphabetically in the Glossary.)

Key Thought
Helpful tips are placed in these boxes, plus advice for making the most of the information in the chapter.

Musical Mouthful
Quotes about music are featured in these boxes. Charles Mingus and Frank Zappa are quoted, and I dug up many other thought-provoking—and in some cases just silly—memorable quotations by dozens of other musical luminaries.

Practice Sessions

In addition to the shaded boxes, short sections called **Practice Sessions** feature instructional text and music examples. Practice Sessions help you master the basic skills of piano and keyboard playing.

Part 1

Overture: So You Want to Play the Piano

Before beginning your study of the piano, you should know what you're getting into. Fortunately, you're getting into a long and glorious tradition of great music played on a noble instrument. Even if you aspire to play jazz standards or pound out Billy Joel tunes, you are participating in this enduring tradition.

In Chapter 1, I begin by explaining why the piano has been so popular for centuries, and the reasons it's such a good choice as a home instrument. Then, in Chapter 2, I take you on a little historical tour that puts the piano (and digital keyboards) in the perspective of a timeline. It's a pretty interesting story! Chapters 3 and 4, the two "Anatomy" chapters, take you on a different sort of tour—inside the keyboard instrument of your choice. Finally, in Chapter 5, I round out the part by explaining why the keyboard is arranged the way it is, with white and black keys, while beginning to show you the basics of music.

Chapter 1

Why Play the Piano?

In This Chapter

➤ The unique qualities of the piano sound

➤ Dynamic range and pitch range of the piano

➤ Connecting music with inner creativity

➤ Why keyboard instruments are great for learning music

If you are reading this page (and something tells me you are), you may have recently decided to start playing the piano. You may have even bought a piano—or an electronic keyboard—for that very purpose.

On the other hand it's possible that, although the idea of playing the piano may have crossed your mind, you haven't made any firm decision or acquired an instrument. Some doubts and hesitations may stick in your mind. Why not take up the Irish concertina instead, or the Bulgarian bagpipe? Or, more seriously, guitar or bass?

No instrument is better than another. I believe it is the music that has grandeur, nobility, and transcendence, and I cast a friendly eye over all its instruments. Still, as egalitarian as I am, the piano has some unique features that make it a wonderful choice for someone just learning about music. This chapter describes the characteristics of the piano and the unique values of learning music. In this chapter, I explain why the piano has so often been, since its invention, the home instrument of choice for adults and kids.

Soothing the Soul

One of the great delights of the piano is so obvious, it's easy to overlook. I'm talking about the sheer sound of the instrument. The tone of a piano strikes a perfect balance between different types of sonority. That is to say, the piano tone isn't too loud or too soft, too heavy or too light, too sharp or too blunted—or too much of anything that makes for tedious listening over a long period.

For many years I was a music producer, working primarily with electronic instruments that were able to mimic *acoustic* instruments. Part of my work involved creating new sounds within these digital instruments, and evaluating the sound creations of other people. The ideal was to create a tone that could be played effectively on an electronic keyboard, and that was pleasing to the ear through the whole course of a song. Many times during the labors of sound creation, I would wonder why I could never come close to formulating something as effective as the natural sound of a piano. During those times it seemed like the piano represented the perfect sound, never to be equaled even by the wonders of technology.

Music Speak

Acoustic instruments is a fancy way of referring to musical instruments that don't get plugged in. Every instrument in the orchestra is an acoustic instrument. Electronic guitars and keyboards, by contrast, require electrical power to make a sound.

Music Speak

Dynamics refer to the loudness of sound and music. Pianists talk about the dynamics of a piece, meaning that some passages are played loudly, and others softly. **Dynamic range** indicates the limits of loudness and softness contained in a piece, or capable of being played by an instrument. The piano has one of the largest dynamic ranges of any instrument.

What makes the sound of a piano so great? Several factors go into the beauty and effectiveness of the piano tone, and most of the time we take them for granted. Here's what's really going on when we listen to piano music, and why our ears like it so much:

➤ Pianos have incredible *dynamic* range. The dynamic range of an instrument is the difference in volume between its softest and loudest tones. Pianos can be played with remarkable softness, though it takes some practice to master the art of playing quietly. At the other end of the scale, pianos make quite a racket when played forcefully with both hands. This wide dynamic range makes the piano capable of great musical drama and excitement, as well as intimacy and peacefulness. Thanks to its tremendous dynamic range, the piano is an instrument of many moods.

➤ Pianos have the biggest *pitch* range in the music biz. What is a pitch range? No, it's not a big field for baseball hurlers to practice their pitching skills. An instrument's pitch range is defined by the lowest and highest notes it can play. With some instruments, the pitch range depends on the player—like the expert trumpeter who can squeeze out higher notes than other trumpeters. With the piano, the range is defined by the instrument's eighty-eight keys, and eighty-eight notes is a mighty pitch range. The piano can growl ferociously in the nether regions of its low range, while simultaneously tinkling ethereally among its highest keys.

➤ Pianos have an inexpressible expressiveness. (If that's not a confusing phrase, I don't know what is.) By that I mean the piano's tone is capable of great poetry, musical articulation, and emotional expressiveness, but in a way that's hard to describe. Tone is sometimes described in colors, and the piano offers a greater palette of tonal colors than most other instruments, especially under the hands of an expert player.

In short, many people say that piano music soothes the soul. When that is the case, it is partly due to the great music composed for the instrument. But just as important, it is the beautiful, fluid, dynamic, and lyrical tone of the piano that causes its listeners to melt.

Creativity and Other Mysteries

It isn't scientific, but I have to come right out and say it: Playing music is good for your soul. Of course, playing any instrument brings out innate musicality that may be lurking in your inner being, as well as creative impulses that you may not be in touch with through other means.

It has been said that music is the universal language. Though there are cultural differences among various types of music around the globe, music is generally and immediately understood by anyone. Music has a unique ability to reach directly into some inner portion of our selves, bypassing our brains. That's why listening to music—really listening, not just experiencing the ubiquitous background of pop-flavored musical formulas we are subjected to constantly—can be a shortcut to our emotions. Perhaps music even shortcuts to our very souls.

If just listening to music can be a transcendent experience, imagine how playing music may add another dimension. Two aspects of playing music make it uniquely valuable:

Music Speak
Pitch refers to the highness or lowness of a note. Women can sing higher pitches than men. (Except for men who don't mind sounding ridiculous.) **Pitch range** is defined by the highest and lowest possible note of an instrument, a human voice, or a piece of music. Tubas have a lower pitch range than piccolos. (They also make more noise when dropped out a fourth-story window.) Pianos have a larger pitch range than any non-keyboard instrument.

➤ Playing music, even somebody else's composition, is inherently creative. You are *making* the music happen, even if you didn't compose the piece. That particular expression of the piece would never happen if it weren't for you. When you play a piece, you are contributing a portion of beauty to the world, even if you're the only person listening. Like baking a cookie recipe or following a needlework pattern, playing a music piece gets the creative impulses flowing.

➤ The physical part of playing an instrument has its own satisfactions and rewards. When you engage your fingers and arms in the process of making music, the emotional and physical aspects of musical art come together in an almost addictive synergy. This phenomenon is especially true when playing the piano, which is more of a whole-body experience than many other instruments. The tactile component of pressing the keys and working the pedals, combined with the emotional component of hearing music issue forth from your efforts, adds up to a very gratifying experience.

You may or may not dabble in making up your own pieces on the piano, or creating musical compositions using the recording features of digital keyboards. But creativity in music establishes itself long before actually composing a piece. From the first time you sit in front of your instrument and begin experimentally pressing keys, you are involved in exploring your inherent creativity.

Musical Mouthful
"When I hear music, I fear no danger. I am invulnerable. I see no foe. I am related to the earliest times, and to the latest."—Henry David Thoreau, *Journal*

The Uniqueness of All Keyboard Instruments

The piano has been the instrument of choice in homes since it was first invented. (Please see Chapter 2 for a quick and easy history of the piano and other keyboard instruments.) Because the piano is admittedly not the easiest instrument in the world to learn, the question naturally arises: Why has it been so popular for so many years?

The piano, as well as other keyboard instruments, is uniquely versatile. First of all, keyboard instruments are the only instruments played with both hands. That is to say, with both hands producing notes. Most other instruments are *held* with both hands, but can only produce one note at a time. As long as we're on the subject, let me take you on a brief survey of other instrument types—seeing their limitations fosters an appreciation of the piano's adaptability.

Music Speak
Melody is a sequence of notes strung together into a tune. Melodies are often the most important part of a musical piece, certainly in popular music.

Music Speak
Harmony is the musical underpinning of a piece. Harmony is usually created by clusters of notes played together, called chords, that provide a context for the melody. You may not notice the harmony when you hear a song, or sing it in your mind. But without the tune's harmony, the melody would be harder to learn and remember.

Music Speak
Rhythm refers to the beat of music, and its movement through time. Quick rhythms create music that makes you tap your foot quickly, and slow rhythms are more langorous, used in ballads and torch songs.

➤ **Bowed string instruments.** Violins, violas, cellos, and contrabasses fall into this group. These instruments work by dragging a long bow (strung with thin filaments traditionally made of hair) across tuned strings, while pressing the points of the strings against the intrument's neck to produce different notes. Bowed strings usually produce one note at a time, but can play certain combinations of two simultaneous notes. They are basically *melody* instruments.

➤ **Strummed string instruments.** Other instruments like the guitar, banjo, ukelele, mandolin, bass guitar, and twelve-string guitar have tuned strings that are plucked and strummed with one hand. The other hand presses the strings against the neck to produce notes and chords. Because all the strings can be played at once, unlike bowed instruments, strummed instruments are good for playing chords. They are both melody and *harmony* instruments.

➤ **Wind instruments.** There are two basic types of wind instruments: brasses and woodwinds. Brasses include trumpets, trombones (all seventy-six of them), tubas, and French horns. Woodwinds include flutes (even though modern flutes are made of metal), piccolos (ditto), oboes, English horns, and bassoons. All these instruments operate by blowing air through the mouth to produce tones, and manipulating mechanical valves on the instrument's body to get specific notes. Wind instruments are restricted to single notes, and are for melody only.

➤ **Percussion instruments.** Any instrument that is hit belongs in the percussion family. Here's a surprise for you: the piano is a percussion instrument, because its strings are hit by internal hammers when you press keys. (Electronic keyboards don't work that way.) Most percussion instruments are drums, blocks of wood, bells, chimes, rattles (which are actually shaken more than hit), and cymbals. With the exception of tympani (tunable drums) and tuned blocks of wood (xylophones), percussion instruments don't create notes. They are primarily *rhythmic*, not melodic or harmonic.

Unlike all these instrument classes, pianos and keyboards merge all three aspects of music—melody, harmony, and rhythm. While the complexity of playing many notes with all ten fingers makes the piano a challenging instrument, the payoff is being able to play the full range of music. A guitar can play chords, a trumpet can make a melody, and a drum set can keep the beat. But only a piano can put it all together in one instrument. When you think about it, pianos put an amazing amount of musical power into your hands.

The Great Teacher

Playing music should be, above all, fun and emotionally rewarding. If you're taking up music as an adult, you probably don't yearn to relive the music classes from grammar school, or ancient, unwelcome piano lessons from your youth. Nevertheless, I must point out that the piano (and other keyboard instruments) is an incredible tool for learning about music generally.

Music theory—the notes, scales, keys, and other technical details of how music works—is rather on the abstract side. Music theory is book learning compared to the softer, more artistic side of actually playing an instrument. But the piano brings music theory right under your hands, because the keyboard layout makes learning about notes, scales, and keys a graphic and tactile experience. The arrangement of black and white keys makes it easier to perceive the *design* of music theory, and its logic.

> **Music Speak**
> Repertoire is the collected works for any instrument. The piano repertoire includes great music from most of the composers in classical and jazz traditions, as well as the work of modern composers who are not so easily categorized.

Many times over the years, I've observed that piano players have an advantage in understanding music theory, which players of single-note or percussion instruments lack. So as you're enjoying the pure pleasure of playing a great instrument, you can have the satisfaction of gaining a foundation in a new language—the language of music theory.

Following the Footsteps of Immortality

Because the piano is such a great instrument in so many ways, it makes sense that most of the great classical composers were (and are) attracted to it. This is perhaps the finest reason to play the piano—there is so much great music written for it! Much of the classical *repertoire* is rather difficult to play, requiring skills that take time to develop, but there is also beginning-level music composed by Bach, Beethoven, and other masters. (See Chapter 20 for some recommendations.)

> **Key Thought**
> A good deal of the "piano" music we hear today was actually written for earlier keyboard instruments, such as the harpsichord or clavichord. Bach couldn't write for the piano because the instrument did not yet exist!

Even if you're not after classical music, the piano is the repository for the greatest compositions in many music genres, from jazz to new age. You can even play transcriptions of operas or symphonies—normally performed by orchestras.

All in all, the piano is a uniquely grand and flexible instrument.

The Least You Need to Know

➤ The piano has unique characteristics that make it satisfying to play, and an excellent tool for learning the rules of music.

➤ Playing music is as much a creative enterprise as composing music.

➤ Keyboard instruments are unique because they allow you to play all three elements of music: melody, harmony, and rhythm.

➤ Most of the great classical composers wrote music for the piano.

Chapter 2

Keyboard Instruments Through the Ages

In This Chapter

➤ A brief history of pianos and keyboards

➤ Learning about harpsichords—the predecessor to the piano

➤ Charting the emergence of the first pianos

➤ Understanding the differences between ancient and modern pianos

➤ Pinpointing the electronic instrument revolution

➤ How computer technology spilled over into music

As with many modern instruments, primitive versions of keyboards have existed for hundreds of years. In fact, Neolithic ape-people practiced the piano in their spare time, and would give recitals in specially built concert caves. All right, so there's no truth whatsoever in the previous sentence. Still, the piano (and by extension, the digital keyboard) has roots stretching back to Renaissance Europe.

The basic idea of piano design comes from the harp, a much older instrument. Harps existed in ancient Greece, long before the birth of Christ. At some point, an enterprising young go-getter named Fred (maybe) conceived of a peculiar notion. Why not build a harp whose strings are not plucked with the fingers, but are plucked by a mechanical device? From this vision was born the idea of a harp operated by keys—the first primitive keyboard. (The strings in modern pianos are not plucked at all, but struck by little hammers. I'll get to that in a minute.)

The idea of fitting a keyboard to a strung harp was envisioned and sketched possibly in the fourteenth century, but certainly by the fifteenth century. (Which, coincidentally, is the last time the Cubs won the World Series.) Following that initial breakthrough, an interesting story of instrument design, innovation, and invention proceeded over the next five centuries. At least, I think it's interesting. If your eyes are already beginning to glaze over, be assured that there is nothing in this chapter that applies directly to playing or learning music. Feel free to skip this chapter. I won't be offended. Really. I'll be fine.

Harpsichords and Clavichords

If you're a fan of Baroque music of the seventeenth and early eighteenth century—Bach and his stodgy contemporaries—you may have heard the sound of a *harpsichord*. The instrument is very metallic sounding, with no variation in loudness from one note to another. The unvarying loudness and clanky tone gives harpsichords an almost robotic sound. In fact, harpsichords were well matched to the music of the Baroque period, which features several melodies playing at once, none more important than the others, all fitting together into a mathematically precise and ornate whole. The fugue, one of the most complex, precise, and scientific musical forms ever invented, comes from the Baroque period. Though Baroque music is usually played on modern instruments, the traditional harpsichord is perfect for conveying the objective, mathematical spirit of Bach and other composers of the period.

> **Music Speak**
> **Harpsichords** were the predecessors of the piano. They had a metallic, unvarying sound. They could not be played loudly and softly as a piano can, and their strings were plucked by mechanical quills, not struck with small felt hammers as a piano's strings are.

> **Grace Notes**
> Oddly, the key colors were reversed on harpsichords, with the broad flat keys (white on pianos) being black, and the shorter, narrow keys (black today) being white.

Though the harpsichord reached its height of expression in the early eighteenth century, small versions of the instrument were around in 1540, having spread from Italy. The early harpsichords were small in scale, containing only as many keys (notes available for playing) as the smallest of today's home electronic keyboards—the kind you find in department stores.

Harpsichords looked similar to today's pianos, but more angular. Whereas grand pianos have smoothly rounded corners and a graceful shape, harpsichords were more boxlike and less wide. Inside the instrument, harpsichords shared the same basic design as a modern piano, in that you pressed black and white keys to make notes. The keys were simple levers that forced a so-called plectrum to raise up and pluck a string with a small quill. It didn't matter how hard or softly you pressed the key; the plectrum always plucked with the same force, and the volume of the note was always the same.

Clavichords, likewise popular in the pre-Baroque and Baroque periods (though not as prevalent as harpsichords), operated a little differently. Like harpsichords, clavichords had standard keyboard arrangements, but the strings were struck, not plucked. Clavichords were very soft instruments, and you couldn't make them any louder no matter how hard you slammed down the keys. Their softness made clavichords inappropriate as performance instruments, and they were used primarily in the home for playing simple pieces, like heavy metal songs.

The Big Breakthrough

Early in the eighteenth century, something important happened. The first Starbucks opened in Venice. Besides that landmark event, a man named Christofori is credited with inventing and building the first piano. (You sometimes see Christofori's name spelled differently, but it should never be spelled "Schwartz.") Christofori's new instrument was called a *pianoforte*, which in Italian combines the words for soft (piano) and loud or strong (forte). The strange name, "softloud," emphasized the big difference between Christofori's invention and harpsichords: the pianoforte could play softly, loudly, and with many shades of volume in between. For a world accustomed to the unvarying volume of the harpsichord, the pianoforte was revolutionary.

Christofori accomplished his breakthrough with two advancements in keyboard design over harpsichords. First, the strings were struck by small hammers, not plucked by quills. The second innovation, which made the first innovation work, was (and still is) called an "escapement mechanism." The escapement mechanism caused the hammer to rebound off the string immediately after hitting it, getting the hammer out of the way and allowing the string to vibrate freely. These two developments distinguished pianofortes from both harpsichords and clavichords, which had a far more primitive and unworkable hammer action.

Christofori produced about twenty of his pianofortes, but they were not a big hit at first. The now-legendary instrument inventor went back to building harpsichords.

The Snowball Starts Rolling

Christofori's abandonment of his own instrument didn't spell the death of the "softloud" by any means. As early as 1730, a mere twenty-one years after the historical date of the first pianoforte, the firm of Kirkman was founded to build the new instrument. During the next hundred years, piano builders proliferated to an astonishing degree in Europe. The composers of the day, taking note of the new instrument's advantages over the clunky old harpsichord, contributed to its emerging popularity by writing music specifically for the piano. Clementi wrote a sonata for the new-fangled piano. Haydn's piano sonatas attracted more attention to the new instrument, and Mozart's piano concertos put it on the map forever.

All of this piano building naturally resulted in some important innovations to Christofori's prototype:

➤ The frame of the piano—basically the harp upon which the strings are strung—was cast in iron starting around 1830. The heavier, sturdier frame is important because it allows the strings to be strung with greater tension, raising the pitch of the instrument and increasing its loudness.

➤ The size of the keyboard increased from between forty-eight and sixty notes to seventy-two keys, then to eighty-four. Modern pianos have eighty-eight keys.

➤ Upright pianos started to be built soon after 1800, probably starting in Philadelphia. (An early example of the American knack for making technology smaller.)

➤ The soft pedal and sustain pedal were relatively early developments, both appearing before 1800. The function of the sustain pedal was first accomplished with a knee lever just below the keyboard, then it was moved to floor-level and operated with the foot, as today.

➤ Over the years, continual refinements to the keys, hammers, and all the small parts connecting the keys to the hammers, were made. The modern piano is much easier to play, much louder, and much more controllable thanks to these myriad improvements.

Key Thought
If you want to hear Baroque music played on its most authentic instrument, the harpsichord, look up the recordings of Wanda Lendowski. Lendowski was this century's greatest performer of Baroque music on its original keyboard instrument, and the best-known harpsichordist of the modern era.

Music Speak
The first pianos were called **pianofortes**, which in Italian means "softloud." Pianofortes were the first keyboard instrument whose volume (loudness) could be altered by playing the keys more or less forcefully.

Key Thought
None of the original pianofortes exist today, at least in playable condition. However, some instrument builders have recreated very early pianos, and some historically enthused performers have recorded eighteenth-century repertoire on those instruments.

In the twentieth century, piano building in the European tradition has been continued by makers such as Steinway, Bosendorfer, and Baldwin. These companies have been somewhat affected by industrial-age factory methods and automated procedures, but still maintain an ethic that hand-crafting of important parts is essential. Japan has gotten into the act with high-quality pianos built largely by machines. Companies like Yamaha and Kawai have established reputations for their excellent instruments, whose strong points tend to be consistency and playability.

The Electronic Revolution

Grace Notes

There are not nearly as many piano builders as in the nineteenth century. Making a piano is mostly a corporate enterprise these days, not a family business. There has been quite a bit of consolidation among piano companies, as in other industries.

In the early 1960s, the electric guitar sprang into public consciousness seemingly overnight. Electric guitars had been used quite a bit earlier, especially in jazz, but the Beatles and other groups did more to shove the new, loud instrument into our faces than any earlier performers. The pop music revolution was also an electric music revolution. Amplified guitars led the parade at first, with portable electric organs and bulky electric pianos following behind. I played a Farfisa portable organ in my junior high school rock band (as well as rhythm electric guitar, I might add), never dreaming that keyboards would snatch the spotlight away from guitars a few decades hence. (Looks like I've just dated myself. Oh well.)

The Fender Rhodes electric piano was the most durable electronic keyboard in the 1970s. I mean "durable" in both a musical and physical sense. The sound of the instrument defined a decade of rock keyboard music.

And the instrument itself, as famous for its back-wrenching weight as for its silvery tones, would survive being dumped out of a skyscraper window. (Whoever it landed on would surely not be so lucky.) Musicians found them indispensible, but hated carrying them around to performances.

Musical Mouthful

"Electrical instruments . . . will make available for musical purposes any and all sounds that can be heard."—John Cage, "The Future of Music: Credo" (1937)

In the late 1970s some enterprising instrument manufacturers created more portable keyboards. These new instruments were easier on the back, but you paid a price musically for keeping your vertebrae intact. Developed in the wake of scientific breakthroughs in sound synthesis, the new type of keyboard could create a number of strange sounds and special sonic effects, but none of the new sounds was destined to take an enduring place among musicians.

Enter the computer revolution. It didn't take long for the technology of personal computers to spill over into the instrument technology. Digital keyboards made their first big splash with an instrument by Yamaha called the DX-7. Capable of producing an infinite number of synthesized sounds, none of which sounded much like a real instrument, the DX-7 became one of the most popular electronic instruments ever, with its sound immortalized on (seemingly) every pop recording of the 1980s. The DX-7 heralded a power shift in the world of electronic instruments, as the banner was passed from the guitar to the keyboard.

Today, the modern keyboard player can choose among a stupendous array of digital keyboards and related music-making devices. Check out **Anatomy of Digital Keyboards** (Chapter 4)to see how home keyboards work, and **Buying an Electronic Keyboard** (Chapter 26) if you want to get one for yourself. In addition, **MIDI and Home Music Studios** (Chapter 23) spills the beans on how computer music technology is exploited by hobbyists.

The Least You Need to Know

➤ The harpsichord, probably invented in the fifteenth century, was the predecessor of the piano.

➤ The first piano was invented in 1709 by Christofori. The instrument was called the "pianoforte," meaning that it could be played softly and loudly depending on how hard the keys were pressed.

➤ The piano differed from the harpsichord in two main ways: it could be played softly and loudly, and its keys were struck, not plucked.

➤ Pianos have become larger, louder, and more durable over the centuries.

➤ Digital keyboards made their first splash in the early 1980s, shifting the focus of the electronic instrument revolution from guitar to keyboard.

The Anatomy of Pianos

This chapter deals with the basics of how pianos work, and the next chapter analyzes how digital keyboards work. Don't worry: I won't get into overly complicated descriptions of the inner workings of keyboard instruments in either chapter. You won't be able to build a piano after reading this chapter. But you will have a general understanding of why you hear a note when you press a key.

Pianos and keyboards are played in essentially the same way. The main feature of each instrument, the arrangement of keys called the *keyboard*, is identical on acoustic pianos and electronic keyboards. They don't feel exactly the same to play, thanks to different materials and mechanisms used in the manufacture of the instruments, but the order of black and white keys remains the same, and that's the most important part.

It's when you look inside pianos and keyboards that important differences appear. (It's never a good idea to look inside an electronic keyboard, as that would entail taking it apart. Unlike a piano, you can't just lift a electronic keyboard's lid and gaze at the inner workings.) How each instrument works helps explain its musical characteristics. Gaining a complete understanding of what each type of instrument has to offer, from the inside out, is useful in determining which type of keyboard—acoustic or electric—you want to learn. (Of course, there is nothing stopping you from playing both.)

On the outside, keyboards look much more complicated than pianos. They usually have a host of switches and dials that make them intimidating right from the start. Compared to the button-intensive complexity of electronic keyboards, the traditional piano appears to be a piece of cake. ("Piece of cake" is a figure of speech. Do not attempt to eat your piano, spread icing on it, or serve it with birthday candles.) From the outside, a piano looks like a big hunk of wood with a keyboard attached. Of course, if you glance inside a piano, the big-hunk-of-wood theory is shot to pieces, but you don't need to know too much about how the complex inner mechanism works. If you suffer from the dreaded compulsion to know all about everything, please refer to the book, *The Complete Idiot's Guide to Knowing All About Tedious Subjects Like the Inner Mechanism of Pianos*. In the meantime, I'll tell you the fundamentals you need to know about how pianos create their dulcet tones.

Parts of the Piano

Music Speak
The **keyboard** refers to a traditional arrangement of black and white keys that play musical notes. The keyboard may be attached to an acoustic piano or an electronic instrument. Electronic keyboard instruments are usually referred to simply as "keyboards," confusing things somewhat. A keyboard (an electronic keyboard instrument) contains a keyboard (an arrangement of keys), just as a piano does.

Music Speak
The **action** of a piano is the entire mechanism that starts with pressing a **key** and ends with a hammer hitting the strings. Included in the piano action are many finely-crafted wood, plastic, metal, and leather parts that work together, giving the piano its characteristic "feel" and sound. Piano technicians can remove the entire action from the piano case to adjust its parts.

Pianos consist of five basic parts:

➤ **Keys**, which you press to make notes

➤ **Hammers**, which hit the strings

➤ **Strings**, which vibrate when struck by the hammers

➤ The **soundboard**, which amplifies the sound of strings vibrating

➤ The **pedal mechanism**, which enables you to sustain or soften the sound

This section explains each of the six essential parts, boiled down to the basics you need to know for a general understanding.

Keys to the Piano

Piano keys are the things you push down to make sounds. As I explain in the previous section, they are arranged into a keyboard, which is identical among all pianos and electronic keyboards. The keys act as a sort of interface between you and the sound-producing mechanism of the piano.

Piano keys are actually levers. When you press one, a hammer smacks some strings. (Keep reading to learn more about hammers and strings.) However, a piano key is not as simple a lever as you may be imagining. Pressing it starts a series of small reactions in process, using a number of smaller levers, springs, and even a strip of leather. The series of actions that takes place when you press a piano key resembles a Rube Goldberg device that requires nineteen steps to get from here to there. The result is that a hammer hits a string, but a multitude of moving parts contributes to the effort. The entire mechanism, including the key, the intermediate moving parts, and the string-smacking hammer, is called the piano's *action*.

The piano action is the most complex and delicately calibrated part of the instrument. Some of the parts are fragile, and warp, crack, or break more easily than other parts of the piano construction. Piano tuners must know how the action works in order to make adjustments that affect how good the piano sounds and how easily it plays. When a note sticks, it's a problem with the action—one of its parts may be jammed or broken. If some keys seem harder to push down than others, the action needs to be regulated and evened.

Why is the piano action so complex? It didn't used to be so complicated, but pianos didn't used to sound as good as they do today, nor did they have such a smoothly responsive feel up and down the keyboard range. Imagine the simplest possible lever mechanism connecting the keys with the hammers that hit the strings. You would push the key down, forcing a hammer up against the strings. If you held the key down, the hammer would continue pressing against the string, stopping it from vibrating. Such a simple mechanism wouldn't work at all, so the first thing a piano action needs is an *escape mechanism* that lets the hammer rebound off the strings immediately, letting the strings vibrate freely. Other actions of the action's complexity enable the player to have great control over the piano's loudness and softness, and maximize the speed and evenness with which the instrument can be played.

Hammering Home the Sound

At the opposite end of the piano action from the strings are the **hammers**. Hammers actually hit the strings and cause them to vibrate, creating the piano sound. Now, if you're picturing construction hammers in your mind, and imagining them slamming metallically against delicate piano strings, you may wonder why it doesn't sound terrible. In fact, piano hammers are fairly diminutive little strikers whose force is further minimized by a covering of felt. Each hammer is a small device consisting of a wood or plastic shaft topped with a felt-covered striker. If the felt were missing, leaving bare wood or plastic, the sound of the piano would be changed drastically—for the worse. Uncovered wood hammers would make a piano sound unbearably clangy and harsh.

If you've ever seen a hammered dulcimer (a folk music instrument), you can understand piano hammers perfectly. Hammered dulcimer players hold a leather- or felt-covered hammer in each hand, using them to hit strings stretched over a soundboard. With a piano, you don't hold the hammers directly, but manipulate them by pressing the keys.

V-V-Vibrating Strings

The whole point of the complicated piano action, which you use by pressing down keys, is to get those piano strings vibrating. The strings are attached to a metal frame, like a harp (in fact, the metal frame inside a piano is called the *harp*), positioned in relation to the action so the hammers can hit certain strings when keys are pressed.

One reason the piano sounds so rich and full is the number of strings it contains. You might suppose that each key causes a hammer to strike a single string, but in fact most piano notes are assigned three strings each. The hammer hits all three at once.

A basic fact about piano strings, and in fact vibrating strings in other instruments as well, is that thicker strings create lower notes. This is because thicker strings vibrate more slowly than thin strings, and it's a law of acoustics that slow vibrations create lower tones than fast vibrations. Accordingly, the low notes of a piano have thicker strings than the middle and upper notes. Because of the thickness, there is no room for three strings per note, so the lower piano notes are reduced to two strings, then just one string for the very lowest notes.

Piano strings are attached to the harp using *pins*. Pins are metal screws driven into a block of wood, and they can be tightened or loosened with a special piano tuning tool. (The tool is

> **Music Speak**
> Piano **hammers** are the last parts of the piano action, and perform the impactful assignment of striking the strings. When a hammer hits the piano strings, it immediately and automatically rebounds, letting the strings vibrate, which causes the piano to sound. Hammers are covered with felt—the perfect material for producing the sound of piano notes.

> **Grace Notes**
> The felt that covers piano hammers is a soft material, and repeated striking against the metal strings causes it to harden somewhat. If you examine the hammers of a piano that has been played for at least a year, you see grooves worn into the felt by the cutting effect of the strings. Those grooves are harder—the felt is more packed down—than the surrounding material, and the harder felt has an effect on the piano's tone. As a piano ages, the tone becomes slightly louder and more insistent.

called a *tuning hammer*, but you can forget I told you that.) Adjusting a pin causes a string to be more or less tautly strung on the harp, raising or lowering its note. Most notes must be tuned by adjusting the tension of three strings, by adjusting three pins.

The All-Important Soundboard

Music Speak
Piano **strings** are thin metal cords stretched tautly around a frame called a **harp**. When struck by piano hammers, the strings vibrate, and it is the vibrating strings that create a piano's sound.

Vibrating strings, by themselves, wouldn't be enough to make the piano into a musical instrument. At least, they wouldn't make it an instrument you could hear very easily. A string vibrating in the air barely makes enough noise to be heard without some sort of amplification. In acoustic instruments, amplification is created non-electronically using wood. Violins and guitars employ wood to create a box over which the strings vibrate, making the sound more resonant and louder. Pianos use a crucial piece of crafted wood called the *soundboard*.

The soundboard is sometimes regarded as the most important part of a piano. In fact, the soundboard is no more important than the hammers, keys, or strings. But it is one of the most difficult parts to make. A soundboard's wood must be of a certain quality, and cured over time in a certain way. It must be of the proper thickness, and the entire soundboard is curved just slightly. The curvature, called the soundboard's *crown*, is crucial to amplifying the vibrating strings.

The Solution to Bored Feet

Grace Notes
One reason the piano is so difficult to tune is that most piano notes have three strings. The tuner has a daunting task—not only must each note be in tune with all the other notes, but each note must be in tune with itself. If one of the three strings goes out of tune, that note begins sounding sick.

Pianos are played with the fingers, but most pianos also have three pedals for the feet. (Some small pianos have only two pedals, leaving out the middle one.) Although the pedals' primary function is to taunt your feet while you're playing, they also have acoustic effects. Here's what the foot-teasers do:

➤ The right pedal is the *sustain pedal*, and it holds notes after you release the keys. Press any key, then push down the right pedal, and the note continues sounding if you lift the key up. This bit of wizardry works with any number of keys. If you want to really make a racket, use your palms to play every key while holding down the sustain pedal. Congratulations! You've composed your first piece of music. Let's give it an evocative title, like "Ear Meltdown."

Music Speak
The **soundboard** is a large piece of wood placed just a couple of inches away from the strings inside a piano. When the strings are struck by hammers and caused to vibrate, the soundboard picks up the vibration and amplifies it to a volume that is easily heard.

➤ The left pedal is the *soft pedal*, named, astonishingly, because it makes the piano softer. Grand pianos accomplish this feat by shifting all the hammers, which hit the strings, ever so slightly to the side. Because most of the piano's notes have three strings assigned to them, shifting the hammers causes them to hit only two of those strings, lowering the volume of sound. Upright pianos use a different method, shifting all the hammers closer to the strings, so there is less distance between hammer and string, and therefore less striking power. In both grands and uprights, using the soft pedal also changes the instrument's tone, considerably in some cases.

➤ The middle pedal is the most exotic, and the least used. On grand pianos and some uprights, the middle pedal is a *sostenuto pedal*, and sustains whatever notes are being played when it is depressed. (Prozac for pedals!) The unique feature of the sostenuto pedal is that it does not sustain any subsequent notes.

Some upright pianos don't have a sostenuto pedal, but do have a middle pedal. What on earth is it there for? It is a *practice pedal* that makes the instrument drastically softer, much more than the soft pedal. You can use it when you don't want people in the next room to hear you practicing, and is great for apartments. The practice pedal works by lowering a piece of felt between the hammers and the strings, muffling the sound.

Grand and Less than Grand

Pianos come in two basic styles. Grand pianos were invented first, and are horizontal instruments covered with lids that pivot upward to let the sound out. Grand pianos are awkward beasts, to be sure, because they take up too much real estate in many rooms. Upright pianos, the tallest of which are basically grand pianos tipped on edge with a keyboard sticking out the side, solve the space problem, and are cheaper to boot. (Actually, you can boot them for free, but doing so damages the wood.)

Grands and uprights are played identically, but sound different. Most grand pianos, even so-called baby grands, have longer strings than uprights. The long strings give grands sonic power, so their sound is louder and carries further. Imagine a large concert theater like Carnegie Hall in New York City, a vast chamber that seats thousands of people. A concert grand piano, which is nine feet long, effortlessly fills the entire hall with resplendent sound. An upright in the same situation would sound like a puppy whimpering in an airplane hangar.

> **Music Speak**
> The **sustain pedal** is the right-most pedal of the piano, and the pedal used most often. The sustain pedal holds notes even after you release the keys.

> **Music Speak**
> The **soft pedal**, the left-most pedal of the piano, makes the whole instrument softer by affecting how the hammers hit the strings.

> **Music Speak**
> The **practice pedal** takes the place of the middle sostenuto pedal on some pianos. Practice pedals cut the volume of the pianos drastically, making it almost inaudible in the next room. As such, it is a nice feature to have if you and your piano live in an apartment.

Whopping Big (and Heavy) Keyboard

Pianos have eighty-eight keys, which is a lot of keys compared to most electronic keyboards. One other significant quality of a piano's keyboard sets it apart from its digital cousins: the keys are heavier to push down. Now, this may not seem like a big deal, but it gives pianos a unique feeling when played, a responsiveness that takes more work to play—and is very unlike what an electronic keyboard feels like. People who have played only lightweight keyboards have trouble with the extra key weight of a piano, and it's no day at the beach for piano players trying to cope with unweighted electronic keyboards, either. The plastic keys are much harder to control for pianists, because they don't offer as much resistance.

Chapter 4 discusses the various weights of electronic keyboard actions, as well as their different sizes.

The Least You Need to Know

➤ Pianos and keyboards are played essentially the same way, but are built very differently.

➤ You press keys to make notes.

➤ Keys force internal hammers to hit piano strings.

➤ When the strings are struck, they vibrate to make notes.

➤ The soundboard amplifies the vibration of struck strings, letting us hear the instrument's tones.

➤ The sustain pedal keeps notes sounding after you release the keys, and the soft pedal makes the piano subtly softer.

➤ Upright pianos are smaller and less powerful than grand pianos.

➤ Piano keys are heavier and harder to push down than electronic keyboard keys.

The Anatomy of Digital Keyboards

In This Chapter

➤ The three main types of digital keyboards

➤ Understanding the basic features of keyboards

➤ Taking the first steps with a digital keyboard

Around the turn of the century, when someone mentioned a "home keyboard," they probably meant the good old reliable upright piano that could fit in the parlor of just about every American house. Today, the piano is just one of many choices for the parlor, crowded by a wide variety of electronic keyboards, from kiddie-sized toys to sophisticated musical *synthesizers*. Still, the point-of-entry to playing any keyboard instrument is—well—the keyboard: the collection of black and white keys you probably first saw on a piano.

One question I often receive is, "Are digital keyboards replacing the piano?" The worry is understandable. Digital pianos and other keyboards do a decent job of emulating the sound and feel of an acoustic piano, and they often cost much less. In addition, there are important conveniences to digital keyboards missing from pianos. However, I'm glad to report the answer to the troubling question is "No." People are still buying real pianos, and pianists are still performing on them. Digital keyboards are an alternative to the piano, but hardly a replacement.

> **Music Speak**
> **Synthesizers** are a specialized type of digital keyboard, able to mimic acoustic instruments as well as produce unearthly sounds that don't sound like any known instrument.

In this book I invite you to learn the basics of keyboard playing and keyboard-oriented sheet music, regardless of whether your instrument of choice is acoustic or electronic. Because the arrangement of keys is identical on both, the essential musical knowledge is the same. This book doesn't judge one against the other, although I do point out the advantages of each. In this chapter, I intend to take you on a tour of the digital keyboard's anatomy, just as I did with the acoustic piano in the last chapter.

A Trio of Keyboards

There are so many models of keyboard that distinguishing among them can drive you back to the relative simplicity of pianos. To make matters easier, you can categorize all electronic keyboards as three basic types. Why yes, I'd be delighted to describe them; thanks for asking:

Music Speak
Throughout this chapter and in other parts of the book, I refer to both **digital keyboards** and **electronic keyboards**. Practically speaking, they are the same thing, because all electronic keyboards these days are digital. Being digital means that the keyboard uses computer-type circuitry to store and play sounds, unlike the older electronic keyboards of the 1970s.

Music Speak
Home keyboards are small, relatively inexpensive digital instruments with built-in speakers for hearing their sounds.

Music Speak
Professional keyboards do not have built-in speakers. There are two basic types: synthesizers, which create new sounds through internal settings; and samplers, which create new sounds by recording them.

➤ **Home keyboards.** Also known as *hobby keyboards*, this category consists of small, lightweight keyboards with built-in speakers. Home keyboards are popular as first keyboards. Although not as advanced in some ways as *professional keyboards*, home keyboards have become quite sophisticated in recent years, providing a mix of good sound quality and plenty of technical features. Home keyboards are usually very button-intensive, with every technical function given its own dedicated button.

➤ **Professional keyboards.** Professional keyboards differ from hobby keyboards in one crucial aspect; they don't contain built-in speakers, and must be connected to an amplifier to make any sound. Aside from the speaker difference, pro models generally have excellent sound quality, are heavier, and are more expensive. Their technical features focus on internal memory, disk drives, and sound creation settings that improve the instrument's performance in a studio or stage environment. They are like musical computers. Usually, you need to have more skill to operate these machines; there aren't as many easy-to-use buttons as are found on the home keyboards.

The two main types of pro keyboard are *synthesizers*, which create new sounds using internal settings, and *samplers*, which create new sounds by recording them.

Samplers are the most acoustically realistic of all digital instruments, because they reproduce actual recordings of real instruments when you play the keyboard. With enough real instrument recordings stored in its memory chips, a sampler can sound just like a piano one minute, and a flute the next. Furthermore, you can record any sound into a sampler, and suddenly the keyboard mimics that sound perfectly.

➤ **Digital pianos.** Pianos are wonderful instruments, but require lots of maintenance (tuning, dusting, and admiring), and are too heavy to carry around the house (unless you have recently come to this planet from Jupiter, where the gravity is much stronger). Enter the modern solution; the digital piano. Digital pianos are not replacements for real pianos, but they are effective alternatives for a few reasons. They don't require tuning, can be moved more easily, and sound remarkably like the real thing. They usually don't contain as many technical gadgets and buttons as home keyboards, and they don't carry as many different sounds. Nor are digital pianos as sophisticated in certain ways as professional keyboards. They are fairly expensive, and you are mostly paying for high-quality digital reproductions of piano sound.

When electronic keyboards were first becoming popular, the difference between a *home keyboard* and a *professional keyboard* was like a chasm separating two cliffs. Home keyboards were cheap-sounding and amateurish; pro keyboards were state-of-the-art machines. Furthermore, you paid a big price premium for the extra quality of a professional instrument.

Now things are different, and the line between hobby and professional has blurred significantly. The bridge across that once-wide chasm has been built by high-quality home keyboards one one end, and lower-cost professional models on the other. The one feature you can count on to distinguish home keyboards from pro models is the built-in set of speakers.

Basic Keyboard Features

Electronic keyboards are strange instruments, both simpler (in some ways) and more complex (in other ways) than pianos are. At first glance they can be a bit intimidating, bristling as they are with controls, dials, message screens, buttons, and even disk drives. On close examination, some of today's music keyboards look like odd computers—and, in fact, that's not far from the truth. Contemporary music keyboards have more processing power than anyone would have dreamed possible not too long ago. In this book, I'm concerned more with musical power than the number-crunching capacity of keyboards, which is mostly hidden from the user.

What Does This Button Do?—Oops!

Actually, there is absolutely nothing you can do "wrong" by pressing a keyboard's buttons or controls. Oh, you can make bad music, no question about that, and doing so is fun in its own way. But you shouldn't feel afraid to press all the buttons and see what results. The worst that can happen is that an electronic genie pops out of the back panel and pinches your nose, but that is very rare.

A Sound Is a Sound by Any Other Name

Keyboards come with lots of different sounds. It's a miracle of the digital age that one instrument can sound like many other instruments. Maybe it's not a miracle on a par with healing the sick, but it's pretty nifty. The sounds that come preinstalled in a keyboard are referred to as *sounds* (how radically original), *sound programs* (for when you want to sound like a nerd), or *patches* (ooh—that's a keeper). Actually, the owner's manual of your keyboard may assign a name for its sounds, and instrument makers sometimes go to extremes to invent vocabularies that apply only to their instruments—as if what we all need is to learn nonessential new vocabularies in our spare time. Forget the pretensions of your owner's manual and just call your keyboard's sounds *patches* or simply *sounds*.

Keyboard patches are usually assigned buttons, and each button is labeled with the patch's name. The exception is on professional keyboards, where the patches are stored in internal banks, and the keyboard's screen tells you what patch is currently dialed up; you can flip through the patches using a single dial or button. On home keyboards it's much more intuitive: just press the *piano* button, for example, or the *flute* button, and the keyboard's sound changes instantly. Whether the result sounds exactly like a piano or flute depends on the keyboard, but the important advantage is variety.

Music Speak
Digital pianos are computer-age alternatives to real pianos. By storing sampled (recorded) notes from acoustic pianos in their memory chips, digital pianos can sound reasonably like concert grand pianos. The verisimilitude only goes so far, though, and experienced pianists agree that digital pianos are no replacement for the real thing.

Grace Notes
All the basic keyboard features are covered in these pages, though I cannot deal with particular models and controls found on individual keyboards. Most keyboards are basically the same in function, even if the specific dials and controls differ. Read on in this section to get the gist of whatever keyboard you may be facing.

Practice Session

One of the most fun things to do when you first set up a new keyboard is to try out the new sounds. It doesn't even matter if you know how to play anything; anyone can push the keys down. As soon as you plug the keyboard in and turn it on, try playing a few notes. Usually, the sound that keyboards are set to play when you first turn them on (called the *default* sound) is a piano-like tone, or as close to a piano sound as the keyboard can make. Find the sound buttons on the front panel, and start pressing them like crazy. For each button, play a few notes. Before long you'll have a good idea what sounds your keyboard can produce.

Grace Notes

Most keyboards have the same basic features. In reading my descriptions of these common features, don't be distressed if your particular model doesn't seem to match up in one way or another. If your keyboard is lacking in one department, it probably makes up for it in with other features. Some keyboards have great sound, and don't go in much for fancy controls and zillions of buttons. Other keyboards take the opposite tack, offering a cheesy-sounding tone but lots of snazzy control features that make it a gadget-lover's dream instrument.

Music Speak

The instrument sounds that are built into digital keyboards are alternately called **patches**, **sounds**, and **sound programs**. Professional keyboards (and musicians) usually refer to sounds as patches. Home keyboards generally label them just as sounds.

Tiny People Inside the Keyboard

Home keyboards have *auto-accompaniment* features that provide rhythms and harmonies at the flick of a switch. Want to play some disco? How about a fancy bossa nova? These things are really amazing and fun, and even the new musician can enjoy improvising a simple melody over these preset grooves. While some ascribe these miracles to the ability to prerecord rhythm and harmonic patterns on tiny computer chips, I figure the only real explanation is that there are tiny musicians hidden inside the keyboard. While this interpretation may be too scientific for the average person, we must acknowledge that we live in a wondrous age, and many technical marvels are possible.

Auto-accompaniment is one of the most important features of home keyboards, and I refer to it often in this book. You don't ever have to use auto-accompaniment, and if you aspire to learn how to play keyboards with a piano-style technique, it's best to disregard it. But for those interested in making the most of the keyboard's technical features, understanding auto-accompaniment is crucial to making good music. The purpose of auto-accompaniment is to simplify playing to the point where, at the extreme, all you need to do is pick out a melody with one finger. A less-radical use of auto-accompaniment lets you play with more fingers of both hands while filling in some harmonies and the rhythms. Unfortunately, auto-accompaniment doesn't do the dishes.

Following are the basic functions of auto-accompaniment. They are included to varying degrees on different keyboards.

➤ **Musical style accompaniments.** Automatic styles provide complete accompaniments in a variety of rhythms and "grooves," from waltzes to hip-hop, sambas to rock 'n' roll, swing jazz to new age.

➤ **Auto-harmonies.** The musical style accompaniments described above don't necessarily give you any harmonies along with the rhythms. The lack of harmonies makes sense, because the keyboard doesn't know what song or piece you want to play against the musical style, so it doesn't know which chords to put in. (I define and describe chords in Chapter 8.) The auto-harmony feature (which may be called something different on your keyboard) lets you play simple chords with your left hand while picking the melody out with your right hand. The keyboard supplies a harmonic background that matches the chords you're playing, along with the rhythms. (I describe chords and how to use them in Part 2 of this book.)

➤ **Auto-bass.** A simpler version of auto-harmonies, auto-bass lets you play one-note bass lines with your left hand, underneath the melody of your right hand. This feature is commonly called *fingered bass* or *single-finger mode*. The keyboard supplies a moving bass line related to your left-hand notes. In some keyboards, a full harmony is inserted based on the left-hand notes.

Immortal Music Deserves to Be Recorded

I don't mean to put the pressure on you to fulfill your latent musical genius—at least, not right away. It's fun to record even mortal music, and many keyboards let you do just that. We're not talking about tape recording here, but *digital recording* that's built right into the keyboard. Not every keyboard can do this, but most modern home keyboards have some kind of recording feature, called *sequencing*. The recorder portion of the keyboard is called a *sequencer*.

Why the esoteric tech-head names for simple recording? It's called sequencing because you're not recording actual sounds, you're recording sequences of keystrokes as you play. Then the keyboard plays back the keystroke sequence and you hear your performance replicated, for better or worse. Along with the simple keystrokes, most keyboards record how hard you hit the keys, which translates into the loudness and softness of each note, plus the depressions of the sustain pedal (keep reading a little further down to learn about keyboard pedals).

Sequencing systems in keyboards vary from simple to complex. The main complexity involves recording on more than one track, which is intelligently called *multitrack sequencing*. It's not important to know much about sequencing at this point—or ever, if composing and recording aren't your interests. Sequencing has nothing to do with playing well. But recording yourself can be fun, and multitrack sequencers, which let you build musical pieces with several different parts, are great tools for making up music.

Sequencing brings into play some of the most advanced technical features of modern keyboards:

➤ Some home keyboard models contain rudimentary sequencers that don't hold much music and only record on one track; other models pull out the stops with fairly sophisticated recording systems featuring multiple tracks and a floppy disk for storing your creations.

Music Speak
Auto-accompaniment is a feature of home keyboards that provides continuous rhythms and harmonies in preset musical styles. You can play the keyboard while the auto accompaniment is pounding out a rock 'n' roll groove, or swinging to a jazz beat. Most auto-accompaniments let you determine the harmonies with your left hand while playing a melody with your right hand.

Key Thought
I want to emphasize that auto-accompaniment features are found on home keyboards, not on digital pianos (by and large) or professional keyboards. And auto-accompaniment doesn't take all the work out of playing. Automated features are designed to get you playing quickly, but still require some musical understanding to use well.

Music Speak
A **sequencer** is a recording device that keeps track of keystrokes on a music keyboard, then plays them back exactly as originally performed. Recording in this manner is called **sequencing**. Sequencers are built into many digital keyboards, enabling the player to quickly and easily record his or her playing.

Grace Notes

The term "track" comes from the old-fashioned days of tape recording. You can think of a track as a single line of information, such as a melody part or a rhythm line. Multitracking allows you to add additional "tracks" on top of your initial recording without erasing it. In this way, complex compositions can be created out of individual parts.

➤ Professional model keyboards called *workstations* contain more advanced sequencers with editing tools that make the keyboards resemble word processors for music. You can record a music track (remember, you're only recording the keystrokes and pedalings, not the sound) and change it around by correcting wrong notes, placing notes on different rhythmic beats, and other very fancy maneuvers. Non-workstation pro-keyboards don't contain sequencers at all, but can be hooked up to computers that do an even more sophisticated job.

➤ Digital pianos often, but not always, have built-in sequencing. Sometimes they sport disk drives, like computers, for storing recorded pieces. The sequencer in digital pianos tend to have fewer tracks, or just one track.

Oh Joy! A Stick!

I admit it, I'm easily pleased. The stick in question is a joystick, which is found on some keyboard models. What does the joystick do? It varies from keyboard to keyboard, but one common function is to bend the pitch of notes being played, upward or downward. The joystick is one of several accoutrements that come with electronic keyboards and are sometimes inexplicable at first glance.

Here is a rundown of what you can expect to find:

Music Speak

A **workstation** is a professional model keyboard with advanced sequencing capabilities.

➤ **Joystick or pitch-bend wheel.** Most keyboards give you some way of bending the pitch of notes. When musicians take a keyboard solo, especially in electronic jazz and rock, they generally play single notes with the right hand, using the left hand to manipulate the pitch bend wheel (or joystick). Used discreetly, swooping the pitch of certain notes up and down lends a more fluid style to the solo than the keyboard alone would deliver.

➤ **The pedal.** Almost every keyboard comes with a plug-in foot pedal that mimics the right-hand pedal of a piano. Called a *sustain pedal*, pressing it causes any played notes to continue sounding (sustaining) even if you take your hands off the keys. The sound continues until you lift your foot off the pedal, or until the sound naturally fades away, whichever comes first. The sustain pedal is essential to many playing styles, because it helps you connect the notes of a piece smoothly with each other without your fingers doing all the work. (It's harder than you may think!)

Home keyboards usually include a single pedal that you must plug into a jack on the back panel insightfully labeled *pedal*. Professional keyboards sometimes contain an extra pedal jack, which, together with a special pedal connected to it, let you change the keyboard's sound (patch) with your foot. Digital pianos are more sturdy, often carrying complete pedal assemblies hanging down from the bottom of their keyboards, with two or three pedals attached—just like a piano.

➤ **Sheet music holder.** A metal gizmo is sometimes included in keyboard boxes that is used to hold up sheet music so you can read and play easily at the same time. It gets attached to the top of the keyboard's front panel. Crack open that owner's manual to see exactly how your sheet music holder gets attached, if indeed you have one.

Poking It Doesn't Help

If you're new to the world of electronic instruments, the first big lesson is that the darn thing must be turned on to make any sound. That basic fact may seem a little elementary (as Holmes commented to Watson), but you'd be surprised how easy it is to forget the basics when working with modern musical devices. (Of course, I'm not speaking from personal experience; I've never forgotten anything basic, no sir.)

So the first thing to look for is the power button. It's harder to find than you may think on some of the button-and-dial-laden models sold today! If you have trouble turning your instrument on, don't panic — just take a look in your owner's manual for a diagram of all the controls.

If you have an electronic keyboard (assuming you got it from a store, not from a frustrated cousin), you have an owner's manual. That's not saying much, considering the quality of many such manuals. Many people consider them sophisticated, information-age torture devices designed to erode the foundations of modern civilization. Why the emnity? Owner's manuals have a well-earned reputation for being more of a hindrance than a help, thanks to confusing writing, failure to define new words the user needs to know, and basic carelessness in presentation.

To be fair, instrument builders make an honest attempt to include a book that really helps you learn the keyboard for which you've just shelled out big bucks . However, one thing no owner's manual attempts is to teach you music. They are designed only to teach you the function of the instrument's technical features—all the buttons and dials. No problem. I'll teach you the basics of how to play, plus the generic technical features common to all keyboards. Then you can fill in specific knowledge with the manual—and I wish you good luck!

Once your keyboard is turned on, it should begin to speak (with notes, that is). Try playing a key. If you don't hear anything, and you're sure the keyboard's power is on (don't forget to plug it in!), something is definitely amiss. You know the instrument is turned on if you see any lights on the front panel. There is usually a small light right next to the power button, and many models sparkle with other lights next to dials and buttons.

If there is a message screen in the center of the panel, you should be able to read something at this point (though it may not be immortal prose or any other soul-edifying content). If everything is working properly (which it almost always is), you can now play the keyboard and hear sounds. Great! Please play *The Flight of the Bumblebee* at this point. Oh, sorry, I'm getting ahead of myself.

If you've turned your keyboard in and still don't hear anything, these are the most likely explanations and solutions:

> ➤ You have a model of keyboard that doesn't contain built-in speakers. All *home keyboards*, also known as *hobby keyboards*, have speakers in them, as do most digital pianos. But professional keyboards almost never come with speakers, and if you have one of

Key Thought
For a complete rundown of pedal funstions and playing styles, as well as exercises for learning to use the sustain pedal well, see Chapter 17, "Pedals: Where's the Clutch?" For now, all you need to know is that the pedal that came in your keyboard box is a sustain pedal, and needs to be plugged into the back panel of the keyboard to work.

Key Thought
When electronic keyboards first came on the scene, many of the best and most popular manufacturers were (and still are) Japanese, and the manuals sounded as if they had been written by grammar-school students of English. Phrases like "When desiring to make selecting of new sound, pressing button of calling *program change* initiating desirable new tone" resulted in equal measures of hilarity and frustration.

these instruments you must plug it into a keyboard amplifier to hear it. Alternatively, you may be able to attach headphones to the keyboard and listen through them, as long as the keyboard has a headphone jack.

Key Thought
The headphone jack is often located on the front edge of the instrument, near a corner, but is sometimes placed awkwardly on the back panel. Search around and look in the dreaded owner's manual.

➤ You have turned the keyboard on, but failed to plug it in. Don't worry, I won't tell anyone. It's not as big a downfall as, say, neglecting to get dressed before stepping outside, or failing to breathe. However, I understand and sympathize with the humiliation you must be feeling at this moment. The solution, of course, is to plug the darn thing in before your mortification deepens further.

➤ You are the unfortunate recipient of a Transylvanian curse that causes you to disable electronic devices in close proximity. Have you noticed street lights blinking out as you pass them? That confirms it, then. The solution, unfortunately, has something to do with drinking vinegar while sitting on a castle turret under a full moon. Best of luck to you.

The Least You Need to Know

➤ Home keyboards are small, relatively inexpensive digital instruments with built-in speakers.

➤ Professional keyboards are synthesizers and other more expensive instruments that have more advanced features, and cost more money, than home keyboards.

➤ Digital pianos are alternatives to acoustic pianos, and do a fairly good job of imitating the sound and feel of a real piano.

➤ Auto-accompaniment, found on almost all home keyboards, provides preset rhythms and chords that you can play along to.

➤ Home keyboards are sometimes equipped with sequencers, built-in devices that let you record your own playing.

Chapter 5

The Keyboard in Black and White

It's time to approach the keyboard—whether you have a piano or digital instrument—with the intent to play it. The previous chapters have given you some good reasons for playing the piano; a history of keyboard instruments; and a tour of the anatomies of pianos and keyboards. So much for background information. Now it's time to put your hands on the keyboard and start exploring those black and white keys. This chapter gets you started actually playing notes, and Part 2 (immediately following this chapter) launches you into making music.

But wait. Before you approach the keyboard, stand back, squint your eyes, and gaze at it. All those gleaming white keys look a bit like teeth. Why, it's smiling at you—either that, or leering. Let's assume the friendlier of the two possibilities, and regard the keyboard as a welcoming instrument standing ready to deliver beautiful music through your fingers. With that encouraging thought, you can now approach it, confident in your (soon to be forthcoming) ability to tame a willing musical beast.

Key to the Keys

It's hard to believe that such an abstract device as a keyboard can make great music of all kinds. The violin, as an example, is more intuitive: you drag the bow across the strings while fingering the neck of the instrument. It makes sense that the violin would produce music, though it's usually not very musical when somebody tries it for the first time. The keyboard becomes more intuitive as you begin to experiment with it, and this section shows you how to begin.

Higher and Lower

The following figure illustrates a portion of a keyboard.

A 48-note keyboard, showing off the universal arrangement of black and white keys.

The illustration shows a small portion of the keyboard, in the case of a piano, and a larger portion of an electronic instrument, because the electronic versions usually have smaller keyboards. The size of a keyboard is also called its *range*, because it determines how low and high, in pitch, the keyboard can play. The first thing to know about the keyboard is this:

➤ Keyboards play lower in pitch on the left end, and higher on the right.

There, you've learned something important already. Feel ready to jam with Keith Emerson, the legendary rock keyboard player, or show off a Beethoven concerto with the New York Philharmonic? Well, first things first. Let's begin examining how the keys are arranged, and leave Keith (and Ludwig) for a later day.

Practice Session

You can begin exploring the range of your keyboard right away in the easiest possible manner: just press keys randomly. Notice the lower pitch produced by keys toward the left end of the keyboard, and the higher tones of the right-hand notes. You can make a *glissando* by sliding your finger along all the white keys from left to right. (Glissandos are easier to do on electronic keyboards than on pianos.) Play keys far apart from each other and notice the extreme difference in pitch. Then play two notes right next to each other—try a black key and the white key next to it, one after the other—and hear how close they are in pitch. Now try playing two notes together, first far apart, then close. Try many combinations of two notes, letting your ear develop preferences for the results—some two-note combinations are harsh, and others harmonious. Two notes played together are called an *interval*.

Different Ranges in Different Keyboards

Pianos have eighty-eight keys, which means they can play eighty-eight notes, but electronic keyboards have something unique: portability. In order to remain portable (and liftable) for the average person, electronic keyboards cut back on the number of keys—way back, in many cases. The most common size (or range) for an electronic keyboard is sixty notes. A few ultra-portable models have only forty-eight keys. At the far end of the cuteness scale, strap-on keyboards, used for stage-strutting by keyboardists envious of the body moves performed by guitar players, have a paltry thirty-six notes.

A midsize keyboard, falling between the standard sixty-note model and a full piano, offers seventy-six trombones—I mean, seventy-six *keys*, sorry. This intermediate size suits players who feel constrained by playing only sixty notes, but don't want to haul around a full-range, piano-style keyboard.

Stretching Across the Octaves

Keyboard range is often expressed as a number of *octaves*. A single octave is the span from one note to a key twelve notes above or below it. If you play any note, then play the note twelve keys above or below it (be sure to count both black and white keys); you can hear that they sound very similar. In fact, they are the same basic note, existing in different octaves from each other. Play both notes at once (with one or both hands), and it almost sounds like a single note.

Getting back to keyboard size, if you count up from the lowest key to the highest (left to right), registering one octave for each twelve keys, you get the octave range of the keyboard. But I'll save you the trouble:

➤ A piano's range is a little over seven octaves. Plenty of room to stretch out with Rachmaninov or Oscar Peterson.

➤ The intermediate size of seventy-six keys, used by some digital pianos and professional keyboards, represents a little over six octaves—an octave to the skimpy side of a piano.

➤ The very common sixty-note size of most home keyboards is a neat five octaves.

➤ Smaller home keyboards with forty-eight keys provide a cramped four octaves, but we're into easy arithmetic now.

Music Speak
Intervals are the distances between notes on a keyboard. Play any two notes, and you're playing an interval. Intervals are named with ordinal numeral: thirds, sevenths, twelfths, fifteenths, and so on. The size of the interval is determined by how many keys lie between the two notes.

Music Speak
An **octave** is the keyboard distance between any note and the next (higher or lower) same note. The two notes that form an octave are said to be an octave apart from each other.

Practice Session
Finding and playing octaves is a good way to start learning your way around the keyboard. It doesn't matter what note you start with, but to find an octave, you must pay attention to the pattern of black keys. If you select the white key immediately to the left of a group of two black keys, find the next white key (above or below) in the same proximity to the cluster of two black keys. The following figure gives you a couple of examples that you can try right away.

Octaves are a 12-note portion of the keyboard.

Don't worry about the names of the notes at this point; we'll get to that later. Just play the two keys, either together or one after the other, and notice the similarity of the tones. (If you play them together and they don't sound like the same note, you know you're hitting a wrong key!)

Now try finding black-note octaves. Finding the same black notes one octave apart is a bit easier than with white notes, because it's the black keys that form patterns on the keyboard. You can, for example, pick the lowest of any cluster of three black keys, then find and play the same key one octave up or down.

You can stretch this exercise by finding notes two or three octaves away from your chosen key. In fact, it's good to find *every* example of a given note. Choose the white key that lies between the cluster of two black keys, and find every one on the keyboard. Play them all, and notice how—though the pitch changes up and down—it is the same note.

Finally, try playing both notes of the octave with one hand (either hand will do). Don't strain to accomplish the stretch; if you have small hands it may prove difficult, but that's not important. If you can play the octave with a single hand, relax your wrist and forearm while holding both notes, then practice session little exercise:

1. Play a white-key octave with your right hand, using your thumb for the lower note and your pinky for the upper note.

2. After holding it for a few seconds and relaxing your wrist and arm, move your thumb up (to the right) to the next white key.

3. Likewise, move your pinky up (to the right) to the next white key. You are now playing a new octave, and will soon be ready to challenge Keith Jarrett to a jazz showdown.

Music Speak
A **half step** is defined as the distance between one key and its neighbor.

Black and White Keys

The first thing you notice when looking at a keyboard is that there are two types of keys; white keys and black ones. Having digested that crucial fact, you may also notice the pattern with which the black keys are arranged. (See the first figure of this chapter, or, if you're near a keyboard, look at that.) Black keys are clustered in alternating groups of two and three notes. This arrangement is important because it defines the keyboard's layout, making it possible to distinguish one note from another by sight.

Aside from giving the keyboard a recognizable pattern, the black keys do not function any differently than the white keys. Each key represents a note, regardless of its color. At the beginning it's easier to learn the white-key notes and play mostly on them, but more advanced playing uses the black keys just as much as the whites.

This brings us to the next earthshaking fact about the keyboard:

➤ The keys divide the keyboard into increments called *half steps*.

Why in the world are they called half steps, you may ask. Because they are half of whole steps, I would unhelpfully answer. Actually, there's no good reason why the smallest increment of keyboard notes should be half of anything, but that is simply the way it is. The difference in pitch between any note and the very next note (up or down) is called a half step. Play the two neighboring keys at the same time, and you're playing a half step, the smallest interval possible on the keyboard. The following illustration gives you a few examples of half steps on the keyboard.

Grace Notes

Grand pianos and upright pianos have the same number of keys: eighty-eight in both cases. Grand pianos may be very much grander in other respects, such as the ability to dominate a small room so you have to crawl under it to get to the hallway, but they don't have any edge over their smaller cousins in the keyboard range department. Some older uprights—very small models called *spinets*—are missing a few keys at the top and bottom of the range.

Examples of half steps on the keyboard. A half step is the smallest interval that can be played on a keyboard.

Where there are halfs, there are wholes (that's an ancient Irish proverb). If two contiguous keys on a keyboard make up a half step, then logically, adding one more step makes a whole step. Fortunately for logicians, that's exactly how it works on keyboards. Pick any note, and count up (or down) to the second key away, and that's one whole step.

The keyboard can be thought of as an arrangement of half and whole steps, but half steps are the most basic increment. The value of distinguishing half and whole steps becomes clearer when we discuss scales later on. For now, one good thing to remember is that an octave consists of twelve half steps. Accordingly, you can find octave notes in one of two ways:

➤ Look at the arrangement of black keys to orient yourself, as described in the previous sidebar.

➤ Pick any note and count twelve half steps in either direction.

The following figure shows a few examples of whole steps on the keyboard.

Music Speak
A **whole step** is found by moving two keys up or down the keyboard.

Examples of whole steps on the keyboard. A whole step consists of two half steps.

The Least You Need to Know

➤ All keyboards play lower notes toward the left of the keyboard, and higher notes toward the right.

➤ White keys and black keys divide the keyboard into increments called half steps.

➤ An octave is the distance on the keyboard from any one note to a note twelve half steps away. The two notes of an octave are actually the same note, but one is higher in pitch.

➤ The piano's range is a little over seven octaves.

Part 2
Give Yourself a Hand

Learning how to play music involves three distinct areas of understanding.

Part 2 shows you the basics of music and how music is notated, step by step. This part concentrates on playing with the right hand.

We begin at the beginning, with learning the proper way to sit at the piano to maintain good posture and good technique in Chapter 6. Then we introduce the right-hand notes, learning how to find "Middle C" in Chapter 7. Chapter 8 covers fingerings for "accidentals," the flats and sharps that occur in some scales. Chapter 9 introduces the concept of rhythm and basic note values, which is further broadened in a discussion of bars, time signatures, and rests in Chapter 10. Finally, Chapter 11 introduces the world of scales and related keys.

Chapter 6

Sitting on the Bench

When it comes to sitting on a piano bench, you'd think a simple instruction like "Sit on the bench" would be sufficient. That would be the end of the chapter, and we could move on to more interesting subjects, like how to baste an eggplant. But n-o-o-o. I have to go and complicate a simple issue by devoting an entire chapter to sitting down.

Well in fact there is a right and wrong way of sitting at the piano, and I'm determined to spell it out. This chapter explores and explains such crucial topics as posture, positioning yourself to use the pedals, finding the right placement for a home keyboard, and what kinds of piano benches are available. It's not the longest chapter in the book, but if you just don't have the patience for it now, you can always come back later.

A Hundred Ways to Make a Piano Stool

If there are actually a hundred ways of making a piano stool, I don't know them all. But there probably are that many different kinds.

Traditional piano stools are rare these days. I'm referring to the circular wooden stools that spin around, raising and lowering depending on the direction of the spin. You can still find them in used piano stores and, perhaps, old-style saloons.

The problem with those old stools is that they did indeed spin around, making them less than ideally stable for playing the piano. Fun, though.

Grace Notes
Think of the last western movie you saw, recollect the inevitable barroom scene, and cast your mental eye over to the piano. Do you see the little stool the pianist is sitting on? That's the kind of old-fashioned stool that once was used by pianists.

Key Thought
The bench top hinges open, revealing a compartment where kids who are resistant to their piano lessons try to hide the sheet music they should be practicing. It's also a great place to dump year-old magazines if you're too lazy to recycle them.

Key Thought
Leaning forward slightly is a good idea, as it lets you contribute some of your weight into the keyboard—leaning into it—which decreases the work your muscles must do.

Grace Notes
Pianist Glenn Gould would never remove his gloves while playing, because his hands were cold. Instead, he cut out the fingertips so he could keep his hands warm and still have a good touch.

In modern times, stools have been replaced by benches, of which there are three major types:

➤ **Regular old benches.** By far the most common piano seat, the basic bench is basically. . . a bench. Completely utilitarian, the common piano bench is a rectangular, unpadded, bottom-bruising construction of wood. These benches cannot be adjusted in height.

➤ **Concert benches.** The Mercedes of piano seats, concert benches are luxuriously (but firmly) padded affairs with circular knobs on each side of the seat. Turning the knobs raises or lowers the sitting surface. These benches are heavy! As a result, they are also very solid, stable, and durable. Not to mention expensive. Normally, concert benches are not included in the cost of a piano—you must buy them separately.

➤ **Piano chairs.** Some people prefer a curious seat made out of wood, that has a small back on it. The sitting surface is pitched slightly forward, encouraging you to topple onto the keyboard face first. Actually, the slightly tilted sitting surface helps you maintain good playing posture, which is slightly forward-leaning. What then is the chair back for? I told you these things are curious. I have never found it a good idea to lean back in one of those chairs while playing, but it is rather reassuring to wedge the bottom of your spine against the back, bracing yourself. Like concert benches, piano chairs are usually not standard equipment, and must be purchased separately.

Posture Has a Bearing

Your posture has a bearing on good playing. Say, if posture has a bearing, do bears have good posture? Never mind. The important point is that good piano posture makes it easier to play well. Bad posture can actually create tension problems in your hands and arms.

The essence of good posture is comfort, but no slouching. A reasonably straight back is key. You want your torso to be straight and stable, so your arms hang naturally, and your hands rest on the keys with no strain.

Good playing technique is as much a matter of distributing your weight effectively as muscle agility. In particular, loud, forceful playing is accomplished through weight, not muscle. As much as possible, you want your hand, arm, shoulder, and back muscles to remain relaxed.

Where to Sit

The big question is: How far from the piano should you sit? If you watch a lot of pianists, you see a lot of variation in how close the bench is drawn up to the instrument. Some players like to be right on top of the keys, while others push way back and must reach for the keyboard, with their legs lunging forward to the pedals.

Here is the best way to start:

➤ Put the bench a moderate distance away from the piano.

➤ Sit on the bench. Let the forward edge of the bench reach to the halfway point from your bottom to your knee. In other words, looking down, you should the edge of the bench about halfway along your thighs.

➤ Place your hand on the keyboard. Your upper arms should be pointing straight down to the floor, with your elbow forming a ninety-degree angle. If you must reach forward for the keyboard, you're too far back. If the keyboard seems to be in your lap, and you must scrunch your arms back to place your hands on the keys, you're sitting too far forward.

➤ Adjust the bench—not your position on the bench—until that ninety-degree angle of your elbow is acheived.

Playing Footsie with the Pedals

The comfort of your feet is important to the whole question of posture and how to position the bench. In normal playing, the right foot is almost always resting on the right-hand piano pedal. (If you have a home keyboard, there is probably just one pedal. Your right foot is near it, sometimes resting on it. I'll talk more about positioning home keyboards later in this chapter.) If your piano is normal, you can rest the front part of your right foot on the pedal lightly, without pushing it down, with your heel anchored on the floor. That position shouldn't cause much stress to your leg or foot muscles.

Some pianos have unusually high pedals that make the standard resting position uncomfortable. With those pianos, you must angle your foot upward too much, and it's tiring. In those cases, pushing the bench backward helps. If you do end up pushing the bench backward to accommodate high pedals, you need to develop a posture that leans forward more.

What to do with the left foot? Well, there is a pedal for that foot (grand pianos and some uprights even have two other pedals), and you may choose to rest your left foot on the other pedal, which isn't used as much. I like slipping my left foot *under* the pedal. Another option is to bend the left leg so that the foot rests on the floor, behind the right foot's pedal position. That is the standard classical virtuoso position.

Placing a Home Keyboard

Fiddling with your posture is complicated if you're using a home keyboard, because the instrument itself is so adjustable. If you put it on a kitchen counter, you're likely to sit with a different poasture than if you place the keyboard on the floor. (Lying on your stomach is definitely not good playing posture.)

Key Thought
As time goes on and you gain some playing experience, it is natural to make adjustments and experiment with your ideal sitting position. An aggressive posture puts you more on the edge of the bench, with the bench pushed back a bit, so you're leaning forward considerably. A more relaxed position is acheived by pushing the bench forward somewhat, and sitting farther back on the bench's surface.

Key Thought
If a piano has unusually high pedals, you might also try placing a thin book (but not a valuable one) under your heel. A piece of carpeting also works, and doesn't slip around as much as a book does.

Key Thought
If there is one supremely important thing to keep in mind when finding your posture at the keyboard, it is to remember *to relax*. Hands, wrists, arms, shoulders, back, thighs, knees, shins, ankles, feet—the whole chain of movement from top to bottom should ideally be stable, comfortable, and stress-free.

Musical Mouthful
"Give me a laundry list and I will set it to music."—attributed to Gioacchino Rossini

Key Thought
The famous drawback to keyboard stands is that they are not exactly rock-steady. Some of them shake around like a hyperactive chihuahua on caffeine every time you touch a note. Audition the stand at the store before buying it, and get the most stable one you can find—any extra expense is worth it.

Digital pianos are built with their own cabinets, like upright pianos, so you can't change a digital piano's altitude. Use the above recommendations for sitting in front of your digital instrument, just as if it were a real piano.

Home keyboards, the light and portable little devils, can be placed just about anywhere. Here are some suggestions:

➤ On a table. (I know, I know—if I keep giving out such great advice I'll win some kind of prize.)

➤ Your desk. Small keyboards fit on large desks without disrupting things too much, and this is a viable alternative if you're thinking of hooking your keyboard up to your computer (see Chapter 23).

➤ The big problem with tables and desks is that they are a little too tall. Piano keyboards are slung rather low, almost touching your lap when you sit in front of them. Tables and desks are considerably higher, and force you to angle your forearms upward to place your hands on the keys. This position may not seem problematic at first, but it will strain you in the long run, believe me. You can't advance to more difficult keyboard music with that posture.

➤ The best keyboard alternative is a keyboard stand, conveniently sold at the same store (most likely) at which you got the keyboard. Stands put the keyboard at a good height, and furthermore, are usually adjustable.

The Least You Need to Know

➤ There are three types of piano benches: unpadded wood benches (commonplace), padded concert benches (luxurious and expensive), and angled piano chairs (funny-looking but useful).

➤ Start by sitting so that your arms form a ninety-degree angle, and your back is fairly straight.

➤ Rest your right foot on the right-hand pedal, with your heel on the floor. The left foot can stay back, or rest on the left-hand pedal.

➤ Home keyboards can be placed on tables and desks, but they are too tall for long-term use. Keyboard stands are shaky, but place the keyboard at the correct height.

Chapter 7

Learning the Right-Hand Notes

In This Chapter

➤ Learning the notes from A to G

➤ Finding middle C

➤ How notes are placed on the music staff

➤ Learning how sharps and flats work

This chapter is all about music notes: how to find them, what they're called, how they relate to each other, and how to begin playing them in a musical way. A note is a musical tone, representing a certain *pitch*. I could be very technical about how a pitch is determined by soundwave frequencies, but you'll be relieved to know I won't describe all that. The important thing to know about pitch is that it is how high or low a note is.

I believe in starting simple, so in this chapter I only present the right-hand notes. In fact, all the chapters in this part are restricted to right-hand notes throughout the examples and instructions. Don't worry about whether starting with the hand that is naturally dominant. Right-handed and left-handed folks play the piano exactly the same way. Learning to play a keyboard is such a specialized skill that "handedness" becomes quickly irrelevant. So for now, perhaps you can bake cookies with your left hand while your right hand starts learning music.

Knowing the Letters

Music notes are named by letters of the alphabet. But don't worry: you don't have to learn twenty-six different notes. There are only seven basic notes, which get expanded to twelve notes when you add *sharps* and *flats*. I describe how sharps and flats work in Chapter 8; this section teaches you the first seven basic notes.

Because there are seven notes, it stands to reason that you only need to know seven letters of the alphabet. Conveniently, it's the first seven letters you need to know: A through G. Each letter is a note, and there are no notes beyond G (H, M, or S, for example).

Music Speak

Pitch is defined two ways: as relative or absolute. *Relative pitch* indicates the relation of a note (higher or lower) as compared with another note. *Absolute pitch* is defined as the fixed position of a note within the entire range of all possible notes.

You may wonder how this can be, because any keyboard has many more than seven keys. Good question! The answer is that the letters are used over and over. Chapter 1 discusses octaves on the keyboard; an octave is the distance between two notes twelve keys apart (counting both white and black keys). Every octave uses the same seven notes, plus the sharps and flats (but don't worry about the sharps and flats yet).

This brings us to the first important thing to know about keyboard notes:

➤ Every note exists several times across the keyboard.

What distinguishes the repeated keyboard notes is their pitch. If you play a D note, for example, low on the keyboard, then play another D note up high (toward the right), you hear the same basic note but higher in pitch. Read on to discover how to do this for yourself.

Finding C on the Keyboard

Key Thought

Throughout this chapter, you'll simultaneously discover where notes are located on the keyboard and in written music.

The best way to start identifying notes on the keyboard is to learn a single note, and become adept at finding all the examples of that note on the keyboard. You might think you should start at the beginning of the alphabet, with the A note, but it's easier in the long run to start with C. C is the most basic keyboard note for reasons that become clearer in later chapters. In this chapter, I show you that, on the printed page, learning C first helps you learn how to read all the other notes.

The following figure illustrates how to find C on the keyboard—in fact, how to find all the Cs. As you can see (no shabby pun intended), C is played with the white key directly to the left of the cluster of two black keys. Don't confuse it with the white key directly to the left of the cluster of *three* black keys—it's an easy and common mistake.

On the keyboard, C is played on the white key immediately to the left of each cluster of two black keys.

Practice Session

With the help of the previous illustration, find and play any C on the keyboard. Find the C that lies above and below the first C. Rather than using the note-counting method described in Chapter 1, identify the surrounding Cs by recognizing their proximity to the clusters of two black keys. Now try playing two adjacent Cs with one hand, using your thumb and pinky—you're playing an octave! While playing all these Cs, notice the tones, and how similar they are. You are actually playing the same note, but in different octaves. This may be a tricky concept to understand mentally, but it's intuitive to the ear. Listen to the differently pitched C tones, and let your ear soak in their similarity.

Lines and Spaces

Now that you know where C is on the keyboard, the next step is to identify it as written music. And the first step in learning what C looks like on the page, is learning the basics of how music is printed. First of all, it's time to learn a word. Printed music is called *music notation*. (OK, so you had to learn two words. Stop complaining.) Music notation consists of four basic items, as I describe in the following sections.

The Staff

The music staff is the group of five parallel, horizontal lines on which notes are drawn (see the following figure). Piano music is written on two connected staffs, one for each hand. Other types of keyboard music sometimes uses just one staff.

Music Speak
Music notation, often called just **notation**, is the written form of music. Notation is what music looks like on the printed page, in sheet music and music books. For the most part, notation consists of round notes placed on the lines and spaces of a music staff, but even guitar chord symbols are music notation. In short, notation is anything written down that tells you what to play on an instrument.

The music staff consists of five lines on which symbols for notes are drawn.

Clefs

Clefs are symbols placed at the far left of every staff, indicating whether that staff contains notes for the lower or upper portion of the keyboard. Although there are several clefs, piano and keyboard music uses just two: the *treble clef* and the *bass clef* (see the following figure). The treble clef is for upper-keyboard playing with the right hand, and the bass clef is for lower-keyboard playing with the left hand. This chapter only shows examples of notes on the treble clef.

Grace Notes
By the way, the plural of *staff* is sometimes written as *staves*, but I use the less elegant form of *staffs*, because I'm trying to cut down on the elegance. It's fattening.

Treble Clef

Bass Clef

Treble and bass clefs indicate which hand should play the notes.

Music Speak
The music **staff** is a group of five parallel lines stretching across the width of a page. Notes representing the keys of the keyboard are placed on the lines and the spaces between lines, indicating which keys to play. In piano music, each hand gets its own staff.

The Notes

Keyboard notes are represented by circular symbols placed on the staff. The notes are placed on either a line, or in the space between two lines (take a look at the following figure).

Each line and each space represents a different note on the keyboard. Knowing about the lines and spaces, and looking at the five-line staff, it's immediately obvious that there are more keys on the keyboard than lines and spaces on the staff, even if you include both treble and bass clefs. The solution to that dilemma is a system of *leger lines* that extend the music staff up and down. Leger lines are small extra lines added above or below the staff as needed. You can see what leger lines look like in the following figure.

Written notes are circular symbols placed on the music staff.

Leger lines show notes that lie above or below the range of the music staff.

Key Thought
Actually, there's no law against playing bass clef notes with the right hand or treble clef notes with the left hand, but generally each hand stays with its own clef.

Expression Marks

In addition to the notes and clefs on the staff, written music is filled with various lines, symbols, and abbreviations that indicate *how* the notes should be played. All the variations that give music its character can be indicated on the printed page. Here's a quick rundown of the basic types of expression marks:

➤ **Dynamics.** Some expression marks tell you whether to play loudly, softly, or some gradation of loudness. Furthermore, there are notation symbols that tell you to gradually get louder or softer.

➤ **Phrasing.** Other expression markings indicate how a portion of music should be "phrased," just as if you were talking. When describing something in words, you may speak slowly and haltingly, or smoothly without any pauses. Likewise, when playing the piano, you may articulate the notes sharply and detachedly, or smoothly and connectedly.

➤ **Tempo.** Tempo is speed, or pace. Tempo marks suggest the proper speed to play a piece. The pace of playing my accelerate or decelerate during the piece (the piece pace?), and there are other tempo markings to indicate speed fluctuations.

Finding Middle C When Reading Music

This is where you begin to put it all together. You know where all the Cs are on the keyboard. Each one of those Cs has its own spot on the music staff. For now, it's important to learn just one, which is traditionally called *middle C*. Middle C is really a piano term, but fits pretty well for digital keyboards.

Middle C is, as you might surmise, the C closest to the middle of the piano keyboard, and the third C from the bottom (left-hand side) of sixty-note (five-octave) home keyboards.

In music notation, middle C hangs just beneath the treble clef staff on a single leger line. (The following figure shows you what middle C looks like.) Remember that written note refers only to middle C, not any of the other Cs on the keyboard. I'll get to the other Cs later.

Middle C appears like this in music notation.

Finding Other Notes

Fortunately, the details of music are fairly logical, at least when it comes to how notes are laid out on the keyboard. Here is what you now know:

➤ You know how to find any C on the keyboard

➤ You know that all the white keys are named after letters of the alphabet.

Music Speak

Clefs are used at the beginning of staffs to indicate which hand should play that staff. The **treble clef** is for the right hand, and the **bass clef** is for the left hand. Actually, in intermediate and advanced piano music, the right hand sometimes plays bass clef notes, and the left hand sometimes strays into treble clef territory. But mostly, each hand stays in its own clef.

Grace Notes

Piano and keyboard music uses treble and bass clefs to notate right-hand and left-hand notes, but other instruments sometimes use different clefs. Viola music, for example, is notated using the *alto clef*, the most common "alternative" clef. Alto clef notes lie between the ranges of the treble and bass clefs, and you never see it in a piano score.

Music Speak

Dynamics is defined as how loudly or softly you play, or the gradations between very loud and very soft.

Music Speak

Tempo is the speed at which you play a piece.

Music Speak
The **phrasing** of music describes how the notes should be played, whether smoothly or detachedly, or a mix of the two.

As the alphabet has a certain order, so do the notes of the piano, moving from left to right up the keyboard. It's logical that the white key to the *right* of any C would be the next letter of the alphabet, which is D. And the white key to the *left* of any C would be the previous letter of the alphabet, which is B.

The following figure shows you how the Bs and Ds of the keyboard are placed in relation to the Cs of the keyboard.

Once you know where C is, you can find the adjacent notes—B and D—very easily. As always, you can find notes either by their relationship to other keys, or by their proximity to clusters of black keys.

Practice Session

Now that you know how to find C on the keyboard, and the two notes directly adjacent to C—B on the left and D on the right—let's have some fun with this new-found knowledge. ("Fun" being a relative term—this probably won't be as much fun as devouring a block of fudge.)

➤ Find every B and D on the keyboard. (Having fun yet?)

➤ Play octaves by finding a B with your left hand, then the next higher B with your right hand. Move each note upward one white key and play a C octave. Move upward one more step and play a D octave. (That's just a hint of the riotous fun still in store for you.)

➤ Find a B in the middle of the keyboard with your right thumb. Place your right index finger on the C next to it, and your middle finger on the D next to the C. Play all three notes at once. (Sounds awful, doesn't it?)

➤ Now play them one after another, up and down again. Repeat the sequence several times, getting the feel of moving your fingers independently on the keyboard.

How much fun was that?! Take a cold shower if necessary.

The logic of how notes are placed on the keyboard holds true in music notation, thank goodness. One of the above illustrations shows how middle C is written on the music staff. You know that D is the next note above C, and that the music staff uses lines, and spaces between lines, to represent notes. The following figure shows you how this logic plays out in finding the D above middle C on the music staff. Notice that D rests in the space between the lowest line of the treble clef staff and the leger line used to indicate middle C.

Key Thought
On many pianos, the manufacturer thoughtfully places its name right above middle C. So, if you look below where the piano brand appears on your piano ("Steinway" if you're very fortunate, "Sears" if you're not), you'll find middle C centered under the name.

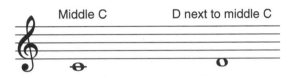

The D above middle C lies in the space above the leger line that C is on.

Returning to the keyboard, you can use the same principle of note placement to determine all the seven basic notes that are played by the white keys (see the following figure). I've kept C as the starting key, and gone upward from there to the next C, showing all the white-key notes of a C octave. You could continue upward (or downward) to the next octave in exactly the same way, repeating the letters of the notes.

Music Speak
Middle C is the C closest to the middle of the piano's keyboard, or the fourth C from the bottom left-hand side of an eighty-eight-key piano.

All seven basic notes, as shown on the keyboard from C to C.

Now back to the written music, so you can see how those keys correspond to written notes. Again starting with middle C, the following figure illustrates what the entire octave to the next higher C looks like on paper.

Key Thought
Middle C is the fourth C up (to the right) from the bottom (most left-hand) note of the piano keyboard.

The seven white keys from middle C to the next higher C, as written on the music staff.

Practice Session

You now know how to find all seven basic notes of the keyboard. Your task now is to experiment with this new knowledge until it becomes second nature. Your goal is to learn the note placements so well that you never have to think about where a note is—you just *know*. It's especially important to be fluent in this regard if you read music, which this book can teach you to do, but even if you don't go the music-reading route, knowing instinctively where the notes are located helps you play better by ear. Here are a few suggestions:

➤ Taking one note at a time, study and recognize its relationship to the pattern of black keys. The F note, for example, is directly to the left of the cluster of three black keys, and this is true for every F key on every keyboard in the world. It never varies.

➤ With each of the seven notes, find every example of that note on the entire keyboard.

➤ Take any five adjacent notes, placing your thumb on the bottom key. Start with this group: C-D-E-F-G. Place your thumb on C, your index finger on D, middle finger on E, ring finger on F, and pinky on G. (Who invented the word "pinky" for that finger, anyway?) Play them in sequence, bottom to top, then back down. Go slowly, and as you play each note, say its name out loud. Notice each note's proximity to the pattern of black keys around it. Now move to different groups of five adjacent keys and repeat the process.

Your First Piece of Music

Key Thought

Notice that the notes proceed alternately on lines and spaces up the staff, and could continue beyond the upper C, extending into leger lines above the staff to notate the entire upper portion of the keyboard.

Here's the first piece of music for you to play in this book. Congratulations on getting this far! There's a lot missing from this musical example—for one thing, there are no timing or rhythmic indications, which I introduce in the next chapter. But why wait for rhythm to begin making music? No reason at all.

Here are a few things to keep in mind as you play the above little piece:

➤ Go slowly. Take all the time you need to figure out the notes.

➤ Use any fingers of your right hand to play the notes. Use just one finger if you want.

➤ Play the piece several times, until you feel yourself getting more comfortable with it, recognizing and finding the notes more quickly.

➤ Try to figure out what the song is. A hint: If a friend named Grace happens to be in the room, you can turn to her and say, "It's amazing!"

A simplified version of the first line of a famous song.

A Second Piece of Music

The illustration below is another piece for you to try. As with the above tune, no rhythmic indications are present, so just pick out the notes at your own speed. What is this melody? It's commonly called "Ode to Joy," and is a melody from Beethoven's Ninth Symphony. (Beethoven contacted me from the spirit world, asking to be included in this book. How could I refuse?)

The Least You Need to Know

➤ There are seven basic notes, which become twelve notes when you add sharps and flats.

➤ Printed music is called music notation, or just notation.

➤ Notes are written on the music staff, which consists of five parallel, horizontal lines. The notes are placed on the lines and in the spaces between lines.

➤ Clefs are placed at the beginning of staffs to indicate which hand should play the notes. The treble clef is for the right hand, and the bass clef is for the left hand.

➤ Notes are named by the letters of the alphabet, from A through G.

Sharps, Flats, and Fingerings

In This Chapter

➤ An introduction to accidentals—sharps and flats

➤ Sharps and flats in music notation

➤ How sharps can be flats, and vice versa

➤ Unusual sharps and flats

➤ How fingerings work

Oh, if only music were played with just seven notes. Things would be a lot easier. Music would also be a lot more boring! None of the songs we like, or the classical masterpieces that have resonated through history could have been composed with only seven notes. (Well, maybe a few of the songs.)

The basic seven notes introduced in Chapter 7 are expanded to twelve basic notes with the help of sharps and flats, called *accidentals*. Those new notes, and their notation symbols, are the focus of this chapter. Read on to see how it all works.

Accidentals Are No Accident

You may have heard of *sharps* and *flats* in music. "That singer is always flat," a friend in a local choir might complain. Classical music enthusiasts are accustomed to referring to pieces by names that may include sharps or flats, such as Schumann's Symphony in B-flat.

Here are the two big facts about sharps and flats, as they relate to pianos and keyboards:

➤ On the keyboard, the black keys are referred to as either sharps or flats.

➤ In written music, sharps and flats are symbols that indicate the black keys of the keyboard, and these symbols are called *accidentals*.

The following sections show you how accidentals work, and how sharps and flats fit in with the basic seven notes (the keyboard's white keys) that you already know.

Whole and Half Steps Revisited

Music Speak
Accidentals are a general name for the notation symbols that indicate sharps and flats in sheet music. Nobody knows how accidentals got their name, so it should just be considered, well, an accident.

In Chapter 5, called "The Keyboard in Black and White," I introduce the concept of whole steps and half steps. Here is a brief review:

➤ The keyboard is divided into half steps.

➤ A half step is the distance between two keys that are right next to each other, whether black or white.

➤ A whole step is the distance between a key and the second key above or below it, whether black or white.

The following figure is an illustration of whole steps and half steps. Whole and half steps are important when it comes to sharps and flats, because sharps and flats are inserted between whole steps to make half steps.

Whole Steps   Half Steps

Whole steps and half steps on the keyboard.

Pinching 'em Upward

Sharps raise any white key one half step upward (to the right). You know, for example, that C and D are two adjacent white keys on the keyboard. They represent a whole step. Looking at them, you can also see that a black key lies between them, dividing the whole step into a half step. That key is called C-sharp (see the following figure).

C D

C#

On the keyboard, C# is C raised one half step.

In exactly the same way as with C and C-sharp, you can name the other black keys on the keyboard. All the black keys lie directly to the right (upward one half step) of a white key. Because you know the names of all the white keys, it's a simple matter to slap a "sharp" after the white key's name, and you have that black key's name.

If that's too convoluted, the following figure shows you an illustration of all the black keys, named as sharps of the white keys to their left.

Music Speak
Sharps are alterations to music notes that raise any individual note upward by one half step.

All the black keys on the keyboard can be named as sharps of the white keys to their left.

Here is a summary of how sharps work:

➤ Sharps raise a note by one half step.

➤ Any black key on the keyboard can be named as the sharp of the white key one half step down (to its left).

Pushing 'em Downward

Just as sharps move notes upward by a half step, flats move notes downward by a half step. The symbol for a flat is "♭." The following figure identifies E-flat as the black key one half step downward (to the left) from E.

On the keyboard, E-flat is E lowered one half step.

But wait a minute! Isn't that the same key, in the above illustration, that you've aready learned to call D-sharp? Yes, and this brings up a crucial fact of musical notation:

Music Speak
Flats are alterations to music notes that lower any individual note downward by one half step.

➤ Black keys can be called sharp *or* flat. A single black key is either the sharp of the white key one half step below, or the flat of the white key one half step above.

How can one key have two different names? The answer is a matter of spelling—musical spelling. In English, there are words that sound the same but are spelled differently, such as *night* and *knight*. In the same way, D-sharp and E-flat sound the same, and are played with the same key—they are just spelled differently when notated in different keys.

The following figure illustrates the two possible "spellings" for each black key on the keyboard.

Each black key on the keyboard can be either a sharp or a flat.

Key Thought
I'll tell you a lot more about how to know whether to call a note D-sharp or E-flat in Chapter 11, called "Unlocking Keys and Scales," in which I introduce keys and key signatures.

With all these different note spellings, the question naturally arises: How do you know what to call a black note? The truth is, the spelling depends on the musical meaning, just as with English words like *night* and *knight*. Musical meaning and note spellings are related to keys.

Here is a summary of how flats work:

➤ Flats lower a note by one half step
➤ Any black key on the keyboard can be named as the flat of a white key one half step up (to the right).

Practice Session

Now is a good time to get hands-on familiarity with the black-key sharps and flats of the keyboard. Here are a few ideas:

➤ Find the sharps for these white keys: C, D, F, G, and A. Play each every example of each one up and down the keyboard.
➤ Find the flats for these white keys: D, E, G, A, and B. Play each one on the keyboard.
➤ Find and play octaves on black keys. Try playing the two notes of the octave with two hands, then with one hand.
➤ Play black keys at random, naming each one as you go. Remember that each black key can be either a sharp or a flat, and determine both names for each key you play.

Sharps and Flats in Written Music

On the music staff, sharps and flats are indicated by symbols placed immediately in front (to the left) of any single note. An additional wrinkle concerning accidentals is provided by *key signatures*, which place certain sharps or flats at the beginning of each music staff.

For now, it's best to learn the sharp symbol and the flat symbol, and how they look when placed before a note. The following figure illustrates they symbols and their placement.

Key Thought
Sharps and flats can be summarized very quickly: flatten down, sharpen up. A-sharp raises (moves to the right of the keyboard) any note by a half step. A-flat lowers (moves to the left of the keyboard) any note by a half step. You can remember that flats *lower* notes by imagining that the note is flattened, as if by a steamroller.

Sharps and flats are placed before notes to be raised and lowered.

The Black Sheep of Accidentals

In exploring sharps and flats, you may have noticed that I left out a few notes. Specifically, the following four notes are missing: E-sharp, F-flat, B-sharp, and C-flat. I left them out to avoid confusion, but I'm putting them in now for the sake of completeness. Those four notes are unusual because—even though they are accidentals—they are played by white keys on the keyboard.

Key Thought
Key signatures are discussed more fully in Chapter 11, "Unlocking Keys and Scales."

Sharps and flats can be white keys? It makes sense when you apply the logic of accidentals. Remember that sharps and flats raise and lower a note by one half step. That rule cannot change, so the four notes listed above all fall on white notes between the gaps of the black-key clusters.

The following figure clarifies how the white key accidentals are possible.

Some accidentals fall on white keys, but those keys are rarely "spelled" with sharps or flats.

Music Speak
Fingerings are choices of using certain fingers to play certain notes of a piano piece. Music notation sometimes labels notes with numbers that indicate which finger should play which note.

Key Thought
Playing the piano with correct *fingering* is a little like rock climbing, where you must plan each foot placement several steps ahead. Without such careful planning, you can find youself in a position where you can't proceed any further, and must retrace your steps. In the same way, playing a piece with bad fingering can leave your hands in a tangle that brings the music to a fumbling halt. Fortunately, when playing the piano, falling off a cliff to a horrible death is extremely unlikely.

The accidentals that fall on white keys are very rare. That's not to say those particular keys aren't played as much as any other keys—they are. But the keys that fall in the gaps between the black-key clusters are rarely *spelled* with accidentals. Nevertheless, it's good to know that the possibility exists, even though you may never encounter such an accidental unless you study advanced classical piano music. Though such spellings may seem to create unnecessary confusion, they preserve the rigorous logic of music notation, without which reading music would be an exercise in chaos.

As if accidentals weren't complicated enough, you'll be delighted to know that *double-flats* and *double-sharps* actually exist. These esoteric accidentals are so rare that it's not worth showing the symbols for them. I'm only mentioning them to uphold my reputation as a pain in the neck. Double-sharps raise any note *two* half steps, and double-flats lower notes by two half steps. Doubled accidentals are used only by emotionally troubled composers who kick cats and are mean to dogs.

Using the Right Fingers

Look at your hands. You've got ten choices when it comes to using a finger on a note. It may not seem like an important decision now, while you're exploring relatively simple pieces. But later it becomes very important, especially on the acoustic piano, and even more especially with classical music. Playing a certain note with the right finger makes it possible to play subsequent notes without disrupting the piece's rhythm. More importantly, playing a note with the *wrong* finger can make it difficult to proceed with the piece. Suggestions about which finger to use are marked in music notation with numbers called *fingerings*.

Some printed music suggests which fingers to use on certain notes, and those markings are called *fingerings*. Fingerings use a simple system that assigns a number to each of your five fingers—the same number system for each hand. Here's how it works:

The thumb (of both hands):	1
Index finger:	2
Middle finger:	3
Ring finger:	4
Little finger:	5

Here's Beethoven's *Ode to Joy*, with right-hand fingerings added.

Fingering numbers suggest which fingers to use, making the piece a bit easier to play.

The Least You Need to Know

➤ Accidentals consist of sharps, flats, and naturals.

➤ Sharps raise any note by one half step, and flats lower any note by one half step. Naturals neutralize the effect of sharps and flats.

➤ On the keyboard, a note may be named either a sharp or a flat, depending on the musical spelling.

➤ Every finger has a number, and these fingering numbers are used to suggest the best way to play notes.

Chapter 9

Whole Notes and Their Offspring

In This Chapter

➤ Counting in music

➤ Keeping the beat with whole notes, half notes, and quarter notes.

➤ Keeping up with fast notes and dotted notes

Music is not just notes—it consists of notes played at a certain time, in a certain rhythm. Every note you play lasts for a certain length of time, relative to other notes and the overall speed of the piece. In written music, every note on the music staff has a *time value*, indicating how long you should hold it. (This is very helpful, or you'd be holding down notes through the night.)

Every piece you play proceeds at a certain speed, called the *tempo*. A piece's tempo may be defined precisely by written instructions on the sheet music, or it may be vaguely defined with leeway for interpretation on your part. However fast or slowly you play a piece, the time value of the notes determines how long each note is held in comparison to other notes.

This chapter spells out how to understand rhythms and the timings of notes as written on the music staff. Chapter 7 explained the notes themselves, including how to name them and where they appear on the staff and the keyboard. (You're only coping with right-hand notes for now.) So that chapter dealt with the *where* of notes, and this chapter will deal with the *when* of notes.

Music Speak
Tempo is the speed of music. It's mostly classical music that refers to fast tempos and slow tempos, but it's also a general term for all kinds of music, and the speed with which it's played.

Counting in Music

In Chapter 7, called "Learning the Right-hand Notes," you can see several illustrations of the music staff with notes on it. There are even a couple of well-known melodies for you to play with your new-found understanding of notes, written music, and the keyboard. However, none of those illustrations is complete, because there are no rhythmic or timing indications. In those earlier illustrations, the notes are placed on the staff in a steady stream, with no instructions for how long each note should be held.

Grace Notes
You're probably beginning to notice that some words I use in this book, like *tempo*, aren't English words. I'm sure you didn't expect to be learning a new language in addition to a new instrument! For reasons known only to certain ascetic monks living in the Himalayan foothills, Italian has for centuries been the traditional language of classical music notation.

Key Thought
For the beat-a-holics in the crowd, there is a handy instrument called a *metronome* that mechanically keeps a rigid, perfect beat. The metronome can help tell you when you've strayed too far away from the central beat or pulse of the music.

Music Speak
A **metronome** keeps you "on tempo" by clicking audible beats while you play a piece. By setting the metronome to a faster or slower tempo, you can keep up the pace or stop yourself from rushing the pace. Metronomes come in mechanical and electronic models.

The duration of notes is measured in *beats*. Here are a few crucial facts about beats:

➤ A note may last a certain number of beats, or a certain fraction of a single beat.

➤ The speed of beats in any piece is determined by the piece's tempo. A piece with a slow tempo has a leisurely pace of beats: One . . . two . . . three . . . four. A piece with a quick tempo has faster beats: One-two-three-four!

➤ Whether fast or slow, beats are always regular. Beats tick by at a completely even pace.

Learning to count beats evenly is an important part of playing music with a good sense of rhythm. Fortunately, foot-tapping is a universal skill. In fact, tapping a foot while playing was considered good form when ragtime was developed in the urban south of early twentieth-century America. The idea was that the quirky rhythms and jazzy note values of ragtime could be played better by keeping a beat clock going with the foot throughout the piece. In fact, tapping was allowed, but foot-*stamping* was considered even better.

When you tap your foot you may notice that the beat is not absolutely even or perfect. No one can keep tapping a mechanical, perfect beat forever! A little variety is actually desirable; the flow of music should not be like the steady drill of a sledgehammer. On the other hand, wandering too far off the beat is not recommended.

Note Values

When I speak of *note values*, I'm referring to the time value of a note—in other words, how long you hold it down or play it. The note value is always measured in beats and fractions of beats.

Here are the three crucial facts that will send you sure-footedly down the path of understanding note values and rhythm in music:

➤ The largest note value is a *whole note*. Makes sense, right? After all, what could be larger than a whole? Every other type of note is a fraction of the whole. There are half notes, quarter notes, and on down to very small fractions of that original whole note.

➤ Whole notes are worth four beats. It doesn't matter for now how fast those beats are—that depends on the tempo of the piece. No matter whether a piece is fast or slow, every whole note in the piece is held for four beats.

➤ Every other type of note—half note, quarter note, and others—is worth less than a whole note. No other note type can be worth a full four beats, so every other note value is worth either fewer beats or a fraction of one beat.

Whole notes look like plain circles in written music. Placed on lines or spaces in the music staff, they are round, unfilled circles—as shown in the following figure.

This is what whole notes look like on the music staff. Whole notes are counted with four beats.

Practice Session

Time to begin counting! Now, don't be self-conscious. The best way to learn counting is to do it out loud. Under your breath is fine if you're nervous about eavesdroppers (though once an eavesdropper realizes what a tedious exercise you're practicing, that person will drop eaves no longer). The following figure shows the most boring piece of music ever written. (Thank you very much, but no autographs, please.)

A good piece for insomniacs. Boring maybe, but a good exercise. Count four beats for each note.

Yes, as you can see, the above masterpiece is one whole note repeated several times. Forget about its mind-numbing musical quality and go for the educational value. Play this "piece" with any finger, counting four beats for each note: "one-two-three-four, one-two-three-four, one-two-three-four," and so on. The first count ("one") comes exactly when you press down the key. It doesn't matter how quickly or slowly you count. What *does* matter is that you count evenly, like a clock. If tapping your foot helps, tap away. Feel free to repeat this exercise with a different note—the immortal qualities of the music won't be diminished, much.

Now try the counting exercise a little differently. I'm about to ask you to do something a little subtle, but important. As you play each note, count four beats as before. This time, emphasize the first beat like this: "ONE-two-three-four, ONE-two-three-four." If you're muttering the counts aloud, mutter louder on the first beat. If you're tapping a foot, tap hard on the first beat, or use your heel on that beat. Try to really *feel* the emphasis on the first beat. Feel the other beats flowing out of the first beat. Let the first beat be the anchor for the whole note.

Once you get the hang of counting through the notes of that simple non-piece, move on to the following composition.

C   D   E   D   C

This piece won't make me immortal, but it'll make you a better counter. Use any fingers on the notes, and count four beats for each one.

The above piece isn't heading for the Smithsonian as an example of great American composition, but it's slightly more diverting than the first exercise. The goals are the same as before. Play the notes with any finger (or fingers), counting four beats for each note. Count evenly. Then try the piece with a strongly emphasized first beat.

Congratulations—you're counting! You're very close now to playing some real music.

Wholes, Halves, and Quarters

Grace Notes

I know, I know—this is beginning to sound like a math lesson. Truthfully, music and mathematics are related, but you don't have to be good in math to play music, that's for sure. I'd be sunk if an aptitude for math were a requirement for playing the piano. Playing with good rhythm is a musical ability, not a mathematical ability. But learning about how music works requires understanding note values, beats, and fractions of beats. Once you understand how it works, your musical intuition takes over and makes the whole experience much less mathematical.

You've learned that a whole note has the largest note value of four beats. Now let's start dividing it up. This is where basic arithmetic comes in handy, but only temporarily. You don't need to perform mental calculations to play music, rest assured. Once you learn note values well enough, and can identify them instantly when you see them in written music, playing with good rhythm becomes instinctive.

The first division of the fat and regal whole note cuts it in half, and the result is two half notes. (See the following figure.)

Whole Note = 2 Half Notes
4 beats = 2 beats each

One whole note, equal to four beats, is evenly divided into two half notes, worth two beats each.

The total beat count of the two half notes must equal four beats (the value of a whole note), so each half note naturally gets two beats. Just as with whole notes (and every other type of note), it doesn't matter how fast or slow the piece is—every half note gets counted with two beats.

The next figure illustrates what half notes look like on the music staff. Notice that they resemble whole notes in that they use unfilled circles, but the *stem* sticking up (or down) gives them away as half notes.

Half notes on the music staff. The stem goes up from notes on the lower portion of the staff, and down from notes on the upper part of the staff.

Time to divide again, like cell mytosis you learned about in biology class. (Are you sorry now you slept through it?) Take the half note, worth two beats, and divide it in half, and what do you have? Two notes that are half of a half—quarter notes! Yes, we're delving deeply into fractions now. Quarter notes are counted with half the time value of half notes, so naturally they get one beat each.

The following illustration shows the value of quarter notes.

Half Note = 2 Quarter Notes

2 beats = 1 beat each

Quarter notes are worth half the time value of half notes.

The next figure illustrates what quarter notes look like on the music staff. They look like half notes, except the circles are filled in.

This is what quarter notes look like on the music staff.

Here are a couple of ways to think about how the whole notes, half notes, and quarter notes are divided:

➤ Two quarter notes add up to one half note, and two half notes add up to one whole note.

➤ You can play two quarter notes while holding down one half note. You can play four quarter notes while holding down one whole note. You can play two half notes while holding down one whole note.

Key Thought

The time value of half notes is a potential point of confusion, so I want to emphasize it. It's easy to think that *half* notes get a *half* beat. Not so! Half notes are called half notes because they are *half* of a *whole* note. As such, half notes get half the value of a whole note's four beats. Every half note is counted with two beats.

Music Speak

The **stem** of a note is the stick-like line that extends upward or downward from the circle of the note. Whole notes are the only type of note that doesn't have a stem.

Key Thought

Just as with half notes, quarter notes present possible confusion. The name *quarter* suggests that perhaps quarter notes are worth only one quarter of a beat. Resist that assumption! Quarter notes are worth exactly one beat each.

Practice Session

As a further exercise in our grand project in counting (next week we'll learn all about colors), please look at the following figure.

This counting exercise contains half notes and whole notes. Count evenly and use any finger to play the notes.

I'm not headed for the Grammy awards for the above little piece, but it'll help you develop counting skills. As you can see, the staff contains both half notes and whole notes. Your mission, should you decide to accept it (and you'd better), is to play the notes with any finger, counting steadily and evenly. Remember to hold the whole notes (no stems) for four beats, and the half notes (stems) for only two beats, as you count to four. Count as quickly or as slowly as you like, but keep it even. Tap your foot, unless you have hypersensitive and grouchy downstairs neighbors.

Once you've played the above exercise a few times, move on to the next one, below.

Count evenly while playing this sequence of half notes and quarter notes.

In the above piece, as you can see to your chagrin, half notes share the staff with quarter notes. Again, use any finger to play the notes, and count evenly. It's a good idea to count a little slower this time, because the notes don't get held as long (shorter time values, don't you know), so they go by quicker. As always, the important thing is to count *evenly*, no matter how slowly.

And now the pièce de resistance—the coup de grace—the ultimate thrill—the . . . well, you get the picture. Take a gander at the following figure, and revel in the sight of whole notes, half notes, and quarter notes coexisting on the same staff.

Here you have whole notes, half notes, and quarter notes.

You know what you must do with the above exercise. Count slowly and evenly. Use any finger, and play the notes in their proper rhythm: whole notes get four beats, half notes get two beats, and quarter notes get one beat.

Now that you know a few note values (whole notes, half notes, and quarter notes), you're a much more empowered musician than you were just a short chapter ago. Understanding note values lets you play pieces that depend on rhythm as much as melody, and it gives your playing recognizability. I'm giving you two pieces here that you can play to amaze your friends (and yourself).

The following piece, a written version of "Jingle Bells," should obviously be played in the holiday spirit—if you're reading this in July, some imagination may be required.

Happy Holidays!

The next piece is a melody composed by Mozart, which is now commonly known as "Twinkle, Twinkle, Little Star." (Mozart's original title was "I Think I See a UFO," demonstrating that Wolfgang was way ahead of his time.)

This familiar melody was originally composed by Mozart, specifically for this book. The man had great foresight, and great wigs.

In playing both of the above pieces, here are a few things to keep in mind:

➤ Don't worry about which fingers to use on which notes. For now, just concern yourself with hitting the right notes.

➤ Play the correct note values. Counting is important, and you should do it just the way you did earlier in this chapter. Go slowly and keep the counting even. The count should go up to four, then start over: "One—two—three—four, one—two—three—four."

Dividing the Quarter

You can play a lot of music with just whole notes, half notes, and quarter notes. But it's useful to understand how quarter notes are divided—don't worry, it works exactly the same way as you've already learned, just with smaller fractions.

You know that a quarter note equals one beat. If you divide it in half, you get something called an *eighth note*. An eighth note is worth half of a quarter note's one beat, which means an eighth note equals one-half beat. (Are you flashing back to grammar school math class yet?)

> **Key Thought**
> If you feel confident about your rhythm, stop counting out loud and do it in your head. Even better, forget about counting numbers and just tap your foot. Eventually, you want to drop the number-counting exercise when you play, and rely on your inner sense of rhythm. Foot-tapping is always allowed.

Key Thought
The division of notes and their resulting time values is perhaps the most confusing part of learning music. Consider: an eighth note equals a half beat?! I realize how bizarre it seems at first. There's nothing to do but grin and bear it. Believe me, it does become intuitive after a while, so hang in there. Grumbling inconsolably helps.

The following figure is an illustration of how eighth notes relate to quarter notes.

Quarter Note = 2 Eighth Notes
1 beat = 1/2 beat each

One quarter note is equal to two eighth notes.

Please notice what eighth notes look like; they appear just like quarter notes, except for the little flag-like squiggle at the end of the stem.

Good news: There are two ways to write eighth notes. Twice as much for you to learn! (Sarcasm provided at no extra charge.) The next illustration shows you the alternate way of writing eighth notes, with a horizontal line connecting the stems instead of the flag on each stem. The horizontal line is usually used when consecutive eighth notes appear. The flag is usually used when a single eighth note stands alone, surrounded by other note types.

Eighth notes can be written in either of two ways.

Dotted Notes

I want to introduce one more note type, and then we're through with note values for this chapter. (Whew) You may have noticed something missing in the note types you've played so far. Whole notes equal four beats, half notes equal two beats, quarter notes equal one beat, and eighth notes equal a half beat. Isn't there a note that equals three beats? Yes there is, but it's created with the help of a peculiar little thing that can be applied to any type of note. Read on to see how it works.

Dotted notes are notes with dots placed immediately after them. The following figure shows what a dotted note looks like on the music staff.

Dotted notes add one half the value of the undotted note

Practice Session

Time to flex your power over eighth notes! The following example is yet another in my interminable series of counting exercises, this one utilizing eighth notes.

Count this exercise using the "and" method of counting described in the text.

Playing eighth notes while counting is a little tricky, because two eighth notes (each worth a half beat) fit into one count. In other words, you're counting in quarter-note time values, so eighth notes go by quicker than you're counting. This may not be a problem, but I want to tell you about a counting technique that helps. Simply put, say "and" between each count, like this: "One-and-two-and-three-and-four-and, one-and-two-and-three-and-four-and." Keep the counting perfectly even. Now you're counting off in eighth-note increments, which makes it easier to time the playing of eighth notes. I've written out the count underneath the notes in the above illustration, but don't count on seeing such hints in regular printed music!

After you've worked with the above example for a while, go on to the following illustration, which mixes in all the types of notes you've learned. In both exercises, you are viewing a music staff with a time signature of 4/4, so you're counting to four in each measure.

Try this counting exercise slowly and evenly.

A dot extends the value of a note by one half its inherent value. I know that sounds uncomfortably like a mathematical formula, but you'll quickly begin recognizing dotted notes, and their time values, without having to compute them. Dotted half notes are the easiest example. You know that a half note is worth two beats. If the dot adds half of the note's usual value (half of two beats is one beat), the dot adds one beat to the time value of the half note. One beat added to a half note's two beats adds up to three beats. You would hold down a dotted half note for the same amount of time it takes to play three quarter notes. And there you have a note with three beats! Of course, it's easier to simply learn that a dotted half note equals three beats than to calculate the formula anew each time you see one.

Music Speak
Dotted notes are regular notes (whole, half, quarter, and eighth notes) with small dots after them. The dot extends the time value of the note by one half its original value. A dotted half note equals three beats, and a dotted quarter note equals one and a half beats.

Now try adding a dot to quarter notes. You know that a quarter note equals one beat. If a dot adds one half of the quarter note's inherent value (one half of one beat is a half beat), then a dotted quarter note equals one and a half beats. You would hold down a dotted quarter note for the same amount of time it takes to play three eighth notes. (The above example illustrates how dotted quarter notes work.)

Practice Session

Do you detect a pattern? I introduce a new type of note, then torture you mercilessly by forcing you to into a counting exercise. Of course, you could close the book, but it would only jump up and chase you around the house. You might as well just come to grips with the following figure, which is a little fragment of musical sublimity using dotted half notes.

one two three one   two three one two three   one   two   three   one two three   one two three

Count this one in three, not four.

As with previous insufferable counting exercises, be sure to keep your counting even, and go as slowly as you like. But there is one big change: Now you are counting to three, not four! So your counting now sounds like this: "one-two-three, one-two-three." Try counting to three a few times before you start playing, to get your mind in the rhythm of three.

The following figure uses dotted quarter notes. When counting through this exquisite piece of music, use the "and" method of counting, like this: "one-and-two-and-three-and; one-and-two-and-three-and." That way, the eighth notes fall on a count, either a numbered beat or one of the "ands" between the main beats. Eventually, if you get comfortable enough with it after a several repetitions (it's one of those pieces you love more and more each time you hear it), you can eliminate the "ands," or even do away with counting out loud entirely.

one + two + three + one + two + three + one + two + three + one + two + three

Counting with the "and" method helps deal with dotted quarter notes and eighth notes.

You can find dots after all kinds of notes, but dotted half notes and dotted quarter notes are, by far, the most common types of dotted notes. Your best bet is to treat them each as a specific type of note in its own right, forgetting that the dot is an added feature. A dotted half note simply equals three quarter notes, and a dotted quarter note simply equals three eighth notes.

The Least You Need to Know

➤ Every note lasts a certain number of beats.

➤ Whole notes are worth four beats; half notes are worth two beats; quarter notes are worth one beat; and eighth notes are worth a half beat.

➤ Dotted notes are worth half again as much as the original note.

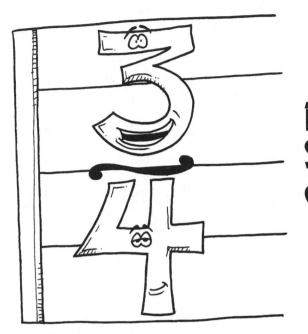

Bars, Time Signatures, and Rests

In This Chapter

➤ Dividing the music staff into measures with bar lines

➤ Letting time signatures determine the number of beats per measure

➤ Taking a breather with rests

Until now in this book, all the musical examples have had a couple of things missing. The previous chapters in this part introduce you to the notes for the right hand; sharps and flats; fingerings; and the different types of notes—whole, half, and quarter.

A couple of things are missing from the musical examples of earlier chapters. The most important is *bar lines*, which organize the music staff into segments. You also need to know about *time signatures*, which tell you how to count a piece. Read on to discover these two important aspects of music notation. Later in the chapter I introduce the concept of *rests*, which tell you when (and for how long) *not* to play.

> **Music Speak**
> **Bar lines** divide the music staff into **measures**, and every measure of a piece contains the same number of beats. All the note values in any measure add up to the same number of beats.

Organizing the Music Staff

Writing out music without bar lines works up to a point. With simple melodies, you can convey the notes and their time values, indicating how to play the melody. But if the music were to get any more complicated, the staff would be a mess.

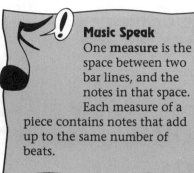

Music Speak

One **measure** is the space between two bar lines, and the notes in that space. Each measure of a piece contains notes that add up to the same number of beats.

Smaller note values, indicating quicker notes, would clutter up the staff and it would become very difficult to understand how the piece should be counted. At that point, the staff would need to be organized in some way, bringing order to the chaos.

Up to this point in the book, I've left out the organizing elements of the music staff for the sake of simplicity. But the fact is, all written music, no matter how rudimentary, contains those organizing features, and this section is where you learn about them. I'm talking about *bar lines* and *time signatures*. I know, it seems like a lot to learn, but this new information actually makes the printed music page more coherent, and easier to understand at a glance. Bar lines and time signatures take some of the work out of counting. So read on, and you're playing will actually get a bit easier. (Boy, is that a flagrant sales pitch, or what?)

Where's the Bar?

Grace Notes

Measures (also called bars, because they lie between *bar lines*) are the fundamental bite-size chunks of written music. In classical music notation, the measures are often numbered, especially in chamber music (composed for two to eight instruments) and orchestral pieces. When rehearsing, the leader of the orchestra or chamber group can instruct the other players to "take it from measure 38," pinpointing where in the piece they should all start playing.

You've probably noticed that we're always counting to four, then starting over. In earlier chapters I never asked you to count to five, or three, or (heaven forbid) to eleven. It makes sense to count to four, because the basic note value—the whole note—always lasts for four beats. Furthermore, every type of note you've learned divides evenly into four: half notes (two beats each) and quarter notes (one beat each).

Wouldn't it be convenient and helpful if written music gave you some indication of when in the piece it was time to start your counting over? In other words, a mark on the page that tells you, "If you're counting correctly, you should be at four right HERE, and should start your count over." Well, there *is* such an indication, and it's called the *bar line*. (Not to be confused with a queue of thirsty people waiting for a frosty cool one.) Bar lines are vertical lines that divide the music staff into sections, each of which equals a certain number of beats. (Four beats for now, but later I show you how the sections can equal different numbers of beats.) The portion of the staff between bar lines is called a *measure* or a *bar*.

The following figure illustrates bar lines and the measures they define.

Measures lie between the bar lines. In this example, the measures equal four beats, and all the note values in each measure add up to exactly four beats.

As you can see, there are several measures on any given staff. Here are the important facts about measures:

➤ There is no theoretical limit on how many or how few measures can exist on a staff, but space limitations and the nature of most musical pieces usually dictates about five to eight measures per staff.

➤ The end of a staff (at the far right) is always the end of a measure, and concludes with a bar line.

➤ The beginning of a staff is always the beginning of a measure.

➤ There can be any number of notes in a measure, but all the note values must add up to exactly the number of beats assigned to the measures. (We are assuming for now that every measure equals four beats. Differently valued measures are introduced a bit further in this chapter.)

Sign of the Times

This is where another crucial element of the music staff is introduced, that lets you understand measures completely. Until now I've diabolically let you assume that measures are always worth four beats, as if four were the cosmic essence of all rhythm. Four is a good number to use for examples, because a whole note equals four beats. But the fact is that the measures of a piece can be assigned any number of beats. The part of the staff that assigns the value of measures is called the *time signature*. The time signature is placed at the beginning of the staff, way over toward the left (see the following figure). The time signature appears only on the first staff of a piece, not on every staff throughout the piece.

> **Music Speak**
> **Time signatures** are placed at the beginning (far left end) of the music staff, and tell you how many beats are in every measure.

This time signature indicates that each measure contains four quarter-note beats.

As you can see in the above figure, time signatures consist of two numbers, one perched oddly on top of the other. Here's what they mean:

➤ The top number of the time signature indicates how many notes exist in each measure.

➤ The bottom number of the time signature indicates what type of note is referred to by the top number.

> **Grace Notes**
> The time signature is sometimes referred to as the *meter*. Like a parking meter that ticks off how much time remains before a cop slams the dreaded summons on your windshield, the meter indicates how to tick off the beats of each measure in your mind. *Meter* and *time signature* are musical synonyms.

Looking at the example illustrated in the previous figure, the top number is 4. That top number indicates that each measure can hold four notes. But what kind of notes? Whole notes, with four beats each? (That would mean each measure contains sixteen beats.) Half notes, with two beats each? (That would mean each measure contains eight beats.) Actually, the bottom number, which is 4, means quarter notes, indicating that the top number is referring to four quarter notes in each measure. (That means that each measure, in fact, contains four beats, because quarter notes are worth one beat each.)

The top number on any time signature refers to the number of notes in every measure, and the bottom number clues you in to what kind of note. When 4 is the bottom number, it means quarter notes. We are sticking with that bottom number for now, because it is the most common and easiest to work with. When the top number is three, it means that every measure holds three quarter notes. When the top number is two, it means that every measure holds two quarter notes. (See the next figure for an illustration of what these time signatures, and measures, look like.)

Grace Notes
Time signatures can get pretty crazy, especially in twentieth-century piano music. A signature like 11/16, indicating that each measure contains eleven sixteenth notes (or the equivalent time value of other note types) is much harder to count than a simple 4/4 meter. Fortunately, exotic meters (time signatures) are just about as rare as a mocha cappucino with the perfect sprinkling of nutmeg. And considerably less tasty.

Three different time signatures, as they would appear at the beginning of three different pieces.

When the time signature is 4/4, 3/4, or 2/4, don't make the mistake of thinking that only quarter notes are allowed in the measures! The time signature represents the total *note value* allowed to be in any measure. It doesn't matter whether that note value is filled in with quarter, half, or whole notes, or even other note types I haven't discussed yet. Look at the following two figures to see different note types filling in the measures.

Here is "Jingle Bells" with a time signature and bar lines.

This is what "Twinkle, Twinkle, Little Star" looks like with a time signature and bar lines.

Taking a Rest

There's no rest for the weary—but there are rests in music! You've got one more important thing to learn about music notation before this chapter is over. Fortunately, it builds easily on the note values described in this chapter. Music has two items of time value: notes, and *rests*. You know what a note is: it's a key on the keyboard that lasts for a certain number of beats. Rests also last for a certain number of beats, but they mark where you *shouldn't* play a note. Rests are used to indicate the absence of notes.

Rests are a big help when you're playing a piece from music. Without these silent markers, it would be harder to count your way through any measure that isn't filled with notes. Rests keep track of the beat even when nothing is sounding, and if you know the rest values you can keep counting through the silence.

You may wonder why rests are necessary. If there are no notes, just don't put any notes on the staff, right? What's the point of any other indicator? The answer is that written music is compulsive in its accounting. Everything needs to add up perfectly. If there are four beats per measure, each staff of the music has to add up to four beats whether there are notes for all the beats or not.

Music Speak
Rests indicate when you should not play. Rests are the opposite of notes, which tell you when to play. Rests have the same time value as notes, and they make measures add up to the right amount of beats when there aren't enough notes.

Rests have certain beat values, just like notes. In fact, rest values are identical to note values, which is to say that for every note there is a corresponding rest. So, there are whole note rests, half note rests, quarter note rests, and eighth note rests. The following figure illustrates what the four basic rests look like, and how their values compare to the different notes.

This is what the basic rests look like, and how they correspond to note values.

The next illustration notates a melody (not prize-winning by any means) with rests. You can see how each rests keeps time with silence, making each measure add up to the right number of beats (four) with a combination of notes and rests.

Notes and rests make each measure add up to the correct number of beats.

The Least You Need to Know

➤ Bar lines divide the staff into measures, and each measure contains the same number of beats.

➤ Time signatures appear at the beginning of the piece, and determine how many beats are in each measure.

➤ Rests correspond to note values, and tell you how many beats *not* to play.

Chapter 11

Unlocking Keys and Scales

In This Chapter

➤ Understanding keys and tonics

➤ Learning about major and minor scales

➤ Introducing key signatures

➤ A brief summary of modes

Music is a highly organized art form. There's plenty of room for experimentation and improvising, but the technical parts of music—how its rhythms, melodies, and harmonies are constructed—is as fastidious as an accountant's checkbook. Chapter 7 introduced the music staff and written notes, showing that every key on the keyboard has a precise spot on the written music page; each hand even has its own staff. Other chapters in this part reveal note types, rests, rhythms, tempos, and measures, showing that written music accounts for every beat in a piece. This chapter affirms the disciplined quality of music's underpinnings by discussing scales, keys, and key signatures.

What Keys Do

Music keys don't unlock anything, but they do affect how listeners hear music, and how players play music. At one time or another you've probably seen a singer who tells her band to play the song up or down a few notes, or who says, "Play it in G, boys." Such an instruction is referring to a key. In music, the key refers to the main note of the piece. The main note can be thought of as a kind of home base, around which the whole piece gravitates. That main note is important enough, in fact, to have its own name: tonic. Sounds like it should go in your drink, but a piece's tonic is its key note. (This is a good time to mention that drinking while playing your keyboard, while possibly fun, can result in lots of bad music.)

Music Speak

In music, the **key** indicates the main note of the piece, and which sharps or flats are needed to play the piece around that central note. The main note is called the *tonic*. Every key has a scale, which is a sequence of notes starting with the tonic note.

How do you tell one key from another? Good question; I'm glad I asked. Keys are identified by key signatures, which are the number of sharps or flats used to play music in that key. Stay with this chapter for a discussion of key signatures a bit later.

A piece's key is not just a theoretical distinction. In most cases, you can actually hear that the tonic note is special, and important to the piece sounding good to your ear. The following figure shows a portion of "The Star Spangled Banner," which you can either play or just look at for the time being. (For once this isn't one of my confounded exercises!)

This version of the American national anthem is a good example of how tonic notes have an anchoring effect on a piece's sound.

Key Thought

I could have written "The Star Spangled Banner" in any key, but any key other than C would have required accidentals (sharps and flats), so C is the easiest key for a simple demonstration. If I had written it in another key, the piece would have started on a different note, and sounded higher or lower. That's why singers request songs in different keys, to match the singer's voice range.

Try humming the above piece to yourself while following the music with your eyes. The point is to see how important the tonic notes are to the piece—each tonic is marked in the music. The piece, as I've written it out in this example, is in the key of C, which means that C is the tonic note. (Every C on the keyboard is equally the tonic.)

As you look at the previous piece and either play it or hum it, notice not only the visual placement of the tonic notes, but also how your ear and your musical sense respond to them. The tonic, C, anchors the piece and gives it a musical home base that sounds right—it feels right. When a tonic falls on the first beat of a measure, it is an especially grounding experience, because the key is driven home all the more strongly.

Transposing music from one key to another is not a skill you need, most likely, which is fortunate because it's quite hard. I'm certainly not going to ask you to do it in this book, unless you spill coffee on the pages, in which case you must transpose "Flight of the Bumblebee" into the key of BZZZZZ. So be careful.

Climbing a Hill of Scales

Keys and scales form a perfect relationship: In order to understand keys, it's helpful to know scales, and in order to understand scales, you have to know about keys. You know that a piece's key is defined by its tonic note. A scale is a sequence of notes that goes from one tonic note to the next tonic note above it. In the key of C, for example, the scale runs from any C on the keyboard to the next higher C.

The following figure shows a C scale, going from middle C on up to the next C. Notice that the scale has seven tones, with the top note, C, being either number eight or number one. Because the upper C is essentially the same note as the bottom C (they are both the tonic), scales are considered to have seven notes.

The scale of C. All scales consist of seven notes, with the eighth note being the tonic, just like the first note.

Practice Session

Using the following figure for reference, play a C scale on the keyboard.

The ascending and descending C scale, written in quarter notes with fingerings.

The first part of the above illustration shows the ascending scale (going up), and the second staff shows the descending scale (going down). I've put in fingerings for you to follow. Keep in mind that your thumb is finger 1, index finger is 2, middle finger is 3, ring finger is 4, and little finger is 5.

Try this exercise in three steps:

1. First, just pick out the notes on the keyboard and get used to what the scale sounds like. Notice how the two tonic notes—at the top and bottom of the scale—really sound like the main note. Going up, the C at the top seems to resolve a question posed by the B preceding it. Going down, the last C sounds like the logical, inevitable conclusion to the scale.

2. Second, forget about rhythm and counting. Just work on the fingerings. Pick out the notes using the correct right-hand fingers, as marked.

   It would be easy to play a scale if we had 7 fingers; unfortunately, God wasn't thinking on that day too clearly, and only gave us 5. For this reason, we have to make a slight accommodation to play a scale smoothly. The tricky part lies between the third and fourth notes of the first measure, where you go from an E with the third finger, to an F with the first finger (thumb). Lift your wrist a bit when playing the E, and slip your thumb underneath to play the F. On the descending scale, you have the same situation in reverse: you must play the descending F with the thumb, and the following E with your third finger. Cross your middle finger over your thumb to play the E.

Both going up and coming down, try to hold down each key until the very moment that you play the next note, resulting in a smooth sound without any gaps of silence between the notes. Keep working on the fingerings until you're pretty comfortable with the scales.

3. Third, play the scales, up and down, with the correct fingerings and in the correct rhythm. There is nothing fancy about the rhythm—it's just a sequence of quarter notes. I've written the scales with a 4/4 time signature, so your counting should be up to four. Go slowly and keep the rhythm even. If you have trouble with the fingerings, try again with a slower count, because it's more important to play with the right fingers than to play fast. With practice, you can build up a little speed.

Major and Minor Scales

Music Speak
Changing a piece from one key to another is called **transposing** the piece. Transposing a piece from C to D, for example, moves it up one whole step. Transposing a piece from G to F moves it down one whole step. You can transpose any piece to any key, and the process moves every note of the piece up or down the same number of whole or half steps.

You know now that scales have seven notes, and they are the sequence of notes between two tonic notes an octave apart on the keyboard. But which seven notes make up the scale? In the case of the C scale it's easy: the scale consists of the seven white keys between any two consecutive Cs. But it doesn't work that way for any other note besides C. If you play the seven white keys between D and D, for example, or F and F, you get a scale that doesn't quite sound right. You're still playing seven notes, but it doesn't have the same natural sound as the C scale. (Don't take my word for it; try it yourself. Just pick out the notes without regard to fingering or rhythm.)

The truth is, there are two important types of music scales, and several other less important ones. (Hey, don't shoot the messenger; I didn't invent this sytem.) The only two scale types you need to know about in this book are major and minor scales. Despite what the names sound like, the major scale is not more important or larger than the minor scale. They each have seven notes, and they each are constructed in a certain way; it is the difference in how they are constructed that distinguishes them. I'll get to the minor scale a bit later in this chapter. For now, the major scale is your focus, because it is the C major scale that you've been playing in this chapter.

What makes a scale a major scale? Aside from natty clothes and a sunny disposition, a major scale is made from a certain sequence of half steps and whole steps. The concept is difficult to convey in words, so cast your gaze over the following figure, which illustrates a C major scale broken down into its steps.

The C major scale, showing whole steps (1) and half steps (¹/₂). Every major scale has the same sequence of whole and half steps.

80

Every step of the major scale (the distance from one note to the next) is either a whole step or a half step. To be precise, just two of the steps in the C major scale (and any major scale) are half steps. The table below shows where the half steps lie in any major scale:

Between notes 1 and 2	Whole step
Between notes 2 and 3	Whole step
Between notes 3 and 4	Half step
Between notes 4 and 5	Whole step
Between notes 5 and 6	Whole step
Between notes 6 and 7	Whole step
Between notes 7 and 8	Half step

Now you know one way to determine a major scale. Just start with any note on the keyboard, and step your way upward using this sequence of whole steps and half steps, playing both white keys and black keys. As I mentioned before, the C major scale is the only major scale that is played on white keys only.

Practice Session

You now know enough to construct major scales beginning on any key of the keyboard. You can try it by referring to the major-scale table, and counting up whole steps and half steps. Start with G, and proceed up the keyboard with this sequence: whole, whole, half, whole, whole, whole, half. (Those are whole steps and half steps.) If all goes well, you are playing a scale with one black key, which is the key of the seventh note, just before the upper G. That note is F-sharp.

Now try one more, this time starting on F. As with the G major scale in the previous paragraph, play up the keyboard with whole steps and half steps in the major scale sequence. This time, you'll play one black key at a different point of the scale—it's the fourth note, which is B-flat.

Scales and Key Signatures

There is another way to determine a major scale besides counting whole steps and half steps, which requires less work but more memorization. This section shows you how, using key signatures.

You know that scales are closely related to keys. The C scale, for example, is the scale of the key of C. Major and minor fit into the scale/key relationship too. The C-major scale is the scale of the key of C major. This leads to an important fact, worthy of spotlighting:

➤ Every key is either major or minor, and every major and minor key has a scale.

Music Speak

A **scale** is a sequence of notes starting with the tonic note of a key, and going up or down to the next tonic note. Every key has its own scale.

Music Speak

Key signatures determine the key of a piece by showing which sharps or flats are necessary to play a scale in that key. Key signatures make their appearance at the beginning of every staff in a piece, and look like a cluster of sharp or flat symbols.

Major keys are still our focus right now, and it's time to move beyond C major to some other major key and its scale. Trying out another major scale brings accidentals (sharps or flats) into play, and leads you right to key signatures. The following figure shows you the F major scale. As you can see, the scale contains one accidental, which is B-flat on the fourth note. Because the F major scale is associated with the key of F major, and because the scale always has one flat (B-flat), the key signature of F major is one flat, or B-flat.

F G A B-flat C D E F

The F-major scale, which has a key signature of one flat.

Here's a handy list of things to know about major keys and their key signatures:

➤ Key signatures are defined by the number of sharps or flats in the scale of that key.

➤ Every major key has a unique key signature, not shared by any other major key.

➤ Key signatures have either sharps or flats, but never a mixture of sharps and flats.

Key Signatures in Written Music

> **Hmm...**
>
> **Key Thought**
> The sharps and flats of key signatures are always added in a certain sequence. The key signature of D major, for example, is two sharps—F-sharp and C-sharp. Those two sharps must be included in the key signatures of every key with more than two sharps. Accordingly, the key signature of A major, which is three sharps, contains F-sharp, C-sharp, and G-sharp. Flatted key signatures work the same way, although the order is different.

Generally speaking, every piece is written in a key. Every key has a signature number of sharps or flats that are needed to make a major scale in that key. Imagine if you wrote a piece in a key that has three sharps: F-sharp, C-sharp, and G-sharp. If you wrote the piece out, you'd have to write in a sharp before every F, C, and G in the piece. Not exactly hard labor in a salt mine, I admit, but still on the inconvenient side. Key signatures show you at a glance how many sharps or flats are in the piece, and which notes the sharps or flats apply to. Key signatures are placed at the beginning of every staff in the piece, and they keep the notes less cluttered with accidentals.

The following figure shows a key signature of two flats: B-flat and E-flat. This particular key signature indicates that every B and E in the piece is automatically flatted to B-flat and E-flat. The two-flat sign at the beginning of the staff constitutes the key signature, and applies not only to the specific B and E notes on those particular lines and spaces, but to every B and E, anywhere on the keyboard, through the whole piece. The key signature flats are placed at the beginning of every staff to remind you which notes are flatted by default.

A key signature of two flats, namely B-flat and E-flat. Key signatures appear at the beginning of every staff in a piece.

A Natural Thing

So what happens when a piece with a key signature of two flats (B-flat and E-flat) has a non-flat B or non-flat E as part of its melody? After all, there is no rule that a melody must use one note instead of another—and believe me, most pieces break their key signatures many times.

In music notation, a certain symbol can be placed before any automatic sharp or flat to override that sharp or flat, returning the note to its natural state. Accordingly, the symbol is called a natural. When a note that is normally a flat or sharp (because of the key signature) is made natural, it is called B-natural (if B is the note). Naturals are accidentals just like sharps and flats.

Musical Mouthful
"You make me feel like a natural woman."— Aretha Franklin

The top staff has a key signature of B-flat and E-flat, and shows how natural sign can neutralize the flats. The bottom staff is a similar illustration using the key signature of F-sharp, C-sharp, and G-sharp.

Following are a few miscellaneous but important facts about key signatures and accidentals:

➤ The key signature of a piece can change during the piece, although this happens mostly in intermediate and advanced classical piano music. When a key signature changes, the new assortment of sharps or flats is inserted at the change, even if it happen in mid-staff. Then, the new key signature is placed at the beginning of every subsequent staff. No matter what, there is always a key signature at the beginning of every staff.

Music Speak
Naturals neutralize previously established sharps and flats. The natural sign is an accidental just like a sharp sign or flat sign. Naturals lower sharped notes by a half step, and raise flatted notes by a half step.

➤ No sharps and no flats is a key signature, too. It is the signature of the key of C major. It means, as we have seen earlier in this chapter, that if you play all the white notes (no accidentals) from C to C on the keyboard, the result is a major scale.

➤ Each key has a unique signature. The uniqueness of key signatures means that only one major key has a signature of three sharps, for example, or two flats. There is no such thing as another key that uses a different set of three sharps or two flats. As an example, remember that F major has a key signature of one flat (B-flat). It is impossible to have a key signature of one flat, using another flatted note, like E-flat or G-flat. A key signature of one flat automatically means B-flat is the flatted note, and it automatically means F major is the key. This means that when musicians refer to the key signature as "one flat," everyone knows it must mean the key of F major, with all Bs flatted.

➤ When an accidental is written before a note (and is therefore not included in the key signature), it lasts for the remainder of the measure before it loses its effect. Take a glance at the following figure for an example of how accidentals last through a measure. After the measure ends, if a composer wants the sharped, flatted, or naturalized note to be played again, the accidental is rewritten.

When an accidental is written before a note, as with the B-flat in this example, the accidental lasts through the measure on that note. After that measure, the note automatically reverts to its natural state.

Practice Session

The trickiest aspect of key signatures is remembering which notes are sharped or flatted throughout the whole piece. Because accidentals aren't used to indicate sharps or flats of the notes in the key signature, you must burn the key signature into your brain's circuitry before starting the piece. Once you get familiar with the handful of basic keys, playing the correct sharps and flats becomes second nature (well, maybe third or fourth nature). For now, it takes more effort to remember the key signature, and effort takes practice, and practice requires . . . exercises! (I know how happy exercises make you.)

The purpose of each of this little bit of torment is to give you practice remembering a key signature. The figure below illustrates the relatively easy key signature of F major—one flat (B-flat). It's a touching piece, so don't be ashamed if it brings tears to your eyes. Don't be surprised if it doesn't, too. When playing the piece, remember that all Bs are flatted unless they have a natural sign in front of them.

With a key signature of one flat, all Bs are automatically flatted in this piece, except when the flat is neutralized by a natural.

A Little Less Major

Most of this chapter deals with major keys, their scales, and their key signatures. But I can't end this discussion without introducing the siblings of major keys: minor keys. Minor keys work similarly to major keys in a couple of important ways:

➤ Minor keys, like major keys, have key signatures.

➤ Minor keys also have scales, called—naturally enough—minor scales.

The main difference between a major key and a minor key lies in the scales. Refer to the previous table in this chapter to refresh your memory of how major scales are constructed from whole steps and half steps. Minor scales are likewise built from whole and half steps, but they are ordered differently. The following figure illustrates the A minor scale, which is the one minor scale (like C major) that doesn't use accidentals. You can see that half steps lie between the second and third tones of the scale, and between the fifth and sixth notes. The following table spells out how to construct a minor scale by counting whole and half steps on the keyboard.

Between notes 1 and 2	Whole step
Between notes 2 and 3	Half step
Between notes 3 and 4	Whole step
Between notes 4 and 5	Whole step
Between notes 5 and 6	Half step
Between notes 6 and 7	Whole step
Between notes 7 and 8	Whole step

Key Thought
Other minor scales use different sequences of whole and half steps, and are called harmonic minor and melodic minor scales. I mention these other two scales just for the sake of completeness, but now that I've mentioned them, feel free to forget them.

The awful truth is that there are three different types of minor scales, but the good news is that you only need to know about one: the scale described by the whole/half step arrangement in the above table. The minor scale in the figure below, and all others that use its sequence of whole and half steps, is called a natural minor scale.

The A-minor scale. Although there are three kinds of minor scales, only one type is important—the natural minor scale, of which this is an example.

Close Relations

Minor keys (and their scales and key signatures) are closely related to major scales. Remember one crucial fact you know about major keys: that each has a unique key signature. It's true (I'm the honest sort) that no two major keys share a key signature, but every major key does share its key signature with a minor key. Major keys and minor keys that share key signatures are said to be related, so that the minor key with the same key signature as a major key is said to be the relative minor, just as the major key is the relative major of the minor key.

Music Speak
Relative minor and **relative major keys** share the same key signature. The major key with a key signature of two sharps (D major) is the relative major of the minor key with a key signature of two sharps (B minor). By the same token, B minor is called the relative minor of D major.

Key Thought
You'll be very glad to know that most piano music is not written in modes, but in the common major and minor scales. It's only a perverse compulsion to be thorough that leads me to include this information on modes.

Grace Notes
Okay, time for a juicy snippet of confusion. You now know that modes are extra scales based on ancient musical systems. What you're about to find out is that major and minor are also considered modes. Major mode consists of all major keys and scales, and minor mode contains all minor keys and scales. "Switching mode" generally refers to a change from major key to minor key, or the reverse.

The easiest major and minor keys to remember, when it comes to being related, are C major and its relative minor, A minor. C major and A minor share a key signature of no flats and no sharps. The two keys also provide the key for determining the relative minor of any major key. If you count downward from C to A, you notice that A is three half steps below C. In exactly the same way, any major key's relative minor can be determined by counting down three half steps from the major key's tonic note.

Scales à la Mode

Some of the smart students sitting in the front row of desks may have heard musicologists refer to modes and wonder how these differ from scales. Well, actually, modes *are* scales, and way back in the medieval era, music was structured around the seven modes rather than the major and minor keys. (You thought learning two scales was hard!) Each mode has a different relation of whole and half steps, determined by the note on which it starts.

Each mode only uses the white keys of the piano. So, the C major scale, which has no accidentals, is known in Mode-land as the Ionian Mode. Similarly, you can play the other six modes by beginning with each note of the C major scale, moving up the keyboard using only the white notes. The following table shows you each of the modes with their fancy Greek names.

D	Dorian
E	Phyrgian
F	Lydian
G	Mixolydian
A	Aeolian
B	Locrian

The modes were okay as far as they went, but they weren't too friendly to added harmonies. A piece that was set in the Ionian mode stayed there and didn't stray into the Dorian mode, for example; whereas a piece written in C major can progress into G major or even A minor. By the early seventeenth century, composers were frustrated with modal writing, and longed to freshen their music with harmonies and key changes. The major and minor scales—equivalent to the Ionian and Aeolian modes—won out the battle of bands, and the other modes fell into disuse.

The Least You Need to Know

➤ Music is composed in keys, and each key is defined by a main note.

➤ Every key has a scale—a series of seven notes leading from the main note to the octave-higher main note.

➤ Every key has a key signature, which is the number of sharps or flats used to form that key's scale.

➤ Keys and their scales come in major and minor versions. Major scales and minor scales are constructed according to a particular order of whole steps and half steps.

Part 3
Give Yourself Another Hand

Part 3 gives the left hand its day in the sun. I'm sure you've noticed that the piano is played with both hands. In fact, that's one of the unique aspects of keyboard instruments—both hands can make notes at the same time. In addition to learning the left-hand notes, the chapters in this part focus on the coordination challenges of playing two-handed music. In addition, I provide a thorough tutorial in chords and other left-hand techniques. Getting familiar with playing and constructing chords makes you a much more capable musician, and enables you to play all kinds of music.

As with Part 2, this part gives you plenty of exercises, framed as Practice Sessions. They are all the more important as you get the two hands working together.

Chapter 12 introduces the notes played by the left hand. Then, in Chapter 13, we put both hands together for the first time! Chapter 14 discusses the joys of accompaniment, and Chapter 15 introduces chord theory, giving you all the chords you need to know.

Learning the Left-Hand Notes

In This Chapter

➤ Finding middle C with the left hand

➤ Learning left-hand notes on the bass clef staff

➤ Exploring time and key signatures in the bass clef

In this chapter, I introduce a whole new dimension to keyboard playing: the left hand. Whether the left-hand notes are useful to you depends on what kind of playing you are interested in. If you have a home keyboard with auto-accompaniment features, you may choose to limit your playing to right-hand notes, supported by the auto-accompaniments afforded by your keyboard. But if you want to explore the full ambidextrous potential of the piano, getting the left hand involved is essential.

Using both hands enables you to play more advanced pieces as well as to accompany yourself. And developing a strong left hand is key to your progress as a pianist.

Middle C for the Left Hand

Chapter 2 introduced the right-hand notes by starting with middle C as a home base. Conveniently, middle C is an anchor for the left-hand notes, too. Just as the right hand plays middle C with the thumb, so does the left hand. When your left-hand thumb rests on middle C, your other fingers extend downward on the keyboard, ready to play its lower half.

Grace Notes
While lefties have to make special adjustments to play the guitar, for example, restringing it to suit their left-handed orientation, it makes no difference whether you are right or left handed when it comes to playing the piano. It's a truly ambitexturous instrument!

When first finding notes for the left hand, you need to become familiar with saying the alphabet backwards. When the right hand plays notes upward from middle C, it's easy enough to recite the alphabet forwards as you play successive notes: C, D,

E, and so on. With the left hand, the order is backwards as your proceed down the keyboard to the left: C, B, A, and so on. The figure below illustrates the keyboard notes extending downward for one octave from middle C.

Middle C is both a left-hand and right-hand note. This illustration shows you an octave of notes (without accidentals) from middle C down to the next C.

Practice Session

Time to give your left hand some hands-on experience with the keyboard. Try placing your left thumb on middle C, letting your other fingers rest on the four keys to the left of middle C. No need to actually play any key yet—though if you did, the roof probably won't cave in. Now place your *right* thumb on middle C, without removing your left thumb. That's right—both thumbs are sharing the key, but just resting on it without playing the note.

Your hands are now resting in the classic "ready" position for playing a keyboard, sort of like resting your fingers on a computer keyboard, ready to type. From the middle C position, your hands are best poised to leap into musical action.

Keeping both hands resting in the ready position, thumbs resting on middle C, play the keys downward with your left hand, starting with the thumb and proceeding to the little finger, then reverse directon back up (see the following figure).

Play these left-hand notes with the fingerings indicated. Remember that left-hand fingerings mirror right-hand fingerings—finger number 1 is the thumb.

Now try getting both hands into the act. Start from the bottom—the little finger of your left hand, which should be resting on the F key—and play each note all the way to the little finger of your right hand (resting on G). When you get to middle C, play it twice on the way up—first with your left thumb, then with your right thumb. On the way down you also play it twice, first with the right thumb. Take your time, and don't worry about rhythm or counting. Just play each note clearly, and release each key as you play the next key. The following figure spells out the notation for this exercise.

This exercise uses all your fingers. Play the notes slowly up from your left-hand little finger to your right-hand little finger, then back down, using the fingerings shown here.

Here's one more thing to try. This exercise is exciting (assuming you're as easily excited as I am) because it starts you playing with both hands at once. Start by playing middle C with *both* thumbs pressing the key down. Using both thumbs on one key may seem like wasted effort, not to mention cramped conditions for your thumbs as they squeeze onto a single key, but it helps your coordination.

Now play both index fingers at the same time—your left index finger should be resting on the B below middle C, and your right index finger should play the D above middle C. Then move on to the middle fingers, then the ring fingers, then the little fingers.

The figure below shows you what this exercise looks like on paper. Don't worry in the slightest about rhythm and counting—just concentrate on playing the notes with both hands simultaneously. Remember to release the keys when you play the next keys. As shown in the illustration, when you get to the little fingers, turn right around and work your way back to the thumbs on middle C.

Time to play with both hands at once! Middle C is shared by the thumbs of both hands.

Congratulations: you're now a two-fisted keyboard player!

Left-Hand Notes on the Staff

Key Thought

The thumbs aren't always used to play middle C, but using them now, as you begin to bring the left hand into play (pun fully intended, I'm afraid), helps center your hands on the keyboard. With both hands resting lightly on the keys, each thumb placed on middle C, your hands are in a sort of "home position" from which they can scoot upward or downward as the music demands.

Now that your left hand is finding its way around the keyboard, you need to know how to recognize left-hand notes as they are written in music notation. Learning the left-hand notes introduces the two clefs—treble clef and bass clef—used in keyboard and piano notation. The treble clef is used for right-hand notes, and the bass clef holds the left-hand notes (the following figure illustrates the two clefs).

In real-life playing, you sometimes reach down to the bass clef notes with your right hand, and there's no law saying your left hand can't play treble clef notes. But for most practical purposes, each hand usually stays on its own clef.

The treble clef (for right-hand notes) and bass clef (for left-hand notes).

Music Speak

A **clef** is a symbol placed at the beginning of the staff to indicate the position of the notes on it. The most common clefs are the *treble (G clef)* or *bass (F clef)*.

Music Speak

A **double staff** consists of the treble and bass staffs connected together, to indicate two lines that are played simultaneously.

The bass clef staff works exactly like the treble clef staff, in that notes are placed on lines and in spaces between the lines. In fact, the staffs are identical (five horizontal lines each), but the clefs make the note placements different. A note placed on the middle line of the treble clef (B) is not the same as a note placed on the middle line of the bass clef (D).

The treble and bass clefs are divided around middle C. You've already learned that middle C on the treble clef is the note hanging beneath the staff on a single leger line. Middle C also exists on the bass clef, and is notated as the note resting *above* the staff on a single leger line (see the figure below). Pretty darn symmetrical, huh? Thank you very much—I wish I could take credit for the notation design, but it was invented several centuries ago when I was only seven years old.

Middle C (Right Hand)

Middle C (Left Hand)

Middle C can be notated on both the treble clef and bass clef.

This is a good time to join the two music staffs into a single, double staff. Huh? Come again? A *single double staff?* That's right: In piano music, and some keyboard music, the left-hand staff (bass clef) and right-hand staff (treble clef) are joined together with bar lines that extend vertically down through both staffs. To emphasize the bonding of the two staffs, a bracket on the left end of the double-staff joins them together.

As mentioned above, the two staffs (treble and bass clef) are identical in how they function, but note placements are different. This is undeniably more difficult than if the note placements were the same. If they were the same, you'd only have to learn one staff, then apply that knowledge to both hands. As it is, however, you must learn how to read the staffs independently. This is perhaps the trickiest part of learning to read piano music, but like anything else it just takes some experience and practice.

To start, look at the following figure, which spells out all the notes of the bass clef down to the first leger line beneath the staff. You can use this illustration whenever you need a refresher course in reading the bass clef.

Key Thought
When you think about it, there can be no other way to notate two-handed playing. Because both hands are often playing at the same time, you must be able to read the notes for both hands at a glance, so one staff must be positioned under the other. It's only natural that the bass clef staff (left hand) be positioned underneath the treble clef staff.

The bass clef notes, and where to find them on the keyboard.

To aid you in learning the bass clef notes, I offer a mnemonic device. This particular mnemonic device is based on the notion that remembering a phrase is easier than remembering a bunch of notes. So, if you take the notes of each of the bass clef lines, bottom to top, they can form an acronym for a memorable phrase. The notes are: G (bottom line), B (next line up), D (middle line), F (below the top line), and A (top line). Here are a few phrases sure to help you remember the order of bass clef lines:

➤ Good Boys Don't Fly Away

➤ Gregarious Babbling Dwarfs Flee Aghast

➤ Gaudy Baubles Demonstrate Futile Agendas

➤ Ghouls Betray Demons, Forestalling Adversity

➤ Gradually But Doggedly, Felicia Advanced

Hope that helps.

Grace Notes
Occasionally, more than two staffs are used to notate piano music. Such an abundant use of staffs is present only when the music is too complex to fit onto the normal two staffs. Orchestral scores connect many staffs, sometimes more than two dozen, to accomodate all the different instrument parts. On the other end of the scale, pop music for piano and keyboards is often notated on a single staff that holds the melody, with chords written above it for the left hand to play.

Practice Session

Now that you know the basics of the bass clef (the bass basics, so to speak), it's a good time to get some hands-on practice (practical practice?) with reading the bass clef and playing its notes on the keyboard. You may remember that I annoyed you with such exercises in Chapter 2, using the treble clef. It might be a good idea to connect the two chapters in your mind, and review the exercises in both chapters now.

First, take a look at the following figure:

A left-hand playing exercise that may, or may not, move you to tears. Probably not.

If no other piece in this book brings you to cathartic tears, this one will. I'm expecting critics to hail this exercise as a landmark of keyboard composition, worthy of its place in the immortal pantheon; either that, or the critics will ignore it completely. Anyway, get out the tissues and start playing. I've marked fingerings, and the exercise is written in rhythm, so you have a chance to put it all together.

Start by forgetting the rhythm and just figuring out the notes, and playing them with the correct fingers. Once you've got the hang of the notes, start counting and playing in rhythm. As always, go slowly and play evenly. Continue practicing the exercise until you can play it in the correct rhythm and with the correct fingers. It doesn't matter how fast you count and play—slow as molasses is fine.

Just for fun (all right, so I'm not exactly a party animal), the following figure gives you another exercise.

This tune may be recognizable as "Here Comes the Bride," which has an alternate title of "Don't Step on the Bridal Train." I've presented the the piece for the left hand with fingerings. It's important to pay attention to the fingerings on this one, because the range covers a full octave—greater than the natural five-key span of your left hand. Again, start by learning the notes and fingerings, then add your counting to play the piece in the correct rhythm. Remember, slow is good. Slow is your friend. Mr. Slow is always there for you.

Time and Key Signatures in the Bass Clef

What's left to round out your understanding of the bass clef, and the left hand's participation on the keyboard? Practice, of course, is what really helps both hands become facile players. When it comes to reading music and recognizing notes placed on both the treble and bass clefs, it's just a matter of getting used to the look of the double staff as two connected single staffs.

You'll be glad to know that key signatures work just the same on the bass clef staff as on the treble clef staff. However, when it comes to the placement of the sharps or flats of a key signature, the symbols must correspond to where the notes lie on the staff. The following figure makes this all clear.

A few examples of what key signatures look like on the double staff. The placement of sharps and flats corresponds to where the notes are located on each staff.

In the first example, the key signature is one sharp (F-sharp), and you can see that sharp indicated on both clefs of the double staff. However, because the F note is located on a different line in each staff, the sharp sign is likewise placed differently. The second example uses a key signature of one flat (B-flat), and here, too, you can see the difference in placement, corresponding to where B is located on both staffs. The other two examples extend this lesson to key signatures with more than one sharp or flat.

Grace Notes

Just a reminder: The key signature is placed at the beginning of every staff of a piece—that means each clef of a double staff of piano music. The key signature is a constant reminder of which notes are automatically sharped or flatted.

Time signatures are very easy: they are simply repeated on each clef of the double staff. The following figure shows what a complete double staff looks like at the beginning of a piece, including the bracket joining the two staffs, the two clefs, the time signature, and the key signature. Remember: the time signature appears only once, at the beginning of the piece, unless the time signature changes during the piece.

The double staff at the beginning of a piece, showing the time signature and key signature.

The Least You Need to Know

➤ Middle C is the same for the left hand as for the right hand. When both hands have their thumbs resting on middle C, they are in a basic starting position.

➤ The bass clef has five lines, just like the treble clef, but the lines and spaces of the two staffs don't correlate to the same notes. This chapter reviews the bass clef notes.

➤ Time signatures and key signatures appear on the bass clef just as on the treble clef.

Putting One and One Together

One of the adventures of playing keyboards is that you use both hands to make music. Other instruments are *held* with both hands, or one hand is on the instrument's neck while the other hand strums (guitar) or bows (violin), but keyboards are the instruments for playing two different parts simultaneously.

Pianos (and electronic keyboards) are the only instruments that let you play a different note with every finger, all at the same time. Such a multinote capacity isn't the easiest thing in the world to master, but, as my Aunt Frieda used to tell me, "Eggplants don't bounce." Of course, her wisdom has little to do with piano playing. The point is that you can begin slowly when it comes to playing with both hands, and this chapter gets you started.

Starting Simple

The so-called *grand staff*, regal though it sounds, is merely the treble clef staff and the bass clef staff connected in one double staff. You read the grand staff in just the same way as single staffs: from left to right. The left-hand part is on the bottom staff. Bar lines, indicating measures, extend through both staffs, keeping them synchronized according to the rhythm of the piece. The time signature and key signature are the same for both staffs.

Practice Session

Learning to play with two hands involves a couple of distinct challenges. First, there is the sheer physical coordination of using both hands on the keyboard, each playing something different. Then, there is the rhythmic coordination of two musical parts being played at the same time. It's almost enough to drive you to the bongos, but hang in there. These exercises get you started very simply.

The following figure is your first step into the world of two-handed playing. Notice that each hand only plays one note (two Cs an octave apart), and the left-hand part is as simple as it gets. The piece is in 4/4 time, so your counting is to four. Go through the right-hand part a couple of times first. You can also practice the bass clef staff by itself. Then put the two staffs together. Use any fingers to play the notes, and count slowly and evenly.

In this exercise, the right hand does most of the work, and the left hand plays just one note per measure.

The next figure shifts some of the work to the left hand, but doesn't make the two hands do any fancy stuff at the same time. Again, practice each part alone before putting them together, counting all the time. When you put the hands together, keep the counting even, no matter how slow your tempo. I realize these one-note melodies are boring as anything, but if you keep reading you'll get to some more interesting music.

The right and left hands alternate the rhythmic work.

The next exercise gives you something to really sink your teeth in. In this heart-rending piece of music, the right hand moves around a little, while the left hand stays anchored on one note. Because the right hand is playing a melody (though not one likely to make Billy Joel put down his pen), it's important to pay attention to the fingering. In fact, two-handed playing requires good fingering more than one-handed playing, because you can't focus all your attention on either hand.

Practice the right hand first, until you can play it easily, almost without thinking about it. Run through the left hand part once, then put them together.

Practice the hands separately first. Count slowly and evenly while playing. Chewing gum at the same time is courting disaster.

You can wrap up this round of exercises with the next figure. This piece is a round, which, if you remember from your sing-along scouting days, is a kind of repetition piece. In this case, the left hand repeats what the right hand plays first. This little study gives you practice playing two melodies simultaneously, but they are composed so that the two hands are not active at the same time. Be sure to try each part several times before trying to put them together, counting evenly all the while.

In this round, the left-hand part repeats the right-hand part.

Practice Tips for Two-Handed Playing

Key Thought
Learning each part separately is good advice from this point on, because the pieces you will be playing will be more and more complicated. Now is a good time to learn the right method of approaching and learning two-handed pieces. And the good habits serve you well later on.

The big thing to remember about playing a piece that uses both hands is that you don't have to do it right the first time. In fact, you don't have to play all the notes the first time. The best way to learn a keyboard piece is to take it apart, try the parts separately, practice each hand on its own, then gradually put them together.

Following are the steps you should take when learning any new two-handed piece.

➤ **Note the key signature.** Check out the sharps or flats at the beginning of the staffs. They tell you which notes are automatically sharped or flatted throughout the piece. You need to keep the key signature in mind when you're learning the notes.

➤ **Start with the left hand.** This may be a surprising tip, because the right-hand part is usually the more prominent of the two, containing the melody in most cases. But that's exactly why you want to start with the left hand, which is usually the supportive part. In the end, you may want to concentrate more on the right hand, so you need to know the left-hand part very well.

➤ **Find the notes.** Don't worry about the rhythm right away. Pick out the left-hand notes one by one until you're acquainted with where each note lies on the keyboard.

➤ **Learn the fingerings.** If fingerings are marked in the written music, play the left-hand notes with the correct fingers. There may be no fingerings at all, depending on the the helpfulness of whoever prepared the arrangement of the music. In most cases some fingerings exist, giving you the correct finger for certain important notes, and letting you determine the other fingerings based on them.

➤ **Count.** Once you've found the notes and their fingerings, it's time to begin playing the left-hand part with the correct rhythm. Look at the time signature to determine how many beats are in each measure. Use the counting methods of previous chapters, beginning slowly and evenly. A fast tempo isn't important at this stage.

➤ **Look at the right hand part.** Finally, the right hand! Start by finding the notes, regardless of rhythm. Once you've gotten acquainted with the notes, figure out the best fingering with whatever help the sheet music gives you. Once you can play the notes with the correct fingers, begin counting the correct rhythm.

➤ **Put the hands together.** When you can play each hand independently, begin putting them together. You may want to disregard the rhythm at first, and that's fine. However, continue to use the best fingerings for both hands, no matter how slowly and haltingly you need to play. Gradually, even out the rhythm and make it steady with your counting. It's helpful to break up the piece into two- and four-measure chunks, learning each chunk separately, then putting them together into a coherent, whole piece of music.

The Least You Need to Know

➤ The grand staff is simply a treble clef staff and a bass clef staff joined together. Bar lines connect the two staffs.

➤ Piano pieces are notated on a grand staff, with the left-hand part underneath the right-hand part.

Chapter 14

Basics of Accompaniment

In This Chapter

➤ What is accompaniment?

➤ Understanding basic left-hand playing styles, including walking bass, chords, arpeggios, stride, and broken chords

➤ Beginning to use keyboard auto-accompaniments

Traditionally, the left hand's role in playing keyboards is to provide harmony and rhythm for the right hand, which is usually playing the melody. Sometimes the left hand has a more prominent part in the music, but generally, left-hand parts are supportive of right hand melodies.

In classical piano music of the eighteenth and nineteenth centuries, the melody is usually higher than the accompaniment, and is played with the right hand while the left hand performs various supportive musical phrases. In Baroque music of the sixteenth and seventeenth centuries, composed for organ and harpsichord, the left hand is more independent; the music of the era favored many simultaneous melodies.

This chapter concentrates on some of the standard things the left hand does in various types of music. This is also where you begin learning how to use the one-finger auto-accompaniment feature common to many keyboards. Some of the styles and techniques in this chapter are traditional to classical piano music, but still can be played on electronic instruments.

Grace Notes

There are a number of spectacular examples of left-hand virtuosity in the musical literature for classical piano. At least one piano concerto (by the French composer Maurice Ravel) and several solo piano pieces owe their existence to the needs of pianists whose right hands had become incapacitated. Is it cheating to play such pieces with two hands? Maybe not, but I wouldn't brag about it.

What Is Accompaniment?

In music, the *accompaniment* is the part (or parts) that plays along with the main musical part. The accompaniment is usually somewhat in the background (lower in volume), so the main part is highlighted. The main part might be performed by a lead singer, an instrumental soloist, or the right hand of a pianist.

Music Speak
Accompaniment is the musical part (or parts) that is played underneath, and supports, the main melody. In piano music, the left hand usually plays the accompaniment, though in classical music the accompaniment switches between the two hands.

Key Thought
Playing with two hands takes a different sort of coordination than playing with just one. The key, as with anything else, is to start simple and practice. The single-finger style of auto-accompaniment featured on many home keyboards lets you create full-blown harmonies to go along with the rhythms that the keyboard is pumping out, just by playing single left-hand notes. That makes coordination relatively easy, but you still must know the basics of harmony and chords. Of course, if you have a piano, digital piano, professional synthesizer, or some other keyboard lacking in auto-accompaniment bells and whistles, you're in for a left-handed learning curve.

Grace Notes
In the classic small jazz ensemble, the upright bass provides a harmonic underpinning to the piano part by playing notes that emphasize the piece's harmonies. The bass also helps propel the rhythm by playing a steady, even stream of bass notes on every quarter note.

When Tony Bennett, the jazz singer, gives a concert, he is *accompanied* by a pianist, or perhaps a jazz ensemble with bass and drums. When a violinist plays a concerto, she is accompanied by a symphony orchestra. When a lounge singer performs her solo act, she accompanies herself on the piano. The purpose of an accompaniment is to provide the harmony (chords) and rhythm (beats) of the music, in support of the melody (and, in the case of singers, the words).

Not all accompaniment is always subordinate to the main part. In piano music, the left hand sometimes has the more important and melodic part, while the right hand takes a turn in the background. When a pianist is accompanying an instrumental soloist, say a violinist in a sonata for violin and piano, it is not always the violin in the spotlight. Soloists usually receive star billing in such partnerships, but piano accompaniments are challenging and important in their own right, and often include solo passages of great beauty and difficulty. It's useful to remember that *accompany* means "to go with," not "to hide in the shadow of."

Left-Hand Playing Styles

Over time, many styles of left-hand playing have developed. In classical, jazz, and pop music, the left-hand parts have evolved in certain recognizable patterns. While each piece is different, and many pieces in all genres disregard tradition with unique parts for both hands, accompaniment patterns have developed that can be learned, making it easier to learn new pieces in these genres. In jazz and pop especially, where improvisation is just as important (sometimes more important) than slavishly following the written notes, understanding left-hand accompaniment patterns can really help you play those musical styles.

The following sections describe and illustrate some accompaniment patterns in different musical genres.

The Simplest Accompaniment

Some accompaniment styles provide rich, full harmonies in support of the right-hand melody. In jazz, though, it is stylish to *imply* the harmonies with sparse accompaniments made up of single left-hand notes. The meager accompaniment style is reminiscent of, and probably inspired by, the upright bass—an important instrument in the basic jazz ensemble of piano, bass, and drums. The playing style is called *walking bass*, because of its ambling, continuous style. The following figure illustrates the walking bass style of left-hand accompaniment of a jazz tune.

If you don't care for jazz, take heart. Walking bass isn't just for swing and bossa nova music. Furthermore, it can be simplified, making it easier to play, and single-note bass accompaniment can be applied to just about any popular genre. (However, walking bass is not appropriate for classical music.) The figure below shows how a simple, single-note bass line can be used as an accompaniment for a song, in this case "The Twelve Days of Christmas."

The tune is "Fly Me to the Moon," and the left-hand part is a walking bass line. Try playing it on the keyboard, and notice how it sounds like an upright bass part of a jazz group.

This simplified arrangement of "The Twelve Days of Christmas" has a simple, one-note-at-a-time left-hand part. Walking bass implies the piece's harmony with just single notes.

Chords

Chords, which are clusters of notes played at the same time, provide the most all-purpose accompaniment. Chords may seem intimidating to play at first, but you get the hang of them with practice.

The following figure shows how chords can be used to accompany part of the melody of "The Twelve Days of Christmas." Try playing the chords if you like, or go to the next chapter for the complete tutorial (the chord curriculum, shall we say). If you do play them, it's easy to notice that they provide a much fuller, richer sound than single notes in the left-hand part. Chords define a full harmony, whereas single notes just imply that harmony.

Grace Notes

One of the great masters of walking bass in jazz piano playing is Oscar Peterson, the legendary blues master. A virtuoso of the highest order, Peterson's solo playing is as compelling and propulsive as if he were backed by an ensemble including bass and drums. Often, an Oscar Peterson arrangement of a tune begins with a simple walking bass in the left hand, and proceeds to more complex accompaniments.

Another excerpt of "The Twelve Days of Christmas," this time with chords in the left-hand accompaniment.

Key Thought
Chapter 15 describes chords in detail and offers exercises for learning them.

Music Speak
Chords are clusters of notes played simultaneously. Most chords create a pleasing harmonic effect, but strictly speaking, a chord can be any group of notes, regardless of how awful it sounds.

Music Speak
Broken chords are chords whose notes are played one at a time. A left-hand accompaniment style popular in classical music from the eighteenth and nineteenth centuries, broken chords were used extensively by Mozart and Beethoven.

Chord accompaniments can be altered by playing the notes of chords individually instead of as a simultaneous group. Such an accompaniment is called *broken chords*, and comes in a few varieties. In other words, the notes of the chords may be played in a variety of orders: top to bottom; bottom to top; or all mixed up in any number of ways.

The next example shows a few ways that broken chords derive from regular chords. The beauty of broken chords is that they add a rhythmic element in addition to harmony.

Besides broken chords, another way to play chords is to ripple the notes upward in quick succession, which is called an *arpeggio*. ("Arpeggio" is an Italian term, derived from the Latin word for "ripply thing.") Strictly speaking, arpeggios can ripple either upward or downward, but they usually go from the lowest note to the highest.

The next figure illustrates what an arpeggio looks like in music notation: the wiggly line tells you to play the chord as a very quick, almost simultaneous succession of notes. There is no hard-and-fast rule about how quickly the arpeggio is played; the speed, force, and character of the arpeggio depends on the mood of the piece.

Repeated chords are the most common style of left-hand accompaniment. The pop music of the fifties featured such chords hammered out through a song, and the music of subsequent decades is only marginally more sophisticated. The typical style for a piano-playing pop star is to pound out chords while singing a song, with very few melodies issuing from the piano.

Chordal accompaniment is a big part of jazz, like pop, but jazz chords are much more sophisticated, usually use more notes, and describe complex, sometimes challenging harmonies. The master of modern jazz harmony and chord-playing was Bill Evans, a sensitive, introverted, thoughtful musician who helped define what is called the modern jazz harmonic vocabulary. That's a fancy way of saying he invented many of the chords used by jazz pianists for the past forty years. When playing a Bill Evans recording, listen to the quiet chords underneath the right-hand melody.

Chords turn into broken chords when you play the notes individually.

An arpeggio is a chord played with a rippling effect, indicated with a ripply line before it. The chord is played very quickly from the bottom note to the top.

Striding Along

There's a certain kind of left-hand accompaniment style that is a little difficult to play, but sounds great. The style is called *stride*, and there's nothing like it. Stride playing fits better on a piano than on a small electric keyboard, because the left-hand style requires a large range. The stride style is characterized by the left hand bouncing back and forth between bass notes low on the keyboard and chords at least an octave higher.

The effect of stride is rollicking and jazzy, and is the characteristic left-hand part of ragtime piano pieces. Variations of the simple note-to-chord style of traditional stride involve substituting an octave or a chord for the low note. The following figure shows a stride left-hand part for the ragtime piece "The Entertainer."

Grace Notes
Broken chords have been around, as a piano composer's device, for centuries. Mozart used broken chords constantly in his piano sonatas, as did all his composer buddies. Broken chords became a bit more complex in the early nineteenth century with Beethoven and his frat brothers. Then, later in the century, the so-called *Romantic* composers (Chopin, Brahms, Liszt, Schumann, and other members of the Legendary Composers Lodge) used extravagant broken chords that forced the left hand to sweep up and down the lower half of the piano range. Broken chords are predominantly a feature of classical music, but are sometimes found in arrangements of popular music.

Music Speak

Arpeggios are chords played by rippling the notes quickly from bottom to top.

Grace Notes

Arpeggios were often improvised by keyboard players in the Baroque period of the late seventeenth and early eighteenth centuries. In those days, rippling a written chord up or down was an accepted means of adding flair to a piece's performance, whether or not the composer indicated an arpeggio. Later, composers became more strict in their notations, and arpeggios were written out explicitly in piano scores.

Music Speak

Stride is a style of piano playing in which the left hand bounces between bass notes and chords. Stride is used in various types of jazz playing, but was made popular by ragtime.

Ragtime is probably the most popular example of the *stride* style of piano playing. Listen to any recording of Scott Joplin to hear that bouncing left hand—but make sure you get a piano recording, and not one of the many arrangements for orchestra. In a more modern vein, check out the piano stylings of Dave McKenna, a contemporary legend with the best stride left hand in the business.

Using Keyboard Auto-Accompaniments

If you have a home keyboard, as opposed to a digital piano or professional synthesizer, chances are it sports some kind of automated accompaniment with buttons for setting the accompaniment style, tempo, and harmonies.

Basically, auto-accompaniment consists of three aspects:

➤ **Style.** Many keyboards let you choose from many music styles such as swing jazz, various rock beats, waltz, bossa nova, country song, and other musical genres. The styles are defined by rhythms, and when you select a style you hear a rhythm section playing the background parts for that genre. Usually, no notes or harmonies are present in the style: you add them yourself.

➤ **Tempo.** The speed at which the style selection plays is sometimes variable. Ideally, you have some kind of slider or dial that lets you speed up or slow down the style as it's playing. Alternatively, and not nearly as flexibly, the styles themselves are defined by speed, such as "slow rock ballad," "medium rock song," and "fast rock."

➤ **Harmony.** The chords of the accompaniment are selected with your left hand in one of two ways. The first way is, quite simply, to play the chords. As you play them, a bass sound begins playing in the auto-accompaniment, providing a stylish bass line playing the harmonies you define with your chords. In addition, the harmonies are filled in with other instruments like guitar.

The second way is called the *one-finger* or *single-finger* method, and is easier to play but less precise. You just play single notes with your left hand, and the keyboard makes certain assumptions, such as whether the chord you want is a major chord or a minor chord. Every keyboard has its own "intelligence" in the selection of harmonies from the single-finger method, but in most cases major chords are the assumed selection. If you want more sophisticated harmonies, you must switch out of single-finger mode and play actual chords.

Stride playing, as in the left-hand part of this simplified version of "The Entertainer," is typical of ragtime pieces, but is also used in other jazz and pop songs.

Practice Session

If you're working with this book from start to finish—well, first of all, congratulations on your stamina. Second, you should know that Chapter 15 gives you a lot of information about chords that helps you use the auto-accompaiment features of your keyboard. But nothing illustrates like an example, so an example is what you're getting, right here in this chapter. The following figure is one way to play a standard jazz waltz tune using auto-accompaniment. I've written out an arrangement of "My Favorite Things," including left-hand notes for activating the harmonies in the keyboard style. Here's how to go about playing this piece:

Playing the left-hand notes with the "full-fingered" or "chord" setting of your keyboard's auto-accompaniment feature results in correct harmonies for the "My Favorite Things."

1. First, select the *waltz* or *jazz waltz* style from among your keyboard's auto-accompaniment rhythms.

2. Go through the left-hand part, finding the notes. If the keyboard's rhythm style begins playing when you press a key, it means the auto-play feature is turned on; you might want to turn it off while practicing.

3. Now practice the right-hand part. Become fairly fluent with both hands individually before trying to put them together.

4. Play the piece as written, counting each measure in four. Become confident in play-ing both hands together before turning on the auto-accompaniment.

5. Now for the payoff. Get that auto-accompaniment going by pressing the *start* or *play* button. If your keyboard has an auto-start feature, use that—the auto-accompaniment should begin when you play the first note.

As with other exercises, it's better to play this piece slowly and surely, than quickly and unsteadily. If your auto-accompaniment has a tempo or metronome setting, crank it down until it's playing at a comfortable speed and you can play all the notes without falling behind the tempo. You can gradually increase the speed as you repeat the piece, at least un-til you get thoroughly sick of it.

The Least You Need to Know

➤ Accompaniments are subordinant music parts that provide rhythm and harmony for the melody, vocalist, or solo instrumental part.

➤ Walking bass is a jazz-style accompaniment that mimics an upright bass part.

➤ Chords are the most common type of pianistic, left-hand accompaniment. Chords may be altered into arpeggios, which are rippled chords, and into broken chords, which play the chord's notes individually.

➤ Electronic keyboards have auto-accompaniment features that provide chords and rhythms while you play the melody.

Key Thought
DISCLAIMER: Every keyboard brand and model is different, and I can't attempt to describe exactly the features of them all. But, different as the various keyboards are, they have similar characteristics.

Striking a Familiar Chord

In This Chapter

➤ What are chords?

➤ All about intervals, and why you need to know

➤ Learning what triads are, and how to make them

➤ A review of common chords

I've devoted an entire chapter to chords for two reasons. First, because the International Society of Chord Terrorism told me I had to. Second, and perhaps more important, because chords teach you a lot about harmony and keys.

Chords are the next step beyond scales in musical understanding. Every genre of music uses chords. The most popular contemporary styles—rock, pop, and modern jazz—often notate music using chord marking instead of written-out left-hand parts.

Come to think of it, there are lots of reasons to concentrate on chords and get familiar with how they work. This is one of the most important chapters in the book, and is brought to you by our friends in the ISCT.

A Basic Chord Explanation

A chord is simply a group of notes played together. Following are some basic facts about chords:

➤ The notes could be spread across the whole range of the keyboard, but typically are close enough together to be played with one hand. (Sometimes two-handed chords are called for, in which each hand plays a chord at the same time.)

➤ A chord may have as few as two notes, but three-note and four-note chord are the most common. Two-note chords are called *intervals*.

➤ Any combination of notes may combine into a chord, but the purpose of chords is to create a harmonious blend of notes. Accordingly, like chords strummed on a guitar, keyboard chords come in standard combinations of notes that fulfill specific harmonic functions, and define the piece's harmony.

➤ Chords are often used by the left hand to accompany the right-hand melody.

The next figure illustrates what chords look like when notated.

Chords come in all shapes and sizes.

Practice Session

The best way to familiarize yourself with chords is to begin playing them, without regard to their harmonic function. In other words, just get the feeling of chords under your fingers on the keyboard. When you play a chord, it feels almost like grabbing a cluster of notes in your hand. When you get the hang of it, playing chords can feel very satisfying, and sound good, too.

Try playing the two-note chords (intervals) in the figure below. Start by finding each note of the chord independantly, then putting them together. Play each interval several times, until you're comfortable with it, then move on to the next.

Try playing these two-note chords, also called intervals.

I have deliberately written the above exercise without bar lines, because rhythm is totally unimportant. Don't bother counting—just practice one chord, then proceed to the next. Find fingerings that are comfortable for you, feeling free to experiment with different fingerings on each interval.

The next figure gives you some three-note chords to work with. As with the two-note intervals described above, don't give a thought to rhythm or counting. (There are no bar lines.) Find the individual notes first, then slowly put them together until you're playing all three at once.

Take your time finding these three-note chords. Keep your arm relaxed from fingers to shoulder, and use the fingerings provided.

The trick to playing chords is to keep your hand and wrist relaxed, but firmly in the position of the chord, so you can lift your hand and drop it down on the chord. It's a lot to ask for, I know! As always, practice is everything. In this exercise I've indicated good fingerings, and using the correct fingers helps keep your hand in a good position for lifting up and dropping down on the chord.

Some of the chords in the exercises included in this Practice Session require you to play black keys for the sharps and flats. When playing a black key and a white key simultaneously, move your whole hand toward the black keys, so that your entire arm moves closer to the base of the keys. Moving your hand like that is especially important when playing a black key with your thumb, the shortest finger. If you don't move your hand forward, you must twist your wrist to reach the black key with the thumb, and that twisting is not only bad form, but stressful to the tendons in your arm. When you shift your whole hand forward, your fingers can play the black keys at the ends of the keys, and your fingers are reaching the white keys in the middle of the key length.

Triads and Intervals

It's all well and good to play chords from an exercise illustration, but it's more important to understand how chords are created in the first place.

Learning about chords has two stages. First I'll show you the fundamentals of how chords are created in any key, based on any scale. Understanding the fundamentals gives you the tools to construct a chord in any situation, even if it takes a bit of time to work out the notes.

The second stage involves memory, as you become familiar with the basic chords used in most popular music, and no longer have to refer to scales or the chord-construction techniques you've learned. Knowing the chords automatically is the goal, of course, because when you're playing a piece there's no time to stop and figure out the chords—ideally, you know them so well that playing them is almost second nature.

Learning the Basic Triad

By far, the most common type of chord is the three-note chord, called a *triad*. Now, before you start thinking this is going to be too easy, let me notify you that not all three-note chords are called triads—just those whose notes are stacked up in a certain formation. Simply put, this is the formation of a triad: First note of a scale on the bottom, third note in the middle, and fifth note of the scale on top of the chord (see the next figure).

The C-major triad is formed by taking the first, third, and fifth notes of the C-major scale, and playing them together.

Triads are formed by taking notes from a scale, and playing them together. The spaces between the notes are called *intervals*. I've mentioned intervals in earlier parts of the book, but this is where you learn how they work, what the specific intervals are, how to find them on the keyboard, and how they fit into chords. (Whew! All that in one chapter? Yes, thanks to the miracle of modern technology. Or modern book publishing. Modern authorship? Oh, the heck with it—just keep reading.) Intervals and chords are closely related, and it's impossible to learn about one without covering the other.

Intervals of the C-Major Scale

An interval is really two notes, or, more precisely, the distance between two notes. By "distance" I don't mean physical distance on the keyboard, but pitch distance. Pitch distance is measured by the number of half steps between any two notes. You got acquainted with this concept in Chapter 11, and practiced constructing scales by counting half steps and whole steps on the keyboard. Finding intervals is pretty much the same. As with scales, it's best to start in the simplest way possible, which is to restrict yourself to the white keys of the keyboard.

The next figure reminds you of what a notated C-major scale looks like, with each note assigned a number in ascending order.

> **Music Speak**
> An **interval** is the distance between two notes. For example, the distance between C and G is a fifth (G is the fifth note of the C scale).

The C-major scale, with each of the ascending steps numbered.

Armed with this illustration, you can easily form and name intervals by using the bottom C as your bottom note. From C to D (the second note), for example, forms the interval of a *second*. (Intervals are named after ordinal numbers: *second*, *third*, *fourth*, and so on.)

> **Key Thought**
> It's called an octave instead of an eighth.

From C to the third note, E, is a third. C to F is a fourth. You get the picture—just go from the bottom C to any step of the scale, and the interval is defined by the number of the top step. What about C to the upper C? That's one interval you learned about as early as Chapter 5, called "The Keyboard in Black and White": the octave. The octave is the only interval not named after an ordinal number.

Now look at the figure below, to see the intervals of the C-major scale written in music notation.

The intervals of the C-major scale.

Intervals in Other Keys

Admittedly, finding intervals within the C-major scale, when the bottom note is C, is the easiest interval exercise in the world (maybe in the whole galaxy). Your mission is not completed until you can find intervals from *any* note on the keyboard. There are two ways to find an interval from any note:

➤ Construct a major scale from that note, as described in Chapter 11, "Unlocking Keys and Scales," then number its steps and find the intervals just as with the C-major scale.

> **Key Thought**
> When two parts are playing the exact same note, that also is considered an interval, even though there is *no* distance whatsoever between the two notes. The interval is called **unison**, and when two singers or two instrumentalists are singing or playing the same notes, they are said to be singing or playing *in unison*.

The process is exactly the same with all major scales, the only difference being that you end up using some black keys, because C major is the only major scale played on white keys only.

The next figure shows the major scale, and its intervals, for D major. Note that D major has a key signature of two sharps (F-sharp and C-sharp), so those two notes are used in the intervals as well as the scale.

The scale and intervals of D major, which uses two sharps.

➤ Count half steps. Counting half steps is how you find intervals without regard to keys, scales, and key signatures. Intervals are independant beings, and though they relate to keys and scales, they exist separately. It's important to be able to find them separately, and the only way to do that is by counting half steps between the two notes of the interval. Keep reading to see how it's done.

Different Types of Intervals

Counting half steps to find intervals reveals a very interesting fact: Intervals come in different types, just like scales and keys have major and minor modes. There are three main types of intervals:

➤ Major intervals

➤ Minor intervals

➤ Perfect intervals

I should mention that there are two other types of intervals, called *augmented* and *diminished* intervals, but they are part of advanced music theory, and you won't deal with them in this book. You must know about major and minor intervals because they are identified by differing numbers of half steps. I'll get to the half steps very shortly, but for now, please absorb these important facts about major and minor intervals:

➤ Major intervals are one half-step larger (more space between the two notes) than minor intervals. Naturally, minor intervals are one half-step smaller than major intervals.

> **Grace Notes**
> The Society for the Prevention of Interval Discrimination (SPID) has asked me to inform you that *perfect* intervals are really no better than major or minor intervals. The term *perfect* is just that—a musical term with no implication of superiority.

➤ You can turn a major interval into a minor interval by *subtracting* one half step from between the two notes. (Either raise the bottom note or lower the top note.) Conversely, you can turn a minor interval into a major interval by *adding* a half step between the two notes. (Either lower the bottom note or raise the top note.)

The next figure is an illustration of how major and minor intervals are related, and can be turned into each other. The process only works with intervals that can be major or minor intervals: seconds, thirds, sixths, and sevenths.

Major intervals turn into minor intervals by subtracting a half step between the notes, which can be done by lowering the top note or raising the bottom note. Minor intervals turn into major intervals in just the opposite way, but adding a half step between the two notes.

Other intervals (unisons, fourths, fifths, and octaves) are the so-called perfect intervals, and cannot be made major or minor. Take a look at the next illustration.

The perfect intervals—unisons, fourths, fifths, and octaves—can never be major or minor intervals.

Finding Intervals by Using Half Steps

Even knowing how to turn major and minor intervals into each other, the question remains how to find a major third, for example, or a minor sixth, starting from any note. To do that, you need to count half steps. The next table shows the number of half steps between every major and minor intervals in any octave.

Music Speak
A **major interval** consists of two half steps; a **minor interval**, one half step. Only seconds, thirds, sixths, and sevenths can be major or minor intervals. Unisons, fourths, fifths, and octaves are called **perfect intervals** because they cannot be major or minor.

Key Thought

Counting half steps to identify intervals may seem laborious, but after doing it for a while the ol' memory kicks in and you begin to recognize intervals (in their major and minor versions) just by seeing them in music notation or in their position on the keyboard. But for now, counting half steps is the best way to get started.

	Major	Minor	Perfect
Unison	—	—	0
Second	2	1	—
Third	4	3	—
Fourth	—	—	5
Fifth	—	—	7
Sixth	9	8	—
Seventh	11	10	—
Octave	—	—	12

Count up (or down) from any note by a specified number of half steps to find these intervals. Don't count the original note.

Practice Session

The next figure spells out the process of counting half steps to find intervals. Use the illustration to find the interval in each example. Start by finding the bottom note (generously spelled out for you by you-know-who), then count up the half step on the keyboard as indicated. When you find the interval, play both notes simultaneously.

Major, minor, and perfect intervals can be determined by counting half steps.

118

Now it's time to put you to work. In the next example, I've given you the bottom or top note of each interval, and it's up to you to find the other note. Make sure you do this exercise in front of your keyboard, and count the half steps with your finger on the keys. The direction you should count is indicated by the arrows, but for added fun, count in both directions from each note.

E + 7 half steps = ?   A-flat + 4 half steps = ?   C +5 half steps = ?

F-sharp + 2 half steps = ?   B-flat + 4 half steps = ?   F + 11 half steps = ?

Try finding the other note of each interval by counting half steps.

Major and Minor Triads

You've learned that major triads are created with the first, third, and fifth tones of any major scale. But when push comes to shove, it's actually a little cumbersome to figure out an entire scale just to find a triad.

Here's an easier way. Triads, being three-note chords, consist of two intervals, one on top of the other. Here's how major and minor triads are constructed through intervals:

➤ **Major triads.** The bottom interval is a major third, and the top interval is a minor third. That formula gets you a major triad every time, regardless of what note you start with on the bottom. Just count up four half steps from the bottom note (major third), then count three half steps from the new note (minor third), and you have the three notes of a major triad.

➤ **Minor triads.** Making a minor triad is just as easy as a major triad, but the intervals are reversed. Minor triads have a minor third on the bottom, and a major third on top. Pick a note, and count up three half steps to find the triad's middle note, then count four half steps from the middle note to get the top note.

The following shows what happens when you create both a major triad and a minor triad using middle C as the bottom note. You can turn a C-major triad into a C-minor triad by simply lowering the middle note. Conversely, it's no problem to alchemize the C-minor triad into a C-major triad by—you guessed it, Merlin—raising the middle note. Best of all, you can accomplish the major/minor transformation with any triad, just by altering the middle note.

Creating major and minor triads.

Practice Session

Time to practice those major/minor chord shifts that make life so fulfilling! The next illustration presents a few examples of triads, with instructions to change each major to minor, and each minor to major.

Alternate between major and minor triads by altering the middle note.

All you need to do is alter the middle note of each triad. Raise the middle to change minor to major, and lower the middle note to change major to minor. Play the triads on the keyboard, both before and after the change, using the fingerings I've written above each triad.

The Common Chords

Most of this chapter has been devoted to the *theory* of chords: how to construct them, and understanding the intervals that make up chords. All of that music theory stuff is valuable, but this section cuts to the chase by giving you the most common chords used in everyday sheet music. These are the chords you need to get your fingers on quickly when reading a pop music sheet. The chords you should practice are notated in the next illustration, one of the most important illustrations for learning chords.

Common chords used in different keys.

When studying the common chords, please keep these points in mind:

➤ Each sequence of chords is in a different key, with a different key signature. The chords of each example are the most common chords in that key. However, this is not to say that you don't see many other chords in pieces written in that particular key. These examples are not meant to be comprehensive—rather, they are a sort of first-aid kit to chords in the most common keys.

➤ I've included examples for several keys, but not all the keys. Most pop music is written in a few basic keys, but if you browse through sheet music you're bound to find many a song with a different key signature than you see in the illustration.

➤ The chord examples presented here only use three-note chords, but it's easy to notice that some of them look different from the triads shown earlier in this chapter. That's because it's sometimes easier to play chords when the notes are rearranged—for example, taking the bottom note and raising it an octave, putting it on the top of the chord. Such rearrangements of the order in which chord notes are stacked are called *inversions*.

Music Speak
Inversions are different varieties of the same chord, with the notes stacked in different orders.

➤ The chord examples are meant to be played! Don't just look at those chords: Get your hands involved. I've written the examples for the left hand, as that is the hand that usually plays chord accompaniments. Take your time figuring out the notes, and take this tip: Observe how the notes move from one chord to the next.

In the first example, moving from the first chord to the second, the bottom note stays the same, while the middle and top notes each move up. Noticing how the individual notes move makes it a lot easier to find the next chord on the keyboard.

➤ Remember to look at the key signatures! The examples are written just as they would be in sheet music (except there are no bar lines), without reminders of the sharps and flats written as accidentals. The exception to the no-accidental policy is in the minor keys, where some chords must be altered in order to sound harmonically correct.

➤ When the mode (major or minor) is not indicated, major is assumed. (Major is usually the default mode in sheet music.) Minor chords are indicated with a lower-case "m" after the chord name, as in *Em* for E-minor.

Key Thought
The inversions that I've presented here are not the only way to play the inverted chords; in fact, throughout the figure you can find the same chords inverted different ways. You can rearrange the notes any way you please. Whole books have been written about how to construct chord inversions that sound great and are easy to play, but I'm determined that this book should weigh less than fifty pounds. I've given you good inversions for these examples, but feel free to experiment with how the notes are stacked.

The Least You Need to Know

➤ Chords are groups of notes played simultaneously.

➤ Intervals are the distances (number of half steps) between pairs of notes. There are major and minor intervals, as well as *perfect* intervals.

➤ Triads are made by stacking one interval on top of another. Major triads have a minor third on top of a major third. Minor triads have a major third on top of a minor third.

Part 4
Master Class

Playing the piano is such a large topic, I could write a book about it. Oh, wait—this is a book. Well, thank goodness there's room for the chapters in this part, which take you beyond the elementary basics into some of the fun, and slightly more advanced, techniques and knowledge of music and keyboards. In Chapter 16, you'll learn about the details of music notation, for example—the marks, squiggles, and strange abbreviations found on almost all sheet music. Chapter 17 gives you a complete tutorial in using the pedals, including the all-important sustain pedal, which requires a certain technique to use well. (Yes, I provide Practice Sessions for the pedals.)

You may not realize it yet, but practicing is almost as much of an art as performing. In Chapters 18 and 19, I share all kinds of power practicing tips in this part, as well as secrets of playing tunes from "fake books," and improvising left-hand arrangements of songs. When you get in a listening mood, check out Chapters 20 and 21 of recommendations of great piano composers and pieces. And, when you feel like you're at the end of your rope, you can find some great motivational tips and techniques in Chapter 22. Finally, in Chapter 23, I touch on digital music tools, home studios, how computers fit into the scene, and even how to avoid music boredom.

Details of Music Notation

In This Chapter

➤ Introducing sixteenth notes

➤ Tying notes together

➤ Tricky triplets

➤ Getting the hang of repeat signs

➤ Crescendos, decrescendos, and other expression markings

➤ A basic glossary of Italian words found in classical sheet music

Earlier parts of this book deliver the goods about basic music notation. Notes, the staff, rests—they're all covered earlier (in a prose style brilliant enough to awaken slumbering Nobel jurors.) But in fact there is quite a bit more to music notation than the fundamentals—details that may seem inconsequential when you're learning about them, but which are commonplace on the printed music page. Knowing about them really helps turn the circles, lines, and spaces into music.

This chapter gives you all the information you need to understand fairly advanced music notation, as used in classical piano music, jazz, and non-EZ arrangements of popular songs.

Note Groupings and Ties

In Part 2, I introduced note values from very long (whole notes, equal to four beats) to the relatively quick (eighth notes, equal to a half beat). I also described the principle of dotting notes to add half their value. Presumably you've become fairly familiar with all those types of notes, but if you need a refresher course, please review Chapter 9, "Whole Notes and Their Offspring," before diving into this section. Here, I introduce note values less than an eighth note; notes that are tied together; and groupings of notes such as triplets.

Roadrunner Notes

The speed with which a sequence of notes plays is determined by two things: the tempo of the piece, and the value of the notes. Notes with small values, like eighth notes and quarter notes, move along at a speedier clip than notes with large values, like half notes and whole notes. However, everything gets played more slowly in a rock ballad, for example, than in a fast, foot-stomping ragtime number. The quarter notes of a slow piece my end up going by more slowly than the half notes of a fast piece, even though quarter notes have half the value of half notes.

As the heading of this section implies, I'm about to introduce note values that get played very quickly, but only when the tempo allows it. We're going deep into fractions now, dividing eighth notes (worth a half beat each) into pieces.

The following figure shows just how fine we're getting with note values, starting from a single whole note, worth four beats, to a type of note you haven't seen yet: the sixteenth note. Sixteenth notes, being worth half the time rhythmic value of eighth notes, are counted with one quarter beat each.

1 per 4/4 measure		Whole note = 4 beats
2 per 4/4 measure		Half note = 2 beats
4 per 4/4 measure		Quarter note = 1 beat
8 per 4/4 measure		Eighth note = 1/2 beat
16 per 4/4 measure		Sixteenth note: 1/4 beat

The basic note values, from whole notes through sixteenth notes.

Sixteenth notes, like eighth notes, may appear two ways on the music staff. When separated from surrounding notes, they appear with a stem that has a flag on the end—except that sixteenth notes have two flags. When several eighth or sixteenth notes are connected, they appear with horizontal bars linking their stems—and in that case, sixteenth notes have a double horizontal bar.

Now that you know whole notes, half notes, quarter notes, eighth notes, and sixteenth notes, the question naturally arises how far you can go cutting note values in half and arriving at a new type of note. The answer, in theory, is that there's no limit. I have seen 256th-notes on classical sheet music for the piano. Practically speaking, though, sixteenth

Eighth notes and sixteenth notes may appear two different ways on the music staff.

notes represent the limit in normal music notation. You may occasionally see thirty-second notes, which have three flags when separated and a triple horizontal bar when connected. Thirty-second notes appear primarily in classical piano music, which seems to delight in confounding the natural limits of human tolerance for tiny notes. In most keyboard arrangements of popular music, jazz, and classical, sixteenth notes represent the small end of note values.

Tying Notes Together

The rules of written music sometimes get in their own way. For example, when a piece is in 4/4 time, every measure must contain exactly four beats, filled with either notes or rests. But what if a note, played on the fourth beat of the measure, lasts for more than one beat? In that case, the note doesn't end when the measure does, so how does it appear on the staff?

To solve that dilemma, as well as other fascinating challenges in music notation, a feature called a *tie* comes to the rescue. The tie is a graceful mark drawn between two notes whose values are added together. The tie may be drawn across a bar line, or reside within the measure. The effect is that when you see two notes tied together, you play only the first note, but hold it for the rhythmic value of both notes. Here are a few examples of ties.

Here are a few things to remember about tied notes:

➤ Ties are mostly used across bar lines to extend the duration of the last note of a measure into the next measure.

➤ Ties are also used within a single measure to add the note values of notes that couldn't be written as a single note.

➤ In some cases, ties are used when not absolutely necessary, as in tying together two quarter notes instead of writing a half note. Ties are used this way to make the piece's notation easier to read for one reason or another. Sometimes tying two notes makes it clearer how the note is held against whatever is happening in the other hand.

> **Music Speak**
> **Sixteenth notes** have half the time value of eighth-notes, or a quarter of a beat. They are indicated by a stem with two flags on the end.

> **Music Speak**
> **Tied notes** are connected by a curved line, indicating that the time value of the two notes is added together. You only play the first note, but hold it for the duration of both notes.

> **Grace Notes**
> There is no limit to how many notes can be tied. In all cases, no matter how many notes are tied, only the first note actually gets played, but it is held for the duration of all the tied notes.

Ties add together the note values of two (or more) notes. You play only the first note, but hold it for the duration of both (or all) tied notes.

Practice Session

Understanding how ties work in theory is fine, but you need to practice them so you don't get thrown off when you see a tied note on sheet music. Actually, that's just my excuse—my real purpose is to torment you with further exercises. But these practice pieces are useful, I promise.

The following example is another piece destined for induction in the Boring Music Hall of Shame. I want to start you off with an exercise that doesn't complicate matters by making you search for notes. The point here is to count accurately, and play the tied notes correctly.

Play the right hand and left hand separately, as they are two exercises. Count slowly and evenly.

The above exercise is for separate hands; the time signature is an easy 4/4; and the key signature is an equally easy no sharps or flats. Remember to count in groups of four beats, and to start slowly and evenly. After playing the right-hand piece several times, try the left-hand piece. The two pieces are not meant to be played together.

The next exercise raises the stakes by putting both hands in action at once. Start by learning the right hand, then get familiar with the left-hand part. When you can play each hand comfortably and without faltering, try putting them together slowly. Evenness is more important than speed. If this piece moves you to sentimental tears, you obviously don't listen to enough music.

Try each hand separately first, then put them together.

The next one is actually a pretty piece of music, but I can't take credit for it unless I was Frédéric Chopin in a previous life. The exercise is an adaptation of a piano piece by Chopin, and gives you a good workout in tying right-hand notes. I've kept the left-hand part simple to let you focus on the job at hand, which is counting the right hand correctly. Practice the right hand first, and repeat it several times, counting carefully, until you're comfortable with it. Work out the two hands together, first without counting, then in the correct rhythm.

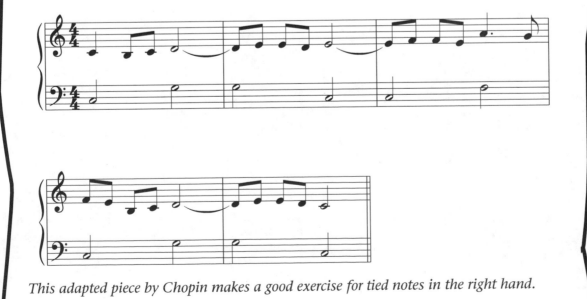

This adapted piece by Chopin makes a good exercise for tied notes in the right hand.

Triplets

I'm not talking about babies here, although if you have the squirming variety, congratulations. The *triplets* I'm referring to are clusters of notes grouped in threes, that create a peculiar rhythm. Triplets are usually formed from quarter notes or eighth notes, but are sometimes sixteenth notes, and in theory can be *any* type of note. A triplet is market on sheet music in a pretty obvious way; with a numeral 3 above or underneath the cluster of three notes. Here's some examples.

Triplets are groups of three notes, marked with a numeral 3. A triplet's note value is equal to two of the three notes.

Music Speak

A **triplet** is a group of three notes grouped into a certain rhythm. Quarter-note triplets are played in the time value of a single half note, and eighth-note triplets are played in the same number of beats as a quarter note.

Key Thought

I can't beat around the bush about one crucial fact: counting triplets is difficult. It's something you have to get a *feel* for. Triplets are played perfectly evenly through the whole triplet. The result is a syncopated rhythm that seems to go against the rhythm of the piece, and yet fits into it. Triplets are definitely cool-sounding, but it takes practice to play them effectively.

What makes triplets special, and tricky, is their note value. One triplet is equal to two of the three notes in the triplet. Therefore, an eighth-note triplet is equal to two eighth notes, or one beat. (A single eighth note is worth a half beat.) A quarter-note triplet is equal to two quarter notes, or two beats. (A single quarter note is worth one beat.) The illustration below clarifies the rhythmic value of triplets.

The rhythmic value of triplets.

Practice Session

The only way to learn triplets is to play them. The first figure below is a very basic exercise, but helpful if you really learn it well. I've provided the counting points in the illustration, to help you count through the triplets. The two parts of the exercise show you the rhythmic difference between quarter-note triplets and eighth-note triplets. (The eighth-note triplets are twice as fast, so you can fit twice as many into a measure.)

A simple exercise for playing quarter-note and eighth-note triplets.

Ready for another exercise? The next figure mixes quarter-note and eighth-note triplets for a truly frustrating—I mean, a highly educational—experience. Play slowly, because the eighth-note triplets go by pretty quickly if your tempo is too fast. Count a *slow* four before you start, then proceed with the piece. I've indicated the timing of the counts to help you cope with the triplets.

Play this exercise slowly, as it mixes fast eighth-note triplets with slower quarter-note triplets.

Play It Again

Imagine if you were composing a piece of music—a popular song, for example (at least you hope it will be popular). As with most pop songs, repetition is crucial to the catchiness of your masterpiece. Verses and choruses both must repeat several times to drive home the sublime musical meaning.

But how tedious it is to notate the same portions of the song over and over again! Fortunately, composers through the ages have been there before you, and a solution is in place. Music notation has something called a *repeat sign* that indicates when a portion of a piece should be repeated. Here's what a repeat sign looks like.

The special bar line at the end of the staff, with the odd dots on each staff, is a repeat sign. When you reach a repeat sign, return to the beginning of the piece and play it again.

Music Speak

Repeat signs bracket portions of a piece that should be repeated. Repeat signs make music notation more compact, especially in pop music, since the repeated portion doesn't have to be written out a second or third time.

Grace Notes

Repeat signs save time and paper by telling you what parts of a piece to play over again. The reiterated portions can be as short as a single measure (though that is very rare) or as long as the entire piece, which is likewise rare in popular music. Repeating an entire piece is not too uncommon in classical music, though, demonstrating without question that the great masters of the past were just lazy bums.

Repeat signs work very simply. When you run into one as you're playing a piece, bounce right back to the beginning and start again. That is, unless you've passed a *reversed* repeat sign on your way through the piece. The following piece shows what a reversed repeat sign looks like. It indicates the place at which you start over when you reach the normal repeat sign. In other words, the portion of the piece between the two repeat signs—first the reversed sign, then the normal repeat sign—is the portion of the piece that gets repeated.

Did you notice something else about the previous piece? Around the repeat sign, the measures are delineated and marked 1 and 2. Those numbers stand for *first ending* and *second ending*, and indicate which measure is played when you repeat the portion. Here's how the musical example of the previous piece works:

1. Play the first ending when you first play through to the repeat sign

2. Go back to the reverse repeat sign and replay the four-bar portion of the piece.

3. This time, as you approach the repeat sign, you skip the first ending entirely (don't play that measure) and play the second ending instead.

Repeat signs and multiple endings are very common in popular sheet music. In fact, I hesitate to break the news, but I must: there are even third endings. Many pop songs have verses or choruses that repeat three times, so it makes sense that the music notation would indicate that repetition somehow. The example below illustrates how third endings work. In most cases, you play the same measure for the first and second ending, then you play the third ending on your last time through the repeated portion.

In this example, you would replay the portion between the repeat signs, playing the measure marked 1 the first time through, and replacing it with the measure marked 2 the second time through.

First, second, and third endings.

Expression Markings

Music is subtle; notation is cut-and-dried. Music is flexible; notation is rigid. Music is horizontal; notation is vertical. Expression marks help bring the life of music into the dry notes and bars of music notation. Expression marks indicate when to get louder and softer; when to play faster or slower; when to pause; when to play smoothly or sharply; and, in the case of classical sheet music, when to dig out an Italian dictionary to see what the heck those strange words mean.

Dynamic Markings

In music, *dynamics* refers to volume—in other words, how loudly or softly to play. The dynamic range of a piece is indicated in the sheet music by abbreviations of Italian words, even in modern popular music. (Some arrangements of pop music forego the traditional Italian for plain English.) The following table illustrates the dynamic indicators used in music notation, the full Italian words they stand for, and what they mean.

Dynamic markings in music notation

What you see	What it stands for	What it means
pp	*pianissimo*	Very soft
p	*piano*	Soft
mp	*mezzo piano*	Medium soft
mf	*mezzo forte*	Medium loud
f	*forte*	Loud
ff	*fortissimo*	Very loud

These dynamic markings are used to generally indicate the volume of a section of a piece. When it comes to dynamic fluctuations within sections, from one measure to the next, other indications come into play. Called *crescendos* (get louder) and *decrescendos* (get softer), these two important expression markings are illustrated in the following figure, using their abbreviated forms.

In addition to *cresc* and *decresc*, the same indications can be given with symbols. You usually see the symbols when the composer (or arranger) wants to indicate a precisely timed crescendo or decrescendo, since the symbols can be stretched as long, or compressed as short, as needed. The spelled-out abbreviations, on the other hand, are more general indications that the piece should get louder or softer, without telling you exactly when the dynamic destination is reached.

Crescendos and decrescendos tell you when to play louder or softer.

Crescendos and decrescendos may be indicated by symbols that define how gradually you should increase or decrease your playing volume

Pass the Dictionary

At the beginning of most pieces is some indication of the tempo and spirit with which the piece should be played. In classical music, traditional Italian expressions are used, whereas in twentieth-century pop music and jazz English expressions are used. You don't need any help from me interpreting an English expression like "Slowly" or "With bounce." But the Italian words used in the classics need some translating. Here are many of the most common tempo markings and what they mean.

Music Speak
The **crescendo** sign indicates that you should play gradually louder; the **decrescendo** sign indicates to gradually play softer.

Italian tempo markings in classical piano music

What you see	What it means
Lento	Very slowly
Andante	Moderately slowly
Allegro	Happily
Allegretto	Lightly; not as fast as *Allegro*
Presto	Quickly
Vivace	Very quickly
Dolce	Sweetly
. . . ma non troppo	. . . but not too (slowly, quickly, or whatever)

Music Speak
Metronomes are mechanical devices that audibly tick the beats of a piece, and can be set for a certain number of beats per minute.

As you can see, Italian tempo markings indicate attitude as well as sheer speed or slowness. In classical music, interpretation of the written music is important, and conveying the spirit of the music is more important than adhering slavishly to a certain tempo indication.

Some composers (and many editors of classical music collections) enhance the Italian tempo markings with specific metronome settings to indicate exactly how fast the piece should be played. When you see such an indication at the start of a piano piece, if you have a metronome you may set it at the required point and even practice the piece with the metronome on to keep the tempo.

Miscellaneous Expression Markings

Music notation is filled with expression markings that attempt to bring life to the notes. In addition to dynamic markings and tempo indications, symbols above, below, and around the notes indicate subtleties in the performance of the piece.

Slurs (But Not Insults)

Probably the most common expression marking in music notation, the *slur* is a sweeping, graceful indicator that helps you phrase the notes of a piece musically and smoothly. (Slurs are also called *phrase marks*.) Whether you're looking at classical or popular sheet music, if the playing level is at least intermediate, slurs are all over the page.

Music Speak
Phrase marks, or slurs, indicate when groups of notes should be played without any breaks between the notes. The effect of a slurred phrase is smooth and seamless.

Slurs indicate unbroken musical phrases. By "unbroken," I mean that the notes within a slur should be played very smoothly, with each note lasting exactly until the next note is played. You shouldn't let little spaces of silence intrude between the notes within a slur.

Here's what slurs look like. Phrase marks can apply to both left-hand and right-hand parts, but usually appear over single-note lines, as opposed to chords.

When interpreting these phrase marks, imagine that you're a singer (unless you really are a singer, in which case no imagination is necessary). Singers need to take a breath every so often during a song, and the notes that are sung before taking a breath are all part of the same musical phrase. Keyboard music can be thought of in the same way, as a series of phrases.

Play the notes within the slurs in a smooth, unbroken manner.

Slurs, or phrase marks, indicate where the unbroken phrases are. As you play melody parts shown with slurs, imagine singing them (or actually sing along while you play), and don't take a breath (or break the phrasing of your playing) until the end of a phrase mark.

> **Music Speak**
> **Legato** means smooth playing, without undue breaks between notes.

Legato and Staccato

Another word for playing smoothly is *legato*. Yes, another Italian word. Playing phrase marks well is called *playing legato*. In fact, the word itself is used sometimes in classical sheet music to indicate a generally smooth approach to a piece or a passage within the piece. There may also be phrase marks in a legato piece (or passage), even though the overriding instruction is to play smoothly.

The opposite of legato is *staccato*, and there's an indication for that, too. Staccato notes are shown with little dots underneath or above them. When you see those dots, make an effort to play the opposite of an unbroken, smooth, legato style. Play each note shortly, letting your finger bounce off the key as soon as you play it.

> **Music Speak**
> **Staccato** means sharp, detached playing, with breaks between the notes.

Staccato notes are indicated by dots above or below the note, and are played detachedly, each note separated from the notes around it.

The Least You Need to Know

➤ Sixteenth notes are worth one quarter beat, and get played twice as rapidly as eighth notes in the same piece.

➤ When two or more notes are tied together, even across a bar line, only the first note is played. But it is held for the counting value of all the tied notes combined.

➤ Triplets are groups of three notes indicated by the numeral 3. A quarter note triplet has a time value of two beats, and an eighth note triplet has a time value of one beat.

➤ Repeat signs tell you which portions of a piece to repeat, without writing that portion a second time.

➤ Crescendos tell you to gradually play more loudly, and decrescendos indicate gradually softer playing.

Chapter 17

Pedals: Where's the Clutch?

In This Chapter

➤ Understanding the three pedals of a piano

➤ Plugging in and using the sustain pedal of an electronic keyboard

➤ Practicing with the sustain pedal

➤ How pedal markings are notated in sheet music

You play the piano with your hands, right? Well, that's only partly true. Sure, you make the notes play with your fingers, but a big part of any pianist's sound comes from the feet. Working the pedals is an important part of playing the piano, and even most home keyboards include one of the piano's three pedals.

Keyboard pedals came into being at around the time the piano was invented. Before the piano, early keyboards like the harpsichord (I'm talking about centuries ago) didn't have pedals—they were hands-only instruments.

The piano changed everything. The earliest pianos, though not as powerful-sounding as modern pianos, nevertheless had a much more sustaining sound than harpsichords or clavichords. Pedals were added to the piano to take advantage of its sustaining power.

Pianos have three pedals, which I briefly describe in Chapter 3, "The Anatomy of a Piano." Most electronic keyboards only have one pedal, which works like the right hand piano pedal, and is the most important pedal. (Digital pianos often have two pedals, and occasionally three.) This chapter is devoted mostly to learning how to use that most important pedal, which is called the *sustain pedal*.

Plugging in the Pedal

Pianos are big, totally integrated mechanisms with the pedals built right into the machine, as it were. Actually, the piano's pedal mechanism *can* be disassembled and removed, but when you buy a piano it comes to your home either with the pedals attached or with a helpful technician who'll put the darn things on for you. It's not an operation to be attempted by someone without experience in piano maintenance.

Digital pianos sometimes create more of a headache than their acoustic counterparts. The pedal mechanisms of digital pianos usually come packaged separately, and the appearance of a solicitous technician is entirely dependant on the generosity of the store from which you bought the instrument—and, in most cases, extremely unlikely. If you are stuck with putting together your new digital piano's pedal assembly on your own, I wish you good luck, the grace of the electronic instrument god, and long-suffering patience. The only thing that may prevent you from throwing your new digital piano out the window in frustration is that it's too heavy.

Home keyboard owners have it easy. Their instruments may not sound as much like a real piano as a digital piano does, but at least attaching the pedal is a breeze. The first thing you must do is find it. The pedals of small keyboards are themselves rather on the small side, so you might have to rummage through the box for a while. The pedal has a longish cord attached to it, with a plug at the end. The pedal itself is usually a small, black device with a rubber bottom that's placed on the floor under the keyboard. Home keyboard pedals are not attached to the main instrument with a wood or plastic construction—it's just a dangling cord connecting the pedal to the keyboard.

Once you find the keyboard pedal, simply place it on the floor where your right foot naturally falls when you sit at the keyboard. The part of the pedal that depresses should face your seat. Then plug the cord into the back of the keyboard, into the jack marked *pedal*.

Some keyboard pedals suffer from their small size and light weight, skittering easily across the floor as they are used, requiring facility with a modern keyboard skill of retrieving the pedal with your feet while you play. With practice, you can get so orthopedically dextrous that nobody will notice you swiftly pulling the pedal back in its place as you play your tunes. I have found a couple of tricks useful:

➤ Wrap the pedal chord around something so that there is very little slack. In other words, keep the pedal on a short leash. If the keyboard is resting on a table, use one of the table legs; if the keyboard is on a keyboard stand, use whatever part of the stand is handy to wrap the cord.

➤ Place something heavy on the floor behind the pedal, as a roadblock. If you've placed the keyboard against a wall, that's ideal. If the keyboard is against open space, you must decide whether you want a possibly unsightly pedal-stop cluttering up your floor.

Trying Out the Pedal

The sustain pedal has a unique function: it holds your notes for you. You still must do most of the work playing, of course, but the sustain pedal makes it much easier than it would be otherwise. When you depress the sustain pedal, any notes you subsequently play, plus any notes you're holding down when you depress the pedal, continue sounding even if you lift your hands off the keyboard.

It's pretty convenient when you think about it, as it lets you sound as if you had more than ten fingers, or more than two hands. You can play a massive chord low on the keyboard, then move both hands to the upper range to play there, and the low chord is sustained as your hands take their new playing position.

The best way to get acquainted with the pedal is to simply try it randomly. I'll get to specific pedaling technique a bit later in this chapter. For now, just experiment. Sit comfortably at the piano; if you're using an electronic keyboard, the pedal should be under your right foot when your leg is bent at about a ninety-degree angle.

Play a note, and while still holding down the key, depress the pedal (that's the right-most pedal on the piano). Release the key, and thrill to the sustained sound of the note being held by the pedal. (It's all right if you're not exactly thrilled.) Play other notes with the pedal still down, lift your hands, then release the notes by lifing your foot from the pedal.

When working the pedal, it's important keep your right heel on the floor. Press the pedal by pushing down on it with the ball of your foot, and release it by pivoting up from your heel. It should take only a slight motion to press and release the pedal, though some piano pedals require more effort.

Practice sustaining random notes on the keyboard, concentrating on minimizing your foot motions when controlling the pedal. Efficiency is key, because you don't want to expend a lot of body movement on the pedal. There's no need to lift your foot *off* the pedal.

Piano players have an easier time of it when getting the feel of the pedal, because piano pedals offer more resistance and spring than keyboard pedals. Furthermore, piano pedals are higher off the floor, making it less tempting to lift the foot way off the pedal.

Pedal Technique

The purpose of the sustain pedal is to connect notes together for a smoother-sounding playing style. The purpose is not, as you may suspect from your first experiments, to create a cacophony of endlessly sustaining notes clashing with each other. Using the pedal effectively takes some practice, and practice is the goal of this section.

There are no universal, hard-and-fast rules about when to use the sustain pedal and when to lay off. To a large extent, using the pedal is a personal decision that has a big effect on your playing style. Sparse use of the pedal contributes to a dry, clear style, while a heavy foot creates more liquid-sounding music. Using the sustain pedal too much causes a muddy blur of notes, while using it too little results in musical discontinuity and ungraceful phrases. These pages show you a basic pedal technique that will stand you in good stead; from there you must use your own ears and musical taste.

Key Thought
It's possible to use the sustain pedal too much, the result being a muddy-sounding mess of notes blending into each other. The important thing to remember is to lift the pedal from time to time, clearing away the notes it was holding. How often should you lift the sustain pedal, and when should you press it down in the first place? The next section, Pedal Technique, gives you some rules and exercises.

Key Thought
You may, in time, develop a preference for a pedal position that stretches your leg out, but the easiest way to start is with the ninety-degree angle. Piano players and most digital piano players don't have a choice, because the pedal mechanisms are in a fixed position.

Key Thought
Piano pedals may seem *too* far off the floor, especially if you have small feet or if the piano lives on rollers that lift the whole instrument up. If the pedal forces your right foot into an uncomfortable position, simply place a book or some other object (pets are not recommended) under your heel.

Suggested pedaling is sometimes marked in piano notation, using two symbols you should be aware of. The first symbol is simply an abbreviation of pedal: *Ped.* It means: push the sustain pedal down! The second symbol is the pedal-off asterisk, which indicates releasing the sustain pedal. Both symbols are illustrated in the following figure.

The pedal-on and pedal-off notation symbols usually appear beneath the double staff, underneath the left-hand part, and more often in piano music than keyboard arrangements.

Pedal markings give suggestions of when to use the sustain pedal.

> **Grace Notes**
> Pedal notations sometimes consist of only the *Ped.* abbreviation, without any pedal-off asterisks. The missing asterisk doesn't mean that you should never lift the pedal up, however. It just means that you should *change the pedal*—an expression meaning lift the pedal quickly and depress it again—every time a *Ped.* notation occurs. Occasionally, the asterisk is used alone, without the *Ped.* abbreviation.

Pedal notations are fine, and helpful in giving a basic indication of when to pedal. In all cases, though, you must use your own taste in deciding when to sustain notes with your foot. In this section I want to introduce you to a basic pedaling technique that is useful on any type of keyboard or piano. There is one fundamental, most important trick to good pedaling:

➤ The crucial technique of good pedaling is holding the pedal down, sustaining a note, until just *after* you have played the note on which you're releasing the pedal.

In many cases you are holding the pedal through the playing of several notes, not just one. The point is to release the pedal a split second after playing a note.

Here are two alternating notes, too far away from each other on the keyboard to be played smoothly without using the pedal.

Play this pedaling exercise with just one hand. Then try it with the other hand.

Try the first part of the above example with the right hand. It doesn't matter which fingers you use—you can even use a single finger for both notes. Don't worry about counting, either, as this is strictly a pedaling exercise. The lower note is middle C, and the upper note is the second G above middle C. Play the first note and immediately depress the pedal. Lift your hand from the keyboard and play the upper note. The moment you play the G, lift the pedal and depress it again in a quick up/down motion. Lift your hand and go back down to middle C, once again using the quick up/down of the pedal the moment you play the note.

Continue in this fashion several times until you're comfortable using the pedal this way. Whever you're ready, proceed to the second part of the exercise, which is for the left hand. Use the pedal in exactly the same way. The upper note in the left-hand exercise is middle C, and the lower note is the second F below middle C.

> **Key Thought**
> Waiting until just after playing a note is tricky, because the natural impulse is to release the pedal just *before* playing the a note. But releasing the pedal just before playing the next note introduces a small moment of silence between the two notes, giving the music a choppy sound. Holding the pedal down until just after playing a note blurs the two notes together for an instant, but the effect is pleasing and smooth.

Practice Session

Time to exercise your new pedaling skill in a musical manner. The first illustration in this Practice Session is a little piece for the right hand that will in all likelihood resonate throughout musical history in its poignant beauty. Either that, or it is totally insignificant. Whichever is the case, your destiny is to learn it with the pedal markings I've provided.

I have used the *Ped.* abbreviation to indicate the quick up/down pedal motion I describe in this chapter. Because your foot is probaly not depressing the pedal before the first note, that particular marking obviously means just *down*. (The truth is, when playing the piano, I often depress the sustain pedal before playing a single note, in which case the first marking would be an up/down.) Likewise, the last pedal indication can mean just *up*.

The pedal marking of this right-hand exercise indicates a quick up/down pedaling motion.

When you get thoroughly sick of the above exercise—I mean, when you've mastered its subtle intricacies—move onto the next one.

This left-hand part, and its pedal markings, are typical of classical music pieces.

This exercise is also for pedaling technique, but should be played by the left hand. As with the previous exercise, the pedal markings indicate the quick up/down of the pedal. The left-hand part written in the above figure is typical of accompaniment parts written by Mozart and Beethoven in their easy-to-intermediate piano sonatas.

The final exercise of this Practice Session puts both hands together in the famous opening passage of a Mozart sonata for piano. (I've adapted it slightly to make the notes simpler to learn, because you have your hands full—or your feet full—getting the pedaling correct.)

A simplified excerpt of a Mozart sonata. Practice the pedalings while playing the left hand alone, then add the right-hand part.

Approach this exercise gradually and in parts. Try the right hand first, alone and without the pedals, just figuring out the notes. I've given you right-hand fingerings. Then move to the left-hand part, working out the notes without the pedal. The next step is to play the left hand alone *with* the pedal. Because the left hand has more notes, use it to learn the pedaling part. Finally, add the right hand melody. Go as slowly as you want, building up speed ever so gradually as you repeat the exercise. (Don't speed up while you're playing the piece.)

Using the sustain pedal on a piano has an added acoustic effect besides sustaining any notes you play. The pedal mechanism lifts the entire damping mechanism off the strings, which normally stops the strings of unplayed notes from vibrating when you play. All the strings of the piano are free to vibrate when you depress the sustain pedal, and many of them do, ever so slightly, when you play even a single note with the pedal down. The vibration of unstruck strings is called *sympathetic vibration*, and it adds a subtle but unmistakable richness and sonority to the instrument's sound.

> **Music Speak**
> **Sympathetic vibration** refers to unplayed strings vibrating "in sympathy" with one or more others that are played.

You can test this yourself by playing a single note with the pedal up, then playing it again with the pedal down. Alternate a few times to hear the difference.

Keyboards, on the other hand, don't have strings, and the pedal effect is much simpler. The sustain pedal on electric keyboards and digital pianos simply sustains notes that are played, without enhancing the sonic effect of the instrument as a whole. This phenomenon is one reason digital pianos cannot sound precisely like the real thing.

Using the Piano's Other Pedals

Most of this chapter discusses the sustain pedal, because that's the one pedal of the piano used by electronic keyboards. Cleary, it's the most important pedal, used by keyboard players in all styles and genres. But this section focuses on the two other pedals that lie underneath pianos.

The left-hand pedal is called the *soft pedal*, and does just what the name implies it should do: It makes the piano softer. Of course, you can make the piano softer with your hands by simply playing the keys less forcefully, but the pedal makes the piano sound like you've just thrown a blanket around the whole instrument. The tone changes, and the notes become less sharp, and slightly muffled.

> **Grace Notes**
> Most classical performers use the soft pedal very sparingly, if at all, because the change in tone is undesirable in most pieces. One musical genre in which the soft pedal attains importance is New Age piano music, in which "soft pedal artistry" places an emphasis on producing tonal shadings with the soft pedal down.

The degree of difference made by the soft pedal varies from one piano to another. With some instruments it's hardly noticeable, while in others the soft pedal makes a startling difference in tone and volume.

The middle pedal on grand pianos and some uprights is called the *sostenuto pedal*, and is similar to the sustain pedal, but with a crucial difference. The sostenuto pedal sustains notes, but *only* those notes whose keys are depressed when you push down the pedal. As those notes are continuing to sound, you can play the piano without other notes "sticking," and even use the sustain pedal normally. This feature lets you play a two-handed chord in one part of the piano range, then play other music above or below it while the chord sustains, without muddying the air with a discord of notes clashing against each other.

> **Music Speak**
> In classical piano music, very occasionally, you see a notation marking indicating use of the soft pedal. That marking is the phrase *una corda* (Italian for "one string") written into the music. By and large, though, players use the soft pedal whenever they desire the softest touch possible in a delicate musical passage.

The sostenuto pedal is not used very much, and some pianos don't have one. Smaller uprights with three pedals have a middle "practice" pedal that inserts a strip of felt between the hammers and the strings, muffling the sound of the piano drastically. It's great for apartment dwellers or anyone who's self-conscious about practicing loudly enough to be heard.

The Least You Need to Know

➤ Every piano has a sustain pedal (the right-hand pedal) and a soft pedal (on the left). In addition, some pianos have a middle sostenuto pedal. The sustain pedal is the most important, and it makes notes continue to sound after you've released the keys. The soft pedal makes the piano a bit softer and changes its tone. The sostenuto pedal sustains an initial note or group of notes, but then lets you play subsequent notes normally.

➤ Most electronic keyboards come with a sustain pedal, which must be plugged into the back of the keyboard.

➤ Pedal markings in sheet music are indicated with the abbreviation *Ped.*, and sometimes, with an asterisk.

Power Practicing

In This Chapter

➤ What are the goals of piano practicing?

➤ Isolating the most difficult part of a piece

➤ The importance of practicing slowly and playing evenly

➤ Making things harder for easier playing

➤ Learning to relax your hands and arms

➤ The value of recording your own playing

Playing the piano is an art. Successful art depends on practice. In a sense, art *is* practice. We hear of great performers "practicing their art." I propose in this chapter that practice is an art of its own. I have practiced piano (first) and keyboards (later) for almost my entire life, and I've learned that ten minutes spent practicing *well* is worth more than an hour of practicing badly. This chapter explores habits of good practicing.

Repetition is the most common form of practice. If you want to do something well, after all, it makes sense to do it over and over again, until the performance is almost automatic. But there is a difference between rote repetition and constructive repetition, and that is the difference this chapter is all about. All practice involves repetition, but the value of your practice depends on what other techniques are layered onto the sheer repetition of musical passages. Read on to learn some fresh practicing techniques.

The Goal of Practicing

What is the purpose of practicing, anyway? Throughout this book I present exercises that are primarily geared to learning the basic elements of playing and notation. The exercises are not entire pieces in most cases, and they are not oriented toward eventual performance. Now, I don't mean to imply that public performance should be anybody's goal, necessarily. But even if you're playing for personal satisfaction alone, and you'd rather hang upside down from a tree than let anybody hear you perform, being able to play music with some expertise is a great feeling. So, whatever your musical goals, using practice techniques geared toward performance excellence enhances your personal musical art.

Practicing, and practicing efficiently, has several goals:

➤ **Smoothness.** Music needs to proceed unhaltingly to be effective. Pauses in the musical flow are distracting and disconcerting. It's natural, when learning a piece, to stumble over notes and stop to get your bearings. One point of practicing is to smooth out those rough spots until you can play the piece through entirely without pausing.

Smoothness also refers to the continuity and musicality of individual phrases within the piece. Using good fingering helps you play musically and unbrokenly, and practicing involves finding and learning the best fingerings for the piece.

Key Thought
You shouldn't play a rollicking ragtime piece such as "The Maple Leaf Rag" at the same tempo that you'd play a slow torch song like "As Time Goes By," or the whole musical point of the rag is lost.

➤ **Playing the right tempo.** Throughout this book, in the exercises, I emphasize that playing fast is your *least* important consideration. Evenness and steadiness are more important than speed when practicing the exercises. That rule of thumb is generally true with more musically meaningful pieces as well, but tempo is more important with real pieces than exercises.

A piece's effect is conveyed partly by its tempo, and one of your practicing goals is to get the piece "up to speed." Speed isn't much of a concern with rock ballads, slow jazz tunes, or classical piano pieces with the Largo or Lento tempo marking. But faster pieces need to steam along at a good clip, or they just don't sound right.

➤ **Clarity.** It's tempting to fudge your way through a piece, or a part of a piece, that you haven't learned perfectly. Hey, it's not a problem—music is fun, and perfection isn't necessarily the goal. Nevertheless, playing every note of a piece clearly is an ideal, and one of the goals of practicing. Clarity is hardest when a piece throws a lot of fast notes at you, like some classical pieces do when you have to zoom up and down the keyboard with speedy scales or arpeggios. In addition to a glut of notes, using the sustain pedal too much can cause lack of musical clarity. Whatever the cause of muddiness, good practicing technique can help bring distinctness and clarity to your playing.

Musical Mouthful
"To stop the flow of music would be like the stopping of time itself, incredible and inconceivable."—
Aaron Copland

➤ **Expressiveness.** Music is emotional. At some point in your practicing, it becomes time to move beyond the rote learning of notes, to conveying the emotional point of the piece. All kinds of music have sentiment as the core value. Good practicing takes into consideration the emotion of the notes you've worked so hard to learn.

Take Apart the Parts

When learning to play a new piece, there often seems to be too much happening at once. Both hands being asked to play different parts, there's a key signature to remember, plus you must count the rhythm. The best way to cope with a piece's complexites, and begin to master each element of the performance, is to disassemble the piece.

There are two ways to take a piece apart:

➤ Separate the two hands. Expert players can sometimes play a new piece at sight, both hands going at once. But most mortals need to examine each hand separately at some point during the practice process.

➤ Isolate the piece's different portions. Usually, keyboard pieces have easy sections and hard sections. Whether you're working with a jazz chart, the lead sheet of a pop standard, or a classical piano piece, some portion of the music is likely to give you more problems than other portions. Isolating the hard parts and treating them like self-contained exercises is the best way to master them. Many of the tips in this chapter give you ideas for practicing portions of a piece.

Imagine walking down the hall of a music conservatory, a college-level school for aspiring musicians. Practice rooms—small, badly soundproofed rooms with a piano in each room—line both sides of the hall. The sonic atmosphere is a cacophony of conflicting musical passages. As you walk down the hall, the music pouring into your ears shifts, rises, and falls as the nearest rooms become more audible than the others, then fade away as you walk along. If you were to concentrate on each room in turn, there is little doubt what you'd hear. In every room, would-be musicians practice isolated passages of pieces over and over, often one hand at at time. In other words, combining the techniques of separating the hands and isolating the piece's portions is a common and effective way to practice.

Here is a rule to remember when practicing hands separately:

➤ Practice the more difficult hand first.

There are a few reasons for this rule. First of all, the most difficult part requires more time to learn, so it makes sense to start with it. Second, if you can learn the difficult hand well enough to play it semiautomatically, it makes it easy to add the other hand. Thirdly, the facility with which you can play the difficult part determines how fast and smoothly you eventually play the whole portion.

When it comes to maintaining the tempo of a piece all the way through, you can only go as fast as you can play the most difficult portion of the piece. By isolating the hardest passage, and practicing the hard hand separately, you zero in on the most crucial part of the whole piece: the part that sets the pace.

> **Key Thought**
> Just as you want to practice the more difficult hand first, so you want to find, isolate, and attack the most difficult part of a piece first. Don't make the mistake of putting off working on a hard passage precisely because it *is* hard! Use the advice in this chapter to make hard passages easier, then enjoy how relatively easy the rest of the piece seems.

Slow, Slower, Slowest

A primary rule of practicing is: Slow it down. Hard pieces (or parts of pieces) become easier when played slowly, of course, but that's not the real reason for developing a habit of practicing slowly. There are two important reasons for habitually practicing at a slow tempo:

➤ The first reason is evenness. Fast passages with a lot of notes definitely need to be slowed down for practicing. The emphasis, as I've repeated often through this book, should be on playing evenly, not quickly. When practicing, play only as fast as you can stay faithful to the rhythm. Playing with rock-solid evenness—no pauses, slowdowns, or speeding up during the passage you're practicing — is great training for eventually playing the part full speed.

Key Thought

Here's something many keyboard and piano players don't know: Extreme evenness gives the illusion of speed. When playing a hard passage with lots of notes, executing the phrases with rigorous evenness makes it *seem* as though you're playing faster than you really are. This is a secret of virtuosos.

Grace Notes

I remember attending a classical piano class led by the Jorge Bolet, the famous, and quite astounding, piano virtuoso. He constantly exhorted the students who played for the class to slow down their playing of fast pieces. He finally confided, "I'm the slowest player in the world. It only seems like I play fast because I play so evenly." Of course, in the case of Jorge Bolet and others of his skill level, they play both evenly *and* lightning-fast. But the point is that by practicing slowly and evenly, you can both increase your speed and your polish. Keyboard virtuosity is a matter of control, not just raw velocity.

➤ The second reason for practicing slowly involves the natural intelligence of your fingers. Yep, you heard me—your fingers have their own smarts. I doubt if your fingers can balance the ckeckbook without a little help from your mind, but they have a sort of independant memory for motion. Just as you hands seem to tie shoelaces without much thought, using a kind of learned autopilot facility, so it is on the keyboard.

Your fingers can learn music and play it back semiautomatically. Practicing slowly etches music into your finger-memory. Ironically, practicing slowly teaches your fingers more quickly than practicing fast.

When I was a teenager, my piano teacher told me the story of how he prepared a difficult piece by Chopin for a performance. He learned the piece fastidiously, working on it with very slow tempos, concentrating on clarity and evenness. The astounding part of the story is that his discipline was so great that he didn't play the piece at full speed *even once* before the day of the performance, and the concert went without a hitch. Whether this account was an exaggeration meant to impress me is irrelevant. It *did* impress me with the importance and power of practicing slowly, whether the story is literally true or not.

A great tool for slow practice is the *metronome*. Metronomes make a deeply annoying clicking sound, certain to drive you and anyone in earshot to rash acts of violence. The clicking torture is worth it, however, because you can set the metronome to a fast or slow rate of clicking, in very small increments.

Metronomes are practice tools for developing evenness. It's like having a conductor standing next to you, or a teacher rapping on your keyboard with a pencil. The worst thing you can do when practicing slowly is to speed up when the going gets easy, and slow down during tough passages. The relentless, machine-ticking of the metronome helps keep you at one steady speed.

There are two kinds of ticking metronome: electronic and mechanical. The mechanical metronomes use a pendulum device that swings back and forth, creating the ticks. A weight attached to the pendulum stalk regulates the tempo. Electronic metronomes plug in and work their magic with a dial to adjust the tempo. The electronic type is more reliable, ticks more evenly, and is usually more expensive. Digital quartz metronomes are now available, some with built in electronic tuners.

One type of metronome to avoid is the kind that blinks a light at you. The blinking light is fine if the device also ticks, but don't get a metronome that has only the light, as the visual indicator isn't enough to really help when practicing. You've got to hear the tick, or it doesn't do the trick. (I made up that rhyme. Just now. All by myself.)

Making Things Harder

When you're wrestling with a hard keyboard piece, or a hard passage within a piece, what's the thing to do? Why, make it harder, of course. That may seem like advice from a masochist, but it's actually good practice technique, and one used in other disciplines.

Prizefighters, for example, train extensively in ways that don't relate exactly to what they do in the ring: by running, lifting weights, and dieting, in addition to hitting punching bags and sparring with suicidal ring partners. In other words, boxers do *more* than they are required to in the ring, over-training for each fight. In music, eating raw eggs and jumping rope for an hour doesn't help much with those tricky left-hand passages. In music, the same principle can be applied, and is sometimes called *overpracticing*.

Overpracticing takes whatever is most difficult in a piece, or a portion of a piece, and makes it more difficult. By magnifying whatever you find hard, and practicing it that way, you begin to make the original music seem easier to play. And it's more than just appearances: the original music *is* easier to play after practicing it in some more difficult form.

Here are some ways to make difficult types of playing even harder for practice purposes.

➤ One basic method of overpracticing that works in almost all keyboard situations is to exaggerate the movements of your fingers. Consider this technique to be a kind of aerobic exercise for your hands.

Normally it doesn't take much finger movement to push down a key, especially the light plastic keys of an electronic keyboard. When practicing a difficult passage, though, play slowly and lift each finger as high as possible before dropping it down on the note. Gradually, through repetition, increase your speed, but continue lifting your fingers as if they were stepping over high hurdles. It is your *priority* to lift your fingers high, so don't go faster than you can while exercising your fingers this way.

➤ Here's one: jump higher and leap farther. This overpracticing technique is for when you have a difficult leap to execute on the keyboard. A leap is a quick jump from one part of the keyboard's range to a higher or lower part with the same hand. Landing accurately on the correct notes at the end of the leap can be tricky. The solution? Add an octave to the leap. Add two octaves. Make it brutally hard.

Go very slowly when you start this particular form of overpracticing. Be very deliberate as you make the leap and land on your destination note(s). Gradually add some speed to the maneuver, until you're playing it almost at full speed. Use the same fingerings as in the original leap. Finally, when you return to the correct leap as written in the piece, it seems much less treacherous.

Key Thought
Start with the metronome set very slowly, and play the entire passage you're working on at that speed. Then gradually edge the ticking speed higher, playing the entire passage at each new tempo. In this fashion you are soon playing the piece (or portion of the piece) at a performance speed, having polished your evenness in the process.

Grace Notes
Anyone who has ever played with a metronome has had the strange sensation that it's the metronome that's slowing down (rather than the obvious fact that they're speeding up)! It's kind of like the notion that the sun revolves around the earth; your perspective as a player can fool you! Metronomes, however, are machines—they don't speed up or slow down, so if you're falling off the steady "click," you must be at fault!

Key Thought
This technique is especially effective with passages for either hand that involve lots of quickly played consecutive notes. After spending some time overpracticing with high fingers, you should find that the passage zips along pretty well when played normally. Reminder: always play evenly!

➤ Too many notes? Play twice as many. When you have a fast passage of notes, usually in the right hand, with some zig-zagging configurations that make learning and playing the passage difficult, slow down and practice doubling up the notes. That's right—play each written note twice. If that doesn't seem frustrating enough, play each note three times. (Use the same finger for each repetition.)

This particular brand of sadistic overpracticing helps ingrain the position of the notes in your mind and finger-memory, plus it forces you to slow down. Check out the example on page 155.

No Strain, Big Gain

One of the most difficult parts of playing the piano is staying relaxed while learning a new physical skill. Your wrists, arms, and shoulders should be at ease while playing. Like anything else that's difficult, it takes practice. It may seem strange, but relaxation is a keyboard skill that can be practiced just like any of the musical challenges discussed in this chapter.

Here are two ways to encourage relaxation in your hands and arms:

➤ One of the bottlenecks of tension for many keyboard players is the wrist. Ideally, your wrist should be in a state of near-liquid relaxation, enabling you to raise your hand from the keyboard without lifting your forearm. One good exercise for encouraging such relaxation is to, indeed, lift your hand from the keyboard without using your forearm.

Just rest your hand on the keys—don't worry about hitting any particular notes or chords. Now, lift your hand by pivoting upward from the wrist, and drop it down on the keys. After several repetitions, try the same thing with the other hand. This exercise can be extended by dropping your hand down on predetermined notes or groups of notes. The next figure shows what notes to aim for with the right hand, then the left hand. (You can try both hands together, too.)

This one simple exercise can be repeated often—even every day if you like. Gradually, you should notice that your wrist is naturally more relaxed when you play.

➤ The second exercise is really is just a common sense relaxer. Every once in a while, remember to check whether you are in a relaxed state from your shoulders down through your fingers. Adjust your posture by sitting directly in front of the keyboard, both feet on the floor, and your back straight. Are your shoulders hunched? Unhunch them. Are you carrying tension anywhere in your upper body? Do a physical inventory, and deliberately relax any tense spots. Shake your forearms out as if you were doing the French "ooh-la-la" gesture quite vigorously with both hands. In every way you can think of, reestablish your relaxed demeanor before beginning to play again.

ORIGINAL VERSION:

OVERPRACTICE VERSION:

Play with left hand only

Overpracticing leaps requires increasing the size of the leap by an octave (or two). Remember: leave your right hand out of it. Play the overpractice version with just the left hand.

ORIGINAL VERSION:

OVERPRACTICE VERSION:

Overpracticing by doubling notes.

Play these notes and chord by dropping your hand down on the keyboard from the wrist, keeping your arm, wrist, and hand as relaxed as possible.

Musical Mouthful
"You cannot imagine how it spoils you to have been a child prodigy."—Franz Lizst

Key Thought
When aiming for particular notes during the hand-drop, the wrist tends to tighten up, so concentrate on keeping it as loose as possible, even as you form your hand into the position necessary to play the correct notes.

Facing the Music

Most of the practice techniques in this chapter focus on physical concerns like overcoming difficulties in a piece or relaxing your arms for better overall playing habits. Lest we forget the emotional side of music, this last section offers a practice technique designed to improve the expressiveness of your playing. It's a simple exercise, but in a way the most grueling, because it's the most revealing.

Here's the exercise in a nutshell: Record yourself playing. You can record yourself with a portable cassette recorder, or, if you're learning on a keyboard with a built-in *sequencer*, use that. Sound quality isn't the point here, so it really doesn't matter what method you use, as long as you can hear the result and learn from it.

Recording yourself play is difficult for every pianist and keyboardist, regardless of your experience or playing level. Hearing your own playing is hard because it rarely sounds like what you expect. Oddly, our ears deceive us while we're actually playing, leading us to believe we sound like what's in our head, rather than what's truly coming out of the instrument. Because we all have an ideal sound in our head, the truth is likely to hurt a bit. But for exactly that reason, recording is a great tool for improvement.

The time to record is when you've learned a piece well. There is no point in adding insult to injury by recording a half-learned piece, so you can witness objectively how much work you still have to do! Wait until you can play the piece smoothly, all the way through.

Remember, the point of recording is to improve your *expressiveness* in playing, so it should be done when you've gained some mastery over your material. As you listen to your playing, make notes (mentally or on paper) of what you want to change. Here are some considerations you may notice:

➤ Is your playing uneven where you thought it was even? You need to overpractice that passage with the "high fingers" technique described above.

➤ Does the piece sound tentative, as if you lacked confidence in your playing? Make sure your arms are relaxed, and try counting while you play.

➤ Would you characterize the playing as stiff or mechanical? You may be placing too much emphasis on counting, and not playing freely enough. Relax your internal metronome (and turn off the real metronome if you have one) and play the piece with a more relaxed attitude.

Of course, you may notice that your playing is far better than you expected! Whatever the result, it's exciting to record yourself and hear your own playing. You should do this exercise occasionally, as a final check when you've learned a piece.

Musical Mouthful
"I am astounded . . . at the wonderful power you have developed, and terrified at the thought that so much hideous and bad music may be put on record forever."— Arthur Sullivan, on seeing a demonstration of Edison's phonograph

Grace Notes
Everyone has had the experience of hearing their voice on a tape recording and saying, "That can't possibly be me!" The same is true with your playing—what you hear when you're playing may not be the same as what you hear, objectively, when you listen to a tape of your playing!

The Least You Need to Know

➤ The goals of practicing are smooth and even playing, playing at the correct speed, playing clearly, and playing expressively.

➤ The first rule of practicing is to work on a piece in sections, hands separately. Always attack the hardest part first.

➤ It's not necessary to be the fastest player in the world, and playing with great evenness simulates speed.

➤ Find ways to make hard passages even harder. Then when you play them normally, they don't seem so hard.

➤ Check often to see if your hands, wrists, arms, and shoulders are as relaxed as they could be. Take a moment to reduce any tension in your upper body.

➤ Try recording your own playing to evaluate whether the piece really sounds like you think it does.

Chapter 19

Faking It

In This Chapter

➤ All about charts and lead sheets

➤ Tips for "faking" an arrangement of a pop or jazz song

This may come as a surprise, but "faking it" is an honored tradition among piano and keyboard players. However, lest anybody get the wrong impression, I should point out that faking it in music refers to a specific skill when playing jazz and pop music. Laziness in general is not universally respected among musicians!

Jazz and pop music have very different requirements and traditions than classical music. Whereas when playing a classical piece every note is important as written, jazz and pop songs consist of a melody, words (if the tune is a song and not an instrumental piece), and chords. How the chords are played, and the arrangement of the whole song, can be left to the discretion of the player. Improvising an arrangement of a jazz or pop tune is sometimes called *faking it*, and the books that help you do so are called *fake books*.

Music Speak

Fake books are volumes of sheet music for songs. Each song in a fake book consists of the melody, written in music notation, and chord symbols above the notes. Taking cues from the chord symbols, the player must improvise (fake) an arrangement for the song.

This chapter concentrates on the specific skills needed to play music out of a fake book. These specialized books of tunes, when approached with a bit of knowledge and an open mind, let you expand your playing range to a large number of songs instantly. Knowing how to fake it makes anyone a much more competent keyboard player.

How Music Charts Work

The word *chart* sounds so unartistic, like a blueprint. In fact, charts (also called *lead sheets*) are very much like blueprints, showing the schematic structure of a song. A song's chart consists of the melody, notated on a single treble cleff staff, plus chord symbols either above or below the melody. (Words are sometimes present if the tune isn't an instrumental.) Some charts work equally well for guitarists and keyboardists, by placing guitar chord symbols next to the keyboard chord symbols. Keyboardists call the chart's chord symbols the *changes*, as in "What are the changes for this tune?" The following figure shows a chart for "Greensleeves," using piano chord symbols only.

A chart for "Greensleeves," showing piano chords above the melody. This tune is simple, but some song charts have much more frequent chord changes.

Music Speak
Music **charts**, also called **lead sheets**, notate the melody of a song, with chord symbols above the notes to indicate the accompaniment harmonies for the left hand. Charts (lead sheets) are compiled in fake books.

In playing a music chart, use your right hand to play the melody, and your left hand for the chords. If playing the chords is too much to cope with at first, just play single bass notes underneath the chord symbols. Sticking with our "Greensleeves" example, the next example shows the easiest possible way to fake the tune from the chart, playing one bass note for each chord symbol.

The next step is to play full chords underneath the chord symbols, as shown in the following example.

The next step in creating an interesting arrangement from a fake book is to fill in the left-hand part with some embellishments—extra notes or chords—to give the piece interest and rhythmic movement. The first three examples showed the simplest ways of playing a chart, by changing the left-hand part only when a chord symbol appears above the melody. Skilled keyboard fakers keep the left hand playing almost all the time, as if they were reading a complicated arrangement from the sheet music. Playing with complexity isn't required or even preferable in many cases, but in examples such as the "Greensleeves" chart I'm using in this chapter, which has two-measure gaps between most chord changes, there's plenty of room for the left hand to fill in.

The final version—still "Greensleeves"—shows what you can do by playing broken chords instead of solid chords.

Here is one way to play the "Greensleeves" chart shown on page 160. This is the simplest possible arrangement, using single left-hand notes instead of chords.

Fakery Tips to Remember

Here are a few things to remember about playing charts and lead sheets from fake books:

➤ The chords indicated in a chart are just suggestions. True, they are often the best possible suggestions, and represent the chords originally intended by the song's composer. But that doesn't stop musicians from changing them (using what are called *alternate chords*) and inserting additional chords into the chart spontaneously. It takes a good knowledge of chords and some musical experience to substitute or insert chords, but you know the old-world proverb: "The only way to get experience is to go for it, big-time, with utter disregard for consequences." (Those old world folks really have a way with words.)

Music Speak
When in doubt, simplify. Remember, you're faking it! Perfection is not a requirement. If you can't come up with a good chord, just hit the bass note, or even leave the left hand out entirely for a couple of beats until you can catch up with the melody. Using fake books should be fun: don't spoil the experience by stressing out.

Using chords in "Greensleeves."

➤ You can assume that any chord symbol refers to a major chord if not indicated otherwise. Minor chords are indicated with a lower-case "m" next to the chord symbol.

➤ The right-hand part of a chart is open to some leeway as well as the left hand. Charts and lead sheets are meant to give you the bare bones of a song, not tie you to a literal interpretation of the notation. The important thing about playing a chart is to make the song recognizable, and many keyboard players throw in a lot of improvisation in *both* hands along the way.

Using broken chords can spice up a faked arrangement.

The Least You Need to Know

➤ A music chart, or lead sheet, consists of a melody written on a single staff, above which are chord symbols indicating what harmonies should be played with the left hand. If the song has words, they are printed beneath the staff.

➤ Chord symbols on a chart are just suggestions, and you can experiment with using other chords, or playing single bass notes.

➤ When playing a chart for the first time, keep it simple until you get familiar with the song.

Beethoven

Chapter 20

The Rigors and Joys of the Classics

In This Chapter

➤ Discussing the difficulties and rewards of learning classical piano music

➤ Surveying the easy and intermediate classical repertoire

Everybody wants to play the classics—that's what makes them *the* classics! But, seriously, all keyboard players should be exposed to the very best music ever written for the instrument; and you can't deny that Bach, Beethoven, Mozart, Chopin, and the boys were no slouches when it came to composing keyboard music.

Classical keyboard music is mostly either piano or organ music. For this reason, many people feel that classical keyboard music should *only* be played on the piano or organ. But it's a mistake to think that you can't play classical piano music on a digital keyboard. In fact, the twentieth century isn't the first time in music history that a whole new class of instrument has been adopted to play music written for earlier instruments.

When it comes to beginning and intermediate classical music, home keyboards can be pressed into service as effectively as digital pianos. However, advanced piano music cannot be played well on the five-octave keyboard range of home keyboards; nor is it easy to play advanced pieces on an unweighted keyboard. Anyone whose playing progresses to lofty levels will most likely be frustrated with the range and "feel" limitations of home keyboards, and upgrade to a digital or acoustic piano.

Whatever you play, this chapter will introduce the joys—and rigors—of the classical repertoire to you.

Grace Notes

Consider that much of Bach's so-called piano music was composed for the harpsichord, which has a completely different dynamic range, and is played with a different technique, than a modern piano. Yet today the piano is, more often than not, the instrument of choice for playing Bach's harpsichord music.

Musical Mouthful
"Classical music is the kind we keep thinking will turn into a tune."—Kin Hubbard

Grace Notes
In modern times there is a clear division between classical and popular music, never mind genre schisms like jazz, R&B, hip-hop, rock, new age, and many others. Before the twentieth century, classical music appealed to the aristocracy that had the leisure and money to enjoy it, but the great composers also wrote music for the masses. Bach produced church music every Sunday; Mozart composed operas for the popular theater; Beethoven churned out piano sonatas to be played in private homes.

Music Speak
The **interpretation** of a classical piece of music is defined as the individual player's approach to its tempo, dynamics, and articulation/phrasing.

How Classical Music Works

Let's review a few common (mis)perceptions about classical music.

➤ Classical music is high-brow

➤ Classical music is difficult

➤ Playing classical music requires extensive training

While it's true that advanced classical music can be very difficult, and some people do indulge in extensive training to master the genre, there is such a thing as relatively easy classical music for the keyboard, and anyone who can read music can play it.

As to the high-brow nature of the classics, it's worth remembering that some of the music we call classical was the popular music of its day.

One reason classical music has a rigorous reputation is its literalness. In other words, classical music is composed, and must be played, down to the individual note and expression marking. The explicitness of classical music is opposed to the informality of popular composition, which consists of just a melody, words, and chords; the exact arrangement of notes is made up by the publisher and/or the player. When you learn a classical piece, every note must be in its place, whereas there can be quite a bit of fudging and simplifying when you play a pop song, and quite a bit of improvisation when you play a jazz tune.

Adhering to the Letter and Spirit

Why would anyone want to play classical music if there were no room for the player's musical personality? The answer is that nobody would. The fact is, there *is* room for personality when playing classical music. Personal playing style, when applied to a classical piece, is called *interpretation*.

The interpretation of a piece usually affects the following aspects:

➤ **Tempo.** The exact speed at which a classical piece moves is usually left up to the player. Sometimes you see pieces whose tempos are explicitly defined by metronome settings at the beginning, but even those pieces are subject to some variation. In most cases the tempos of classical piano pieces are indicated by vague descriptors such as Allegro (happily) or Lento (slowly). While it wouldn't be appropriate for a Lento piece to be played fast, the indicators are general enough to allow considerable leeway.

➤ **Dynamics.** Even more than with tempo markings, the dynamics of a piece—how loud or soft it should be played at any given point—can be taken as suggestions rather than rules. If you question whether a composer's indications should be disregarded or changed, consider that many dynamic markings you see in classical sheet music—such as crescendos and decrescendos—were placed there by the publisher or editor of the music, not the composer.

All kinds of dynamic indicators infest the notation of most classical music, and if you listen to recordings while following along with the music, you can see that much of is completely ignored. Volume (loudness and softness) is one of the main ways of expressing mood in music, which is the most personal aspect of a performance.

➤ **Articulation and phrasing.** Articulation is the degree to which notes are disconnected from each other, and phrasing refers to the way in which notes are connected. Articulation and phrasing are related concepts, and difficult to learn except through experience.

> **Grace Notes**
> If you were to buy several recordings of a famous classical piece, such as a Beethoven sonata or a Chopin étude, you'd find that in each case the tempo indicator is obeyed with a variety of personal styles that represent slightly different specific tempos.

If you have any recordings of Bach piano music, played by different performers, listen to them with an ear to how the notes are articulated and phrased. Some performers play the lines of notes with the utmost smoothness, seamlessly and without any breaks between the notes. Other players, seeking to distinguish the notes from each other, use a more detached touch that separates the notes from each other. What did Bach want? It's hard to say, since he just wrote down the notes, often without any phrase markings, and since he was composing for the harpsichord which has a more detached sound than the piano. In all cases, classical music is *old* music played on modern instruments, and it is up to the player to make it sound good with whatever techniques and styles are available.

Even the Masters Wrote Easy Music

The question of difficulty in classical music deserves further discussion. While it's true that the reputation for difficulty is largely due to its rigorous notation, I can't deny that a lot of piano/keyboard classics are treacherously hard to play. Some pieces were composed for piano virtuosos, and in the nineteenth century the great piano composers *were* the performing virtuosos of the day, and they naturally wrote music with which to show off their glorious keyboard technique.

> **Grace Notes**
> Playing classical music, with its combination of rigorous notation and personal interpretation, offers a challenge to find a balance between mechanical playing and artistry. You may think that musical artistry is beyond you, but anyone who learns a single piece of classical music has the right to interpret it, and in so doing bring a personal artistry to the fore, even if only for personal pleasure.

Believe it or not, the great classical composers actually wrote some easy music. In some cases they composed for students, in other cases they met publishing requests. As someone who has dabbled in composition myself, I can testify that there is a pure satisfaction in composing simple music for its own sake, as well. Whatever the many reasons, there is a wealth of classical music that doesn't crunch the player's knuckles. Once you've become very familiar with the basics of reading music and two-handed playing, you can graduate yourself to the classics with some easy pieces.

Bach

Johann Sebastian Bach wrote quite a bit of keyboard music for young students, some of whom were his own kids. Bach composed in the early eighteenth century, during the final glory days of the so-called Baroque era of classical music. Baroque keyboard music features composition in which both hands play melodies at the same time, and the two or more (melodies, not hands) fit together into a whole that's more than the sum of its parts.

Grace Notes
One of Bach's most famous collections, the *Clavier-Büchlein für Anna Magdalena Bach,* was a collection of student-level pieces for his second wife to practice her keyboard technique.

Grace Notes
It has been said of Mozart's music that it should be played either in childhood or old age, because only innocence or long experience can bring out the purity of the music. But don't let that stop you from playing Mozart if your age falls somewhere between nine and ninety. The music is refreshing and disarmingly simple.

To explore Bach's music, look for any compilation of pieces for beginning or intermediate players. There are many *preludes* and other pieces that require good counting, but are not fast or complicated. One of the hardest types of piece that Bach wrote is called a *fugue*, which usually has at least three independent melodies played by the two hands that most people are endowed with. Keeping straight three, four, or five melodies with two hands is quite a trick, and requires advanced skill. Stay away from the fugues at the beginning, and enjoy the simpler pieces.

Mozart

After the movie *Amadeus*, most people became familiar, to some extent, with the life of Wolfgang Amadeus Mozart, perhaps the most precocious music prodigy to ever live. Because he composed music from an astonishingly early age, it makes sense that some of his pieces are fairly simple to play. (We might as well disregard the fact that little Wolfgang was also composing operas during those tender years.) Some of his later work is likewise suitable for intermediate players.

Mozart, amazingly, seemed to be born with the capacity to compose mature keyboard music, so there is very little from his pen that is really suitable for beginners. But intermediate players can enjoy some of the piano *sonatas*. Sonatas are composed in pieces, with the pieces called *movements*. Even if some parts of a sonata are a little on the intimidating side, it's fine to play just a single movement.

Beethoven

One of Beethoven's most famous piano pieces, called *Für Elise* (which literally means "for Elise," but which I prefer to translate as "My socks are too tight"), is an intermediate-level piece learned by beginning piano students the world over. Ludwig van Beethoven also composed many *sonatinas*, or little sonatas, for the piano. These sonatinas are mostly easier to play than Mozart piano sonatas, and certainly much easier than Beethoven's thirty-two piano sonatas, which are for advanced players.

Beethoven composed his music a bit later in the eighteenth century than Mozart, and while the two composers sound similar, Beethoven had more fire and brimstone compared to Mozart's limpid innocence.

Chopin

Frédéric Chopin was a great Polish pianist of the nineteenth century who composed in the Romantic style of soaring, all-important melodies (usually in the right hand) supported by flowing accompaniments (usually handled by the left hand). Chopin was undeniably a virtuoso, and wrote some of the most challenging piano music of his century. However, he also wrote for less accomplished players some short pieces.

Look for compilations of Chopin's music for intermediate pianists. Also check out any books of abridgments that have simplified versions of his more difficult compositions—because the melody is a large part of his compositional genius, much of Chopin's music becomes playable and enjoyable when the accompaniment (left-hand) part is simplified.

The French Impressionists

Music and art follow each other throughout the ages. Just as French turn-of-the-century painting took on a *impressionistic* flavor, with fuzzy washes of color and indistinct images, so did classical music have its own impressionistic period championed by Maurice Ravel, Claude Debussy, and many other French composers. Impressionistic music features flowing, watery music with harmonies that sound more modern than in the Romantic pieces of the mid-nineteenth century.

Unfortunately, Ravel and Debussy didn't write much simple music, preferring to explore their respective styles with richly complex piano scores, leaving beginning and intermediate players in the dust of their impressionistic fervor. New players must turn to other composers, some of whom are suggested below:

➤ **Erik Satie.** You may be familiar with Satie's work, or one of his works, without being aware of the composer's name. Satie wrote the so-called *Gymnopédies* that has been used over and over in all kinds of recordings, including rock songs. It is bittersweet, poignant, and—most important— fairly simple to play. It is one of several easy but hauntingly beautiful pieces Satie wrote for the piano. Take note that his work has a broad range that often can't be fit into the five-octave range of home keyboards.

➤ **Charles Gounod.** Gounod lived and composed a bit earlier than the pillars of French impressionism, but his music is still atmospheric without being overly complex. Some of Gounod's pieces are downright simple, and are found in collections of easy French piano music.

➤ **Gabriel Fauré.** Perhaps best known for his evocative *Requiem* for orchestra and chorus, Fauré lightened the mood in some of his piano pices. Though not as simplistic as Gounod or Satie, Fauré's piano music is manageable for intermediate players.

The Least You Need to Know

➤ Classical music is more literal than popular music or jazz, and that's one reason it seems intimidating: you can't fudge it.

➤ Some of the greatest classical composers wrote easy music that beginning pianists can enjoy, including Bach, Mozart, Beethoven, Chopin, and some of the French impressionists.

➤ Classical piano music is sometimes available in simplified arrangements that let you play immortal music without studying for years.

Grace Notes

Chopin was impressed with, and influenced by, folk music from the villages of Poland, and those simple tunes inspired some of his melodies. Chopin composed a series of *Mazurkas* for piano—the mazurka is a type of folk dance. Some of the slower mazurkas are fairly easy to play without any simplification. Chopin's Waltzes are good for intermediate-advanced players, as are the Nocturnes. Pretty much everything else is hard.

Key Thought

I must advise you frankly that impressionistic piano music loses much of its effect when played on electronic keyboards, even digital pianos. Much of the necessary sonority, created by holding the sustain pedal so the strings vibrate freely, cannot be replicated on digital instruments. However, this effect is less important in the simpler music of the period.

Grace Notes

Some of Ravel's and Debussy's music is available in simplified versions. One piece you might want to search out is Ravel's *Pavane pour une infante défunte* (Dance for a Dead Princess), which, despite the morbid title, is one of the loveliest piano pieces ever.

Listen to the Music

In This Chapter

➤ Surveying the phases of classical music through history

➤ Recommendations of classical piano music for listening

➤ Some seminal jazz pianists of our century

➤ A few great classical pianists of the recording era

When you begin to play the piano, it opens a whole new sense of appreciation for piano music—its beauties and difficulties. Perhaps you've been listening to piano music for years, and need no help from me sorting through the piano repertoire. Or, maybe you like jazz but don't know much about classical, or you appreciate new age piano albums but would like to broaden your music collection.

As a budding pianist, it's important to not only listen to yourself play, but to listen to others. Hearing how other pianists approach a work can be quite inspirational and give you new ideas of how to improve your playing. Plus, listening to different pianists can give you a taste of a variety of different styles, so you can better focus your study in areas where you have the greatest interest.

This chapter is a roundup of great piano music through the centuries, and great pianists of the recording era.

Begin With the Baroque

Piano music begins with the *Baroque* era, a European artistic period that lasted from roughly 1600 to 1750. Baroque architecture is highly ornate, and was often expressed in elaborately chiselled cathedrals. Classical music of the period was likewise complex and ornamental, and the predominant keyboard of the period was the harpsichord (see Chapter 2). Why then do I call it the beginning of piano music? Because modern performances of Baroque keyboard music are usually on the piano, not the harpsichord.

Music Speak
The **Baroque** period of music ran through the seventeenth and early eighteenth centuries, and featured complex, ornate music. Typically, composers fashioned multiple melodies to play at the same time, fitting them together with mathematical accuracy in pleasing harmonies. Bach is the most famous Baroque composer.

Baroque music is not very emotional, though it can be stirring. The Baroque style did not feature lovely melodies set against a chordal accompaniment, like a piece by Chopin, a jazz ballad, or a George Winston piano song. Baroque composers fitted melodies against each other ingeniously, forging music of great precision that has a mathematical quality. *Contrapuntal* music, or music written in opposing parts, is the highlight of Baroque compositional style. It is almost abstract in its devotion to a labyrinth of musical rules.

What does it all add up to for the listener? At its best, contrapuntal Baroque music is glorious in its grandeur, and touches your soul with majesty. It doesn't leave you humming a melody for the rest of the day.

Baroque music sometimes sounds dry, like an exercise. Indeed, contrapuntal music really is an exercise in composition. However, the great Baroque composers transcended the technical aspects of their art, and delivered immortal music. (Sounds corny, but it's true.) There are two giants of the Baroque period you should know about:

Bach

Johann Sebastian Bach lived at the end of the Baroque period, and composed contrapuntally even as his younger contemporaries were moving into new, more hip styles of music. Near the end of his life Bach was considered something of an old fogey, and his music was quickly forgotten when he died—only to be revived in the nineteenth century. Bach's profession was writing church music, which he cranked out in weekly batches. Lucky for pianists, he filled in the cracks of his day writing keyboard pieces, many of them small exercises in counterpoint.

Music Speak
Contrapuntal music features separate melodies that sound good when played against each other. (Contra means against.) One of the most mathematical styles of music composition, it has many rules that the composer must follow. (Otherwise the contrapuntal police get you.) Bach was a master of counterpoint music.

His best-known collection of such pieces is **The Well-Tempered Clavier**, a title that needs some explanation. Well-tempered refers to the system of music we are familiar with today, including keys, scales, half steps, whole steps, and the modern method of tuning a keyboard. Music wasn't always composed according to the current system, and Bach celebrated the liberation all composers felt from more primitive systems of music theory by writing a prelude and fugue for every single key, both major and minor. (That's twenty-four keys.) Then he did it again—Book 2 of The Well-Tempered Clavier. (*Clavier* is a generic name for a keyboard instrument.)

Another large keyboard work by Bach is the **Goldberg Variations**, composed to help cure a prince of insomnia—not the most dignified commission in the world for a man destined to be one of the world's greatest composers. Bach also wrote many suites (pieces divided into several short parts), and a few keyboard concertos. And, outside of his output for keyboard, he created an enormous body of orchestral and choral works.

Handel

Georg Frederick Handel was a German Baroque composer who settled in England. Today, his best-known work is the **Water Music**—a series of pieces for small orchestra that you can't help hearing if you tune to any classical music radio station for one day. Handel's compositional style sounds more formal than Bach, and usually more ceremonial. Handel usually sounds like he was always writing for royalty—he very often was. He turned out a number of operas and many symphonies.

When it comes to piano music, check out Handel's **sonatas**. (A *sonata* is a piano piece that usually has three parts, called movements.) If you get into sonatas in a big way, you can even trace how the form developed through the next century in the hands of different composers who I'll tell you about later in this chapter. Handel is the place to start a sonata odyssey.

Classic Classics

Classical music refers to the entire tradition of the strictly composed, refined music practiced by trained musicians for several centuries. Within that long tradition have transpired several phases, or styles of music, as this chapter surveys. The Classic period is one such phase, and it shouldn't be confused with classical music generally. The Classical period extended from the mid-eighteenth century to the mid-nineteenth century (more or less) in Europe.

The styles of Classic composers different from their Baroque predecessors very distinctly. The contrapuntal style of pitting melodies against each other faded out of chic, and a new rigorous tradition took its place. Composers from this period were more concerned with structure than anything else, and stuck fast to their definitions of pieces like *symphonies*, sonatas, and *concertos*. Within the pieces, the compositional style was elegant but less intellectual than the Baroque composers had been. There was more emphasis on single melodies supported by accompaniments.

So what effect does music from the Classic period have on modern ears? Some piano music from that era sounds excessively polite, but the best has a marvelous innocence and purity. Later in the period, the music is earthy, strong, bold, serious, and strict. It is not a musical period known for its overt emotionalism, but it provides many memorable melodies.

Here are some of the composers you should be aware of, and some of their great piano music:

> ➤ **Mozart.** Considering Wolfgang died in his thirties, his prodigious output is all the more amazing. The **piano sonatas** are among the most lucid and limpid piano music ever written. If you need some sonic simplicity in your day, go for the effortless innocence of an album of Mozart sonatas.

➤ **Haydn.** Haydn was an early master of the Classic period, whose music contains lingering traces of the Baroque period. Haydn's **piano sonatas** are much shorter than Mozart's, and less developed. They are somewhat more ornate, and don't have the translucent Mozart genius.

➤ **Beethoven.** Most people have heard of Ludwig, and know the poignant story of his deafness, which occurred during his adulthood and didn't stop him from composing. Beethoven was a gruff composer who brought a kind of peasant earthiness to refined classical forms. If you really want a challenge, make it a project to listen to all thirty-two of his **piano sonatas**. (I know I'm recommending a lot of sonatas in this section. What can I say—it was a ragingly popular musical form back then.) The early sonatas sound like a coarse version of Mozart. The middle sonatas include the famous **Moonlight Sonata** and **Appassionata**—both deservedly enduring in their beauty and power. The late sonatas are phenomenally challenging pieces, both to play and listen to.

➤ **Schubert.** Franz Schubert was one of the most spectacular melodic composers of all time—a hall of famer in the tune-humming department. He wrote many songs for classical singers accompanied by piano, and also—guess what?—**piano sonatas**.

Virtuosity Emerges

The title of this section may be misleading. Keyboard virtuosity was certainly celebrated in the Classic and Baroque eras. But it's hard for us to relate to ancient virtuosity, performed as it was on ancient instruments that were very different from our modern pianos. The music itself was influenced by the instruments. The string-busting virtuosity that we think of today emerged in the nineteenth century during a period called the Romantic era of classical music.

Why Romantic? Melody was king during this period—tear-jerking, swoon-worthy melodies dripping with moonlight that leave listeners weak in the knees and gasping for more. It was during the Romantic period that the melody-and-accompaniment style of composing reached a height of sophistication and beauty.

Romantic piano music was composed for instruments very close in range, sonority, responsiveness, and power to modern pianos, and composers went to town. In fact, the great composers of the nineteenth century were also the most dashing pianists, unlike the twentieth century, during which composition has spun off into a separate and somewhat reclusive art.

There's a lot of exciting music to listen to from the Romantic period. Here are the highlights:

➤ **Chopin.** Perhaps the most famous and beloved Romantic composer, Chopin enjoys a special regard among pianists and piano lovers, because he composed almost exclusively for the instrument. Chopin was himself a great pianist of his day, and he adored the instrument. He is the piano's great champion of the nineteenth century, even of all time.

Chopin wrote no symphonies, no operas, and even his two piano concertos have boring and perfunctory orchestral parts. Where to start with the piano music? Chopin invented forms like **mazurkas**, **nocturnes** (he actually popularized this previously invented form), **polonaises**, and **ballades**. His two sets of piano études (technical studies whose gorgeous musicality transcends their studiousness) are astonishing. If you're new to Chopin, your best bet is one of the many compilation albums featuring a mix of several works.

➤ **Liszt.** A contemporary of Chopin, Franz Liszt was considered the greatest virtuoso of his day, and in retrospect was one of the hottest piano stars of all time. He practically caused riots when he performed in concert. His compositions are less profound than Chopin's but you might want to pick up a compilation CD just to enjoy unbridled, unapologetic, virtuosic flash.

➤ **Brahms.** A very refined woman with impeccable taste once said to me she didn't like Brahms because he had no sense of humor. Reflecting on that critique, I realized it's true—Johannes Brahms has no playfulness in his compositions. By all accounts not a playful man in person, he nonetheless wrote soulful, inspired music for orchestra, combinations of instruments, and piano. The best way to get a handle on Brahms's piano persona is to buy an album that contains many of his short pieces for solo piano. His moods range from quietly introspective to tumultuous and assertive.

➤ **Rachmaninoff.** Sergei Rachmaninoff was born late in the Romantic period, and composed well into the twentieth century, by which time he was rather a throwback to a previous era. A Russian composer, Rachmaninoff recently gained popular allure when his **Piano Concerto #3** was featured in the movie *Shine*, then featured again in David Helfgott's chart-busting recording. That particular concerto has been my favorite since I was a young teenager, so I recommend it. Rachmaninoff is perhaps best known for his concertos, but he also composed many shorter solo piano pieces such as **preludes** and **études**. They are crushingly difficult to play, and it's fun to listen to master pianists dispatch them as if they were easy.

➤ **Scriabin.** Another Russian, and, like Rachmaninoff, born late to the Romantic era. Scriabin's early piano music sounds like a Russian Chopin, but it didn't take him long to develop a highly individual and almost modern style. His later pieces veer almost into atonality—a style of composing that can sound as if the notes were picked at random. Scriabin pushed the envelope, but he wasn't a capricious or trivial composer. His piano music is deeply sensual and evocative. Try an album of **études**, **preludes**, or miscellaneous short piano pieces.

The Impressionists

Around the turn of the twentieth century, the artistic spotlight turned to France, and particularly to Paris. Writers, painters, and musicians gathered to live the bohemian life of cultural elitism in Paris. Classical music entered its next major historical period named for the style that bound painters and composers together: Impressionism.

Music Speak
Impressionism is a style of music that emphasized rich tone color, slow moving harmonies, and almost arrhythmic and amorphous melody lines.

As you can gather from the name, impressionistic art and music was created to convey an impression—not necessarily a concrete impression, and certainly not one based on realism. Paintings from the period are fuzzy and imbued with a wash of colors. Music from those days shares the same sensibility, as harmonies were stretched in new directions and the rhythmic pulse of previous generations became vague. Impressionistic music doesn't generally have a strong beat. Instead, it is a watery-sounding melange of shifting sonorities and evocative harmonies. Some of the pieces from this period attempted to convey, musically, underwater scenes or landscapes. Harmonic rules that had been in place for hundreds of years were thrown out the window, and smashed on the Parisian streets below.

For the listener, impressionistic piano music is extremely moody. It bears a certain resemblance to new age music, but with far greater complexity and sophistication. Impressionistic melodies don't stick in your head, and the pieces definitely don't make you tap your foot. Rather, music from that period sends you on mental journeys filled with lovely and fantastic imagery.

There are two main composers from this period you might want to check out:

➤ **Debussy.** Claude Debussy was influenced by many musical traditions, including jazz. His piano music sounds much simpler than it actually is—his pieces are densely filled with notes, but must be made to sound transparent. He composed preludes and études in the Romantic tradition, but they are on the abstract side and are hard to listen to if you're not already a fan of Impressionism. Instead, try a group of pieces called **Images**.

➤ **Ravel.** Maurice Ravel was an Impressionist with a stronger sense of melody than some others, and as such is a good introduction to the period. His piano music is fastidiously crafted and especially lovely. Look up the **Sonatina**, the **Pavane for a Dead Princess** (morbid title; beautiful piece), **Jeux D'Eau**, and collections of piano pieces. Ravel didn't compose a huge body of works, but each one is a gem.

Jazz—America's Music

Twentieth-century piano music in America has been dominated by a single, diverse, sprawling art form: jazz. Jazz is America's home-grown music genre, born from a confluence of Afro-American spirituals and urban street music early in the century.

Music Speak
Ragtime was one of the first forms of jazz piano, developed early in the century in southern urban centers like New Orleans. Featuring a *stride* left hand, bouncing back and forth between bass notes and mid-range chords, set against jaunty melodies in the right hand, ragtime is joyful and playful music.

Ragtime was the first organized expression of early jazz piano that you can listen to today. The happy, rhythmically syncopated type of music enjoyed a renewal of popularity after the movie *The Sting* was released, featuring ragtime prominently in the soundtrack. Since then, Scott Joplin has been firmly installed on the musical map of the twentieth century.

You can find albums with collected ragtime pieces, called *rags*, by Joplin and others. Scott Joplin was a genius of melody and mood, but any ragtime composer you come across will give you some joyful listening. Ragtime has bittersweet moments, but overall is some of the most purely happy music you can find.

Jazz piano is a subject worthy of several books by itself. For now, I just want to point you to a few jazz piano artists from different points along the jazz spectrum who represent a broad range of listening experience.

➤ **Bill Evans.** The quiet, thoughtful, introspective jazz stylings of Bill Evans are often considered the birth of modern jazz piano. A great innovator, even with his modest playing style, Evans developed the jazz harmonies and chords all jazz players now take for granted. Evans was a great melodist whose improvisations never became abstract or confusing. When playing a jazz standard, he takes you on a melodic journey at the end of which you may not remember how you got there, but you sure enjoyed the ride. Bill Evans recordings make great background music, because they are so unassuming and undemanding. But don't forget to listen carefully from time to time, and appreciate his subtle harmonies and reverant melodic sense.

➤ **Oscar Peterson.** Sheer virtuosity isn't restricted to the classical field, and Oscar Peterson proves it. One of the great technicians of jazz piano, Peterson will stun you with his speed and power, while reaching your soul with a masterful grasp of the blues and traditional jazz. Not much of a composer, Oscar Peterson has built a legendary career playing both solo and in small jazz ensembles. His style and touch are so distinctive that when you've heard him once, you'll probably recognize his playing in the future. He represents a perfect marriage of virtuosity and musicianship.

➤ **Chick Corea.** Chick is what musicians call a "monster." Bringing a stupendous musicianship to the service of both acoustic and electronic jazz, Chick Corea is a legend in his own time who easily crosses from one genre to another. He has even composed several classical works—before Paul McCartney and Billy Joel made it vogue to do so. To hear him as a keyboardist you can get his Return to Forever albums from the 1970s, or, more recently, the Chick Corea Electric Band CDs. As a pianist, check out the Chick Corea Acoustic Band albums.

➤ **Keith Jarrett.** Master of free-form, pure piano *improvisation*, Keith Jarrett made a big splash in the 1970s with voluminous live recordings of his spontaneous playing. The so-called Koeln Album, recorded live in the city of the same name, created the same sort of stir in jazz circles that the Beatles' *White Album* did in the pop world. Jarrett is known for his idiosyncratic performance style, replete with wild swayings on the bench and unselfconscious singing along to his own music. These quirks can be heard on many of his recordings.

A Quick Survey of Pianists

Since the invention of the grammaphone (thanks, Thomas), it has been easy to hear all the great pianists of the current era. What a shame we'll never know what Chopin and Liszt sounded like as pianists! This section points out a few of the legendary twentieth-century pianists, and their musical specialities.

➤ **Rubinstein.** Artur Rubinstein was one of the great Romantic pianists of the mid-century. Well, for most of the century, actually, considering what a long life he lived. Not considered one of the knuckle-crunching virtuosos, Rubinstein specialized in bringing a clear and sweet presentation of the Romantic repertoire. He was one of the great Chopin interpreters of all time. Rubinstein's playing was never encumbered by excess emotion or drippy sentimentality, but was tasteful, to the point, and clear.

> **Music Speak**
> **Improvisation** means making up the music as you play. It is an essential skill in playing jazz piano.

➤ **Horowitz.** Vladimir Horowitz is the recording era's preeminent piano virtuoso—so far. He brought unheard-of power and an almost unbelievable technique to bear, and would routinely shatter modern piano strings as if they were flimsy nineteenth-century models. Horowitz loved to play Liszt, Scriabin, Rachmaninoff, and other Romantic composers of the big, flashy romantic repertoire. He also performed Chopin, but less convincingly. Surprisingly, his concerts usually featured the small, late Baroque sonatas of Scarlatti, and sometimes Mozart pieces. Although Horowitz retired early in his career (only to emerge again later), his recorded output is substantial. Get anything you can find, especially the incredible live performances.

➤ **Ashkenazy.** Another Vladimir, Ashkenazy is now conducting orchestras more than he is playing piano in concert, but his early career was primarily as a pianist. For my money, Ashkenazy's blend of virtuosity and elegance is unbeatable. He has taken a stab at recording across all the music periods, but stick to his playing of Romantic pieces like Chopin and Rachmaninoff.

➤ **Gould.** Glenn Gould is one of the strangest, most idiosyncratic, and genius-laden figures in the annals of classical pianism. His uniquely precise, almost mathematical playing style made him a natural for the music of Bach, and that's primarily what he is known for, though he recorded other composers as well. Stay away from his rare romantic releases, and stick to Bach with Gould. When I first heard Gould's Bach playing as a teenager, I became permanently spoiled, and have never been satisfied with any other pianist's interpretations since. A compulsive musical personality who was most comfortable in the recording studio, Gould's Bach recordings are fastidious, technically brilliant, marvels of clarity, and thrilling in their boldness. He somehow brings a completely modern quality to the music, without sacrificing the antique ornateness of Baroque composition.

➤ **Ohlsson.** Garrick Ohlsson emerged on the scene in the early 1970s after winning the prestigious International Chopin Competition in Warsaw. Not since Van Cliburn won the Tchaikowski Competition in the 1950s has a piano prize winner received such acclaim. Ohlsson didn't didn't attain the rock-star status of Cliburn, but he has continued with a solid career. His playing is breathtaking, featuring a prodigious technical command of the keyboard and an extroverted, devil-may-care style that has left me on the edge of my seat more than once. His personal repertoire is wide-ranging, covering centuries of piano composition. Still known for his Chopin interpretations, he recently embarked on a two-year project to record and perform every one of Chopin's pieces.

> **Grace Notes**
>
> Stories of Glenn Gould's eccentricities abound. Once he sued the Steinway piano company for a large amount when one of its representatives shook his hand too vigorously. He conducted his own chamber orchestra but refused to allow an audience to attend its performances. He always had a glass of distilled water within his reach while playing, and placed a rug under his special, 14-inch-high chair. In 1964, he abruptly quit public performing because he felt the only "perfect" performance could be caught on record. In his recordings, he spliced together several performances in order to achieve this perfection.

The Least You Need to Know

➤ The Baroque era is classical music's first era of the piano.

➤ The Classic era featured Mozart and Beethoven.

➤ Romantic music highlighted beautiful melodies, composed by Chopin, Liszt, Rachmaninoff, Scriabin, and others.

➤ Impressionistic piano music is moody and evocative. The two main Impressionistic composers were Debussy and Ravel.

Staying Motivated

In This Chapter

➤ A few ways to take a break from practicing

➤ How to find a piano teacher

➤ Questions to ask before taking the first lesson

Playing music should be fun, but the truth is that it requires practice, and practicing can be a drag. Ideally, you should always be working on a piece that's slightly too difficult, growing into it in the process. But it's not uncommon to select something a little too difficult, and then long-term frustration can set in. Not a good feeling, nor a productive state of affairs.

Fortunately, you're not in school anymore, and can do what you want. (If you *are* in school, my condolences.) You don't have to keep working on a piece that's too hard, or that you're bored with. You don't have to practice more than you really want to. This chapter provides some tips on staying motivated and keeping the practicing grind interesting and fun.

Keeping It Interesting

There's no denying it—practicing can wear a little thin over the long haul. Much as you may love the piano, and be excited about playing, there are two facts that rub against each other:

➤ Developing skill on the piano requires regular practice

➤ Regular practice sometimes gets boring

What can you do? Well, here are some things you can do:

➤ **Take a break.** Okay, this is a no-brainer, I admit it. When you're sick of practicing, stop practicing. What you may not know—and this is going to sound loony—is that you can actually get better by not practicing. Paradoxical as such a statement seems, there is truth to it.

Key Thought
When you work repeatedly on something with your conscious mind, you can hit roadblocks to progress repeatedly, and never seem to get anywhere past a certain point. If you put the project away for a time, it's as if the unconscious mind continues working on it. Then, when you return to your practice, the playing is sometimes mysteriously easier. I have experienced this odd and fortunate phenomenon so many times that I now rely on it.

➤ **Try different kinds of music.** If you're getting bored with practicing classical pieces, get a collection of pop tunes—maybe oldies from your teen years—and try something completely different. By the same token, if you feel saturated from playing too much popular music, have a crack at some classical stuff, which requires a completely different kind of concentration and skill. (See Chapter 20 for specific suggestions.)

➤ **Stop playing and listen.** Adopting the piano into your life is a two-way street. There's playing, and there's listening. Both thrive on attention and dedication. When you get bored with practicing, you tend to lose appreciation for the piano generally. Listening to favorite piano music—or exploring new recordings—is an ideal way to renew your appreciation. And when it's possible, there is absolutely nothing better than going to a piano concert for getting inspired again.

➤ **Switch instruments.** Switching from keyboard to trombone is good. (Just kidding.) The point I'm making is that if the piano has you under its thumb, and if you have the means, try getting a home keyboard to play around with. The various buttons and electronic features of home keyboards are a lot of fun to experiment with. In the process, you would certainly gain a fresh appreciation for the wonderful aspects of the piano you might have been taking for granted.

➤ **Find a music partner.** The best solution of all to tired practicing is to find a music partner to share this venture with. The person needn't be another keyboard player—in fact, another pianist or keyboardist would limit the possibilities for collaboration. If you know someone who sings, or plays another instrument like flute or violin, you can make music together. Playing with another person, relying on each other to keep the musical flow going, choosing and exploring new music together—these are fulfilling activities that keep the routine from ever going stale.

Finding a Teacher

Hard though it may be to fathom (especially for me), this book may not provide enough instruction for a lifetime of learning. Even if you continue getting value from these chapters for the next, say, seventy-five years, you may want to have a live teacher to stay motivated. Furthermore, it's good to ask questions of someone who can actually answer. (You can try asking questions of this book, but I can't guarantee a response.)

The question is, how do you find a teacher? Here are a few ways to locate one:

➤ Call up a local school and say you want a piano teacher, and you want one now! Well, no need to be obstreperous. Just politely ask if any music teachers on the school faculty give private piano lessons. If there is a music school nearby, all the better.

➤ Check the classifieds of your local paper.

➤ Look on bulletin boards around town—many local teachers use that free means of advertising.

➤ If all else fails, try the Yellow Pages.

For a beginner, there is almost no such thing as a bad teacher, as long as you both speak the same language and the person doesn't have any pathologies you find disagreeable. (Chewing on the curtains during the lesson, for example, would be disturbing.) Nonetheless, you should ask a few questions over the phone before committing to the first lesson:

> **Musical Mouthful**
> "I will gladly give lessons as a favor, particularly where I see that my student has talent, inclination, and anxiety to learn."— Wolfgang Amadeus Mozart (1778)

➤ **How long are the lessons?** Some teachers offer two lengths: thirty and sixty minutes. Others play around with weird times like forty-five or fifty minutes. Some teachers show more flexibility than others. Beginning students do best with half-hour lessons—longer isn't necessary. Don't let a teacher force you into an hour if you don't feel you're ready for such intense lessons.

➤ **Who does the driving?** Most teachers work out of a studio, either in their home or a separate location. If driving isn't a problem for you, going to a studio is preferable all the way around: the teacher probaby has a good piano, lots of sheet music, and you don't have to make sure the house is clean every week. (That would be a big consideration for me.) However, if your schedule or transportation resources make it inconvenient to travel to a lesson, find a local teacher who makes house calls. Many piano teachers still do this, though you might have to pay a bit more for the lesson.

➤ **What kind of music?** Needless to say, the teacher should teach the sort of music you wish to play. Now, if you're a beginner, and simply want help learning your way around the keyboard, then just about any teacher can help you. But even at the beginning a good teacher can focus on tips and tricks that apply to the type of music you eventually want to play. So make sure, at the beginning, that you and your teacher are on the same page.

> **Key Thought**
> Once you've made an appointment for a lesson, don't think that you're committed to this teacher for life. Take a first lesson, and see how the two of you get along. The lessons should be fun, as well as informative. Above all, if you feel self-conscious or uncomfortable learning and playing with this person, find someone else. You should feel completely comfortable and trusting during your lessons.

➤ **How many students, and what ages?** Ask the prospective teacher point-blank how many private students he or she currently is teaching. Make sure they're talking about *private*, one-on-one students, not classroom students. Chances are that a bustling practice indicates a good teacher.

The Least You Need to Know

➤ Taking a break from practicing can be productive, and can actually improve your playing in the long run.

➤ You can find a piano teacher by checking with local schools, looking classified ads, and even in the Yellow Pages.

➤ The best piano teacher can match your schedule, come to your home if you don't have a car, and make the lesson fun.

Chapter 23

MIDI and Home Music Studios

In This Chapter

➤ What in the world is MIDI, and why should you care?

➤ The many types of MIDI keyboard

➤ All about MIDI recorders, also known as sequencers

➤ Keyboardless instruments: tone modules and drum machines

➤ The basics of hooking MIDI devices together

Are you learning on an electronic keyboard? For some people, a keyboard is just the beginning.The beginning of what? Of letting their homes get overrun by digital music-making creatures of all shapes and sizes. Well, it's not necessarily that bad, but there certainly are a lot of fun musical toys out there that enhance the features of your keyboard. This chapter serves as your companion should you be afflicted with hardware lust—a disease I have succumbed to more than once.

Digital music equipment, as part of the computer revolution, brings an astonishing degree of musical power and capability right into the home. For some people it's nothing more than a fun hobby; for others, such equipment brings out musical ability that was hidden for years; and for some people, advanced keyboards and related equipment actually opens up new career doors. This chapter has modest ambitions—it gives you a rundown on what is available, what it does, and why people are buying it.

MIDI, the Essential Acronym

Any discussion of keyboards and home studios must start with the strange musical term, *MIDI*. MIDI is an acronym for Musical Instrument Digital Interface, but don't worry—that's as technical as I'm going to get in this chapter. Actually, you may be somewhat familiar with MIDI, if you've looked at the back of your keyboard or in the owner's manual. The back panel of almost every home keyboard has jacks labeled MIDI, though you may have to squint hard to read the label. If the MIDI jacks are there, the owner's manual certainly talks about how to use them.

Music Speak
MIDI is an acronym for Musical Instrument Digital Interface—a fancy way of saying that MIDI connects keyboards to other keyboards, and keyboards to computers. There are other types of MIDI devices as well, including drum machines, tone modules, and sequencers.

Basically, MIDI lets you hook musical devices to each other for various purposes that I describe in this chapter. The only things you need, in order to use MIDI, are a MIDI cable and a second MIDI device. (Your keyboard is a MIDI device if it has MIDI jacks on the back panel. Keep reading to discover other types of MIDI devices.) There's no limit on the degree to which you can expand a MIDI setup, except perhaps budgetary and space limits.

But what *is* a MIDI setup? In the most general terms, a MIDI setup is two or more connected MIDI devices. The two devices could be two keyboards, a keyboard and a computer, a keyboard and a recording device, a keyboard and a drum machine, or any number of other possibilities.

There are two basic reasons for having a MIDI studio:

➤ **Enjoying lots of different sounds.** If you own a home keyboard or digital piano, you can make it sound like a number of different instruments just by pressing buttons. This is definitely fun, and prompts the more-is-better syndrome to kick in. If one keyboard with a hundred instrument sounds is good, wouldn't the addition of a second keyboard, with one-hundred fresh sounds be better? This reasoning is especially compelling if you grow tired of your keyboard's sounds.

Furthermore, some keyboards specialize in one type of sound, much as digital pianos have excellent acoustic piano sounds, but sometimes fall short when it comes to emulating other instruments. If you have been playing a digital piano for a while, you may begin to crave the tones of a digital synthesizer; if you've been learning on a home keyboard with a cheesy piano sound, you may begin eyeing digital pianos.

➤ **Recording original compositions.** Recording is the second big reason for accumulating space-eating, budget-consuming MIDI gear. For many people, recording is the name of the game with MIDI, thanks to devices that keep track of every keystroke you play, then let you correct mistakes and alter your own performance in many ways. MIDI recorders (which I describe in more detail later in this chapter), have the added enticing benefit of letting you record in simultaneous tracks, just like a professional sound studio. With all the sounds at your disposal thanks to your keyboard(s), and with the multitrack capability of MIDI recorders, home MIDI studios amount to virtual orchestras. And having a virtual orchestra in your home, let me tell you, is a blast. MIDI recording is very appealing to composers, both amateur and professional.

Grace Notes
Many television shows use scores completely created in MIDI studios. The well-known score of *Seinfeld*, combining musical themes with pops and bursts of sound, is one current example.

The Many Types of MIDI Keyboard

I want to make clear right from the beginning that MIDI is not some exotic feature that you must search for when shopping for keyboards. There is almost no such thing as a modern keyboard made today that doesn't have MIDI jacks built in. The presence of MIDI jacks is all you need to see to determine that a keyboard is a MIDI keyboard. Only the very least expensive, ill-equipped home keyboards lack MIDI jacks. Other home keyboards, sporting the crucial MIDI jacks, may differ widely in the features they offer, but they all share one essential ability: they can send and receive MIDI information.

Here are the basic types of MIDI keyboards. (You may wish to review Chapter 2, which also discusses this information.)

Home Keyboards

Home keyboards, also sometimes called *hobby keyboards*, reside on the less expensive side of the keyboard price range. Home keyboards are cheaper, lighter, and suffer from a lower sound quality than professional keyboards described below. These budget keyboards have powerful advantages, though, among them:

➤ Home keyboards are cheap. And light. As mentioned above, you don't break your bank account buying them, and you don't break your back carrying them.

➤ Ironically, home keyboards are easier to operate than more expensive professional models. They tend to have more buttons, and better labeled buttons.

➤ One feature is present in all home keyboards: speakers. Built-in speakers negate the need for an amplifier or headphones when you want to hear what you're playing, which is pretty much always.

➤ Auto-accompaniment patterns may or may not be your cup of tea, but they are a distinctive aspect of home keyboards that add to their appeal. (See Chapter 14, "Basics of Accompaniment," for more enlightening discourse on auto-accompaniment.)

Home keyboards represent a good way to start using digital keyboards, as they normally carry an effective range of features without forcing you to spend money on professional bells and whistles you may never use. Many home keyboards sport an on-board MIDI recorder, and most keyboards include about one hundred instrument sounds. In most cases, the MIDI recorder is not as powerful as its professional-level counterparts, and the sounds don't meet professional studio standards, but the point is that home keyboards get you started in fine style.

Professional Synthesizers

A synthesizer is a kind of keyboard that can create (synthesize) its own sounds. Synthesizers come with a selection of built-in sounds (often called *factory sounds* or *presets*), just as home keyboards do, but you are not limited to the presets. Synthesizers let you create new sounds, or modify the factory sounds, or even buy new banks of instrument sounds from the manufacturer or a third-party company. The result of this flexibility is that synthesizers have a virtually unlimited sound palette if you go to the trouble and/or expense of using its capabilities.

A subset of professional synthesizers is represented by the so-called *keyboard workstation*, which crams many features into an integrated package. Workstations are really three MIDI devices in one: keyboard, MIDI recorder, and drum machine. (I discuss MIDI recorders and drum machines a bit later in this chapter. Patience.) Workstations are great introductions to pro-level keyboards, since they pack so much power into an instrument that often costs about the same as a regular professional synthesizer.

> **Music Speak**
> MIDI is a digital language—basically a specialized kind of computer language. As such, the stuff transmitted through MIDI cables and MIDI jacks is called *MIDI data* or *MIDI information*.

> **Key Thought**
> When it comes to synthesizers, there is some blurring of the line between home keyboards and professional models. For the sake of clarification I am grouping all synthesizers (which are sometimes called *synths*, by the way) as professional keyboards, because the ability to create new sounds is usually a matter of professional interest. However, the truth is that making a new sound is fun no matter what your level of experience, and some inexpensive home keyboards let you "tweak" the factory sounds to some extent. Professional synths give you helpful features like memory slots for storing new sound creations, and even computer-style disk drives for longer term storage.

Music Speak
A **sampler** is a type of keyboard designed to digitally record real sounds; these recordings are called "samples."

Grace Notes
It's easy to confuse samplers with MIDI recorders, but they are not the same. Samplers digitally record real sounds like a flute or a drum. MIDI recorders record keystrokes played on MIDI keyboards. MIDI recorders do not record real sounds at all. I describe MIDI recorders in more detail a bit farther ahead in this chapter.

Key Thought
The sequencer doesn't record actual sounds like a sampler does—so don't bother trying to sing into it. It only records *MIDI data*, which consists primarily of keystrokes, pedal movements, and how hard you hit the keys.

Samplers

Samplers are a unique type of keyboard. The one thing samplers do that no other MIDI instrument does is record sounds. (Recording with a sampler is called *sampling*.) With a sampler, you can record your dog barking, then play the bark on the keyboard. You can record the wind, and play the whoosh. Such sampling escapades may not be the most musical use to which technology can be put, but are fun nonetheless. In professional studios, samplers are used to record real instrument notes, which then are played on the keyboard.

Talk about an unlimited sound palette! With sampling, the entire real world of sound is at your disposal. All you need is a microphone, which plugs directly into the sampler, and you're in the sampling business for fun and profit. (Well, probably not for profit.)

Samplers tend to be more expensive than sythesizers, thanks to their specialized circuitry, plus the built-in hard drives and floppy drives needed to store samples. I should also mention that sampling isn't quite as easy as I make it out to be in the preceding paragraph. Sampling is a specialized studio skill that requires good microphones and lots of technical skill to accomplish effectively. Samplers, though are nice MIDI instruments to have even if you never actually record anything. You can buy samples made by other people and companies, and samplers produce the most realistic instrument sounds of any type of MIDI keyboard.

MIDI Recorders

Earlier in this chapter I have made reference to MIDI recorders. I didn't want to muddy the waters before, but I'll tell you now: MIDI recorders are called *sequencers*. Sequencers get such a nerdy name because they perform the geeky task of recording *sequences* of keystrokes. If you hook up a sequencer to a MIDI keyboard, then play something on the keyboard with the sequencer in Record mode, the sequencer keeps track of every key you play, when you play it, and how hard you play it. After you've finished the recording, you can play back the sequence, hearing your performance reproduced exactly, and even make corrections to the notes.

There are three basic types of sequencers:

➤ **Sequencers built into keyboards.** Some home keyboards have simple sequencers, and professional keyboard workstations have fancier, more advanced sequencers.

➤ **Stand-alone sequencers.** These devices are box-like MIDI components, sometimes called *hardware sequencers*, that sit next to your keyboard, or even on top of it (but not covering the keys), and plug into the keyboard's MIDI jacks. They are usually more powerful than sequencers built into home keyboards, but not as powerful as software sequencers described in the next paragraph.

➤ **Software sequencers.** Software sequencers are computer programs that run on personal computers attached to a keyboard's MIDI jacks. When a computer is part of a MIDI setup, its main function is usually to run the software sequencer. (Most computers don't have built-in MIDI jacks the way keyboards do, so you must buy a *MIDI interface* that brings the computer up to speed with the MIDI realm, and gives it MIDI jacks.) Software sequencers are, by far, the most powerful type of sequencer, and used by MIDI enthusiasts who are serious about composing and recording with keyboards.

Music Speak
A sequencer digitally records sequences of MIDI information for playback and editing. There are built-in, stand-alone, and software sequencers available.

What do I mean when I refer to a sequencer as being "powerful"? A sequencer's power depends on two sets of features:

1. How many tracks it lets you record
2. How many ways it lets you edit your recordings

It is the multitrack capability that makes MIDI a virtual orchestra (or jazz ensemble, or rock band). The more tracks you have to work with, the better—assuming you have enough instrument sounds in your keyboard(s) to fill up all those tracks. Sequencers built into home keyboards sometimes only have one or two tracks, while the sequencers built into professional keyboard workstations have eight or sixteen tracks. (As with professional multitrack tape decks found in live recording studios, tracks tend to be added in increments of eight, for some reason.) By contrast, software sequencers offer at least sixty-four tracks in most cases, and sometimes hundreds.

Grace Notes
Many musicians already use their home computers to make their own digital recordings. Once recordable CDs become available, you'll be able to make and distribute your own albums from your own home studio—all by using your computer!

When it comes to editing music, sequencers are like word processors for music. After playing into a sequencer you can change individual notes; assign an entire track to a different instrument sound; transpose the performance to a different key, and alter the tempo without altering the pitch of the notes. (If you speed up a tape recording, everything gets high-pitched and comically squealy.) Software sequencers have very advanced editing features, plus the big computer screen for displaying the recording's MIDI data in various ways.

Tone Modules

One peculiar aspect of MIDI is that you can hook two keyboards together, and use each keyboard to play the other keyboard's sounds. In other words, you can access the sounds inside of a keyboard through the MIDI cable connecting the two instruments. Since that is the case, you may be asking, why have the second set of keys? Why not just put the second keyboard's sounds in a box, played by the first keyboard? It's a good question, asked by instrument designers several years ago, and that's exactly the solution they chose.

Boxes filled with preset sounds, lacking keyboards, are called *tone modules*. They are modules (hardware boxes) with tones (instrument sounds) inside them, sporting MIDI jacks on the back panel.

Music Speak
Tone modules are like keyboards without the keyboard. What's left? The brain of the keyboard, including all the sounds the keyboard can make. Tone modules are used in MIDI studios with one master keyboard that controls various tone modules and drum machines.

Grace Notes
Most MIDI professional-level instrument manufacturers create tone module versions of their keyboards, so you have a choice. In most cases all the features are the same in the keyboard and module, except, of course, that the module doesn't have a set of keys, and can be played only with another keyboard. You can get tone module versions of both synthesizers and samplers, but usually not of home keyboards.

Music Speak
Drum machines provide drum sounds for people using the MIDI capabilities of digital keyboards. You can hook up a drum machine to a keyboard, and automatically have access to many realistic drum and percussion sounds.

Many MIDI setups contain just one keyboard attached to multiple tone modules. Tone modules take less space than a keyboard, although they usually cost about the same as the keyboard model of the same instrument.

Drum Machines

One specialized MIDI device worthy of mention is the time-honored *drum machine*. The drum machine isn't honored by too much time, come to think of it, but there were drum machines being used in hotel lounge gigs as early as the late 1970s, predating the MIDI revolution. Drum machines do what you would expect; they make drum sounds. Featuring little pads on their top surface, you can play them with your fingers. Drum machines are traditionally used as nifty accompanists that have infallible rhythm, are never late to the gig, weigh less than a single real drum, and don't get upset when you ask them to play softly.

The heart of the drum machine is its built-in sequencer that allows you to prerecord drum patterns in various tempos and styles. Drum machines fulfill the same basic function as auto-accompaniment features on home keyboards, but they generally have better drum sounds. (These days, almost all drum machines use digitally sampled—recorded—drums.)

A related MIDI component to the drum machine is the *percussion module*. Percussion modules are the tone module versions of drum machines, just as tone modules are alternate versions of keyboards. Percussion modules lack the built-in sequencer, and are meant to be used with a hardware or (ideally) software sequencer. Percussion modules are connected with MIDI cables to the keyboard, which accesses its sounds. Accordingly, the pads that drum machines have are missing from percussion modules.

Hooking It All Up

Now that you've bought two keyboards, three tone modules, a sampler, a drum machine, a computer, and sequencing software—well, if you've bought all that, you can't even afford MIDI cables to connect it together.

It's beyond the scope of this book to provide a complete tutorial on connecting all the many types of MIDI studio. But I don't want you to put down this chapter before getting a basic understanding of what the MIDI jacks are for and how to use them. Armed with that understanding and fortified by the literary excellence of the owner's manual that no doubt complements whatever new MIDI gadget you buy, you should be able to hook up a component or two without problems.

Keeping this book in your hand, walk around to the back of your keyboard to find the MIDI jacks. Are you there? Good. Look for the black, circular jacks with six holes in each jack. There should be at least two (possibly three) jacks, labeled MIDI. Once you see them, look more closely at the labeling, and notice that one jack is MIDI IN, and the other is MIDI OUT. Here's what they mean:

➤ MIDI IN jacks are for *receiving* MIDI data.

➤ MIDI OUT jacks are for *transmitting* MIDI data.

Use the MIDI OUT jack when you want to send MIDI data from the keyboard to another device, such as a tone module or sequencer. Just plug one end of a MIDI cable into the MIDI OUT jack of the keyboard, and plug the other end into the MIDI IN jack of the second device. Then, when you play the keyboard, all your keystrokes are automatically sent through the MIDI OUT jack.

Two Typical MIDI Setups

So what is really the purpose of all this? What can these MIDI devices do for your musical life? This section outlines a couple of alternative MIDI setups common among MIDI hobbyists, and describes what they are used for.

Basic Recording

One of the first and most common desires to take residence in the aspiring MIDI-phile's heart is the desire to record music. If your keyboard lacks a built-in sequencer, you may start considering buying a simple hardware device for basic recording. You don't have to cash in your kid's college fund to buy a basic stand-alone sequencer that gives you a few tracks of MIDI recording. Two MIDI cables round out the expansion—one goes from keyboard OUT to sequencer IN, and the other reverses the process from sequencer OUT to keyboard IN. So equipped, your keyboard is suddenly enhanced by the ability to record itself.

Having a sequencer lets you hear what you sound like when playing, which may be a mixed blessing. (I'm not ragging on your playing ability, mind you, I just know from painful personal experience what a surprise it can be to hear yourself perform.) Sequencing is also great for budding composers. You can make up tunes, record them, and save them for your Uncle Posterity. If you plan on saving many pieces, get a sequencer with a disk drive.

Adding a Tone Module

For many people, recording isn't the goal, but having a good selection of intriguing sounds is important. Getting a tone module and attaching it to the keyboard dramatically expands the sounds available to you through the keyboard. It's not the most inexpensive purchase in the world, but if you have a home keyboard with preset sounds that cannot be changed or augmented, you have no choice if you *need* new sounds.

Tone modules have specialties in some cases, making it possible to get a particularly desirable sound. For example, if you're frustrated with the piano sound in your home keyboard, you might consider a tone module that specializes in grand piano samples. Less expensive than a general-purpose tone module (and often smaller), it's a way of classing up the sound of your keyboard in at least one department—piano sound. You could do the same thing in another department by getting a percussion module that specializes in ethnic drums, for example, or rock 'n' roll drum kits.

Grace Notes

Early synthesized drums were the heart-and-soul of '70s-era disco music. Without the ability to reproduce mechanically a steady beat, this music wouldn't have had its characteristic thump-thump-thump accompaniment.

Grace Notes

Some keyboards and all tone modules have a third MIDI jack: the MIDI THRU jack. The MIDI THRU jack performs a specialized function, by taking all MIDI data received at the MIDI IN jack, replicating it, and passing it along through the attached MIDI cable. Use MIDI THRU when you have a tone module or other MIDI instrument positioned between your keyboard and a third MIDI device, like a sequencer.

Here's how the MIDI data is transmitted in such a setup:

Keyboard (MIDI OUT) to

Tone Module (MIDI IN)

Out of tone module (MIDI THRU) to

Sequencer (MIDI IN)

Many people press the home personal computer into use for sequencing. This is practical only if the computer and the keyboard are in the same room, and preferably near the same desk. If you go this route, you need to buy sequencing software, plus a MIDI interface for the computer. Check a local, fairly high-tech music store for information on what's available for your type of computer and budget.

Connecting a tone module to a keyboard is quite simple, and requires only one MIDI cable. Plug an end of the cable into the keyboard's MIDI OUT jack, and the other end into the tone module's MIDI IN jack. Once the tone module is connected to the keyboard, the net effect is a keyboard with expanded and upgraded sounds.

The Least You Need to Know

➤ MIDI is the Musical Instrument Digital Interface, and it allows you to connect two keyboards, or a keyboard with a computer. It's used for recording multitrack compositions, and for creating desktop orchestras.

➤ Almost every modern keyboard is a MIDI keyboard, including home keyboards, synthesizers, and digital pianos.

➤ Sequencers are MIDI recorders that keep track of your keystrokes and pedal movements as you play, then play back your exact performance.

➤ Tone modules and drum machines don't have keyboards, and must be played by a keyboard hooked up to them through MIDI.

➤ MIDI devices are connected using MIDI cables plugged into the MIDI jacks on the back of the devices. If you have an electronic keyboard, it probably has MIDI jacks in the back.

Part 5
Bringing It Home:
Buying an Instrument

This final part is a buyer's guide for pianos and all kinds of electronic instruments. I do not provide a brand-name tour of available instruments, a topic deserving of a separate book. However, I do bring to light all the general considerations you should keep in mind when shopping for a new or used piano, and a new or used keyboard.

Chapter 24 addresses issues in buying a new or used piano, while Chapter 26 does the same for electronic keyboards. In between, Chapter 25 covers everything you need to know about maintaining a piano in your home, including what kind of climate pianos thrive in, where to avoid placing them in your home, and how to find a tuner.

Buying a Piano

In This Chapter

➤ The reasons for buying a piano instead of an electronic keyboard

➤ Whether to shop for an upright or grand piano

➤ How to shop for a used piano, and whether to in the first place

➤ How to maintain a piano in your home

There was a time—not too long ago—where almost every American home had a piano in the parlour. Maybe no one could play it very well, but still it was a fixture in American life. Young people—especially young ladies—would be expected to entertain guests by playing the popular songs of the day, and families would gather round the piano to sing their old favorites.

The day may come when you consider the ultimate keyboard purchase: a piano. This chapter walks you through the general steps of buying a piano, from the "why" to the "how" of it, and from the "which" to the "how much."

Why Buy a Piano?

There are some obvious disadvantages to buying and owning a piano. Pianos are big, heavy, and difficult to move. Pianos are far more expensive than electronic keyboards. To top it off, a piano is a finicky resident in your home, requiring tunings and other maintenance. On the surface, it seems that electronic keyboards and digital pianos are such a convenient alternative that there would be no reason to buy a piano. Yet, pianos have not become the dinosaurs of the musical instrument kingdom. In fact, their popularity has grown during the time that digital keyboards have also become popular. This section describes a few of the reasons why pianos are still the keyboard of choice for many people.

Musical Mouthful
"Music with dinner is an insult both to the cook and the violinist."—G. K. Chesterton

The Real Piano Sound

The most compelling reason for buying a piano belongs to your ears. Technology has come a long way in imitating the sound of acoustic instruments through the use of digital sampling (see Chapter 23), and digital pianos are startlingly similar to real pianos when you first hear them. (Other types of electronic keyboards don't even come close enough for comparisons.) After playing a digital piano for a while, though, it becomes apparent to pianists that a lot is missing from the sound and feel of a piano. There are a couple of reasons why pianos have a superior sound to their digital cousins:

➤ **Real strings and dampers.** The difference between real vibrating strings and samples stored on memory chips is more than just a difference in materials and space. The sound waves bouncing around inside a piano create an acoustically complex sound that cannot, at least at this stage of the technology game, be replicated with circuitry.

The dampers—the felt pads that rest on the strings, and are lifted by the sustain pedal—play a part in the piano's unique sound. When you press the sustain pedal of a piano, all the strings are free to vibrate in response to those rampant soundwaves inside the instrument, creating a sonority that you may not be able to identify while playing, but certainly notice when it's missing. That extra sonority is definitely missing in digital instruments.

➤ **The inner machinery.** The piano mechanism that starts with the keys and ends with the hammers hitting strings is called the piano's *action*.

You, as the player, control this complex mechanism through its interface, which is the keyboard. It may seem surprising, but a good player actually can wield a fair degree of control over a piano's tone depending on how the keyboard is played.

Advanced piano study focuses to a large degree on coaxing the best tone out of the piano by refining the player's "touch" on the keyboard. All of these subtleties of touch are lost on digital keyboards, whose keys trigger on/off switches attached to tone-generating circuitry. Digital keyboards can register changes in volume according to the force with which you press the key, but that's the limit of their responsiveness.

The Mechanical Piano Action

Every piano keyboard has an individual feel to it, reflecting the construction and sheer weight of all the action's parts. When you press a key, you set in quick motion a whole series of mechanical events. Some pianos have a light feel while other are heavy; some actions feel fluid and fast, while others are stiff and demand slower, more deliberate playing.

Digital pianos try to emulate the weight and feel of piano actions, and some of them even replace the plastic keys normally used by electronic keyboards with wood keys. But there is no replacing the complex feel of a real piano action, with its solid "thunk" when the hammer hits the strings, and the tiny recoil of the hammer that you can feel in the key.

These all may sound like tiny details, but they add up to an entirely different experience when playing a piece on a real piano, compared to a digital.

Grace Notes
Pedaling on a piano can be a subtle skill involving half-pedals and other tricks that control how the strings vibrate. Digital pedaling, by contrast, is a simple on/off experience that applies *only* to whatever notes are being played. I should also mention the piano's soft pedal (see Chapter 17, "Pedals: Where's the Clutch?"), which exerts control over the instrument's tone and sonority. Digital pianos often include soft pedals, but they make a simple change to the instrument's volume, not the tonal characteristics.

Key Thought
The action is like a Rube Goldberg device: a long succession of levers and springs that culminates in a felt-tipped little hammer shooting forward (or upward, in the case of grand pianos) and smacking the strings of a note (see Chapter 3 for a description of the piano's inner workings).

Appearance

There's no denying that pianos are beautiful. Even a lover of technology and gadgets would have to admit that a gleaming ebony grand piano makes a more striking impression in a room than a dial-encrusted keyboard housed in plastic. The choice of a piano instead of a keyboard can legitimately be made strictly on its furniture value, aside from all musical considerations. Upright pianos may not have the dramatic appearance of grands, but are still dignified additions to a room.

Educational Value

If you are buying a keyboard instrument primarily for the kids in your household, the piano's tradition may appeal to you for their sake. Pianos have an entirely different educational value than keyboards—and both are worth considering for their respective merits. If you're buying an instrument for your kids, you really must choose between tradition and modernism.

MIDI Pianos

With all this talk about choosing between a digital piano and an acoustic piano, I'd be remiss if I didn't mention a compromise: MIDI pianos. Yes, MIDI pianos actually exist, though they may seem like a contradiction. MIDI pianos are real pianos, with strings, dampers, and everything, but with MIDI functionality built in. It's quite a feat, but some ingenious piano manufacturers have figured out how to turn an acoustic piano into a digital instrument, complete with a disk drive.

A lot of extra hardware is built into the piano, including a system of sensors near the keyboard that register every time a key is played, and turn the keystrokes into MIDI data, just like an electronic keyboard. That data can be sent to a computer or other MIDI device through a MIDI cable, again just like a digital keyboard. MIDI pianos also receive MIDI data, and play back MIDI sequences with a real piano sound—which is bound to be better than any sampled piano.

But MIDI pianos present a couple of problems. First of all, they are very expensive. Enough said on that topic. Second, they are finicky, sometimes needing a lot of regulation and adjustment of the electronic components built into the instrument, as well as the natural piano parts like hammers and dampers. Making it all work together is quite a feat, and though the manufacturers have ironed out the main problems, you still can count on hiring a trained technician more than you'd have to for a simple non-MIDI piano.

The Big Questions

If the day comes that you decide to buy a piano, you are immediately faced with two whopping-big questions: Should you buy an upright or a grand? Ideally, you can resolve these

Grace Notes
One of the most popular piano-variants of the turn-of-the-century was the player piano. Using a punched paper roll, it could reproduce performances at home. There was something magical about watching the keys move up and down by themselves. On more sophisticated instruments, the original pianist's touch could be accurately rendered, as if a ghost were playing the instrument! Today, there are digital player pianos which play automatically off of prerecorded discs.

Key Thought
Although pianos and electronic keyboard each have individual learning challenges, it is much easier for a pianist to play a keyboard than for a keyboardist to play the piano. The difference is due primarily to the heavier action of a piano, which is hard to cope with if you have only played the light actions of keyboards. Of course, piano players are clueless about the auto-accompaniment features of a keyboard, not to mention sequencing and other MIDI learning curves discussed in MIDI and Home Music Studios.

questions before beginning the shopping experience, as it's best to know what you're looking for before placing yourself under the influence of persuasive salespeople. Practically speaking, though, you may find your priorities changing as you see what's available. Even so, following are the main questions to keep in mind at the outset.

Upright or Grand?

Pianos come in two basic design types, and there are big differences in cost, quality and practicality between them. Here are the considerations upon which your decision should be based:

Space

They're not called *grand* pianos for nothing. Grand pianos are big! If you live in a small apartment, squeezing in a grand may be out of the question right from the start. If you have a larger living space, but are targeting a medium-sized room for the piano, you may or may not want the instrument dominating your decor. Fortunately, grand pianos come in many sizes. The term "baby grand" refers generically to small grands, but is not defined by a particular size range.

The following table gives you examples of typical grand piano sizes in four size ranges. The largest range, concert grand, is listed for information only—concert grands are usually not appropriate for home use (unless you want the whole neighborhood to hear you practice).

Grand piano sizes

Range	Piano size
Baby grand	4' 9"–5' 5"
Mid-size grand	5' 5"–6' 2"
Large grand	6' 2"–7' 5"
Concert grand	7' 5"–9' 0"

This table should be taken as a very general reference. Some piano brands may advertise sizes larger than 5' 5", and call them "baby grands."

All grand pianos are measured from the front edge of the keyboard (the part of the piano closest to your lap when you're sitting at the keyboard) to the very end of the instrument, at the point farthest away from you. The width is another measurement to keep in mind: most grand pianos are no wider than sixty inches (five feet) at their widest point, which is the keyboard plus the wood surrounding it. Keeping all these facts in mind, you can do a rough measurement in your room to see how large a piano you can fit. (My experience is that grand pianos tend to look bigger when delivered than you think they will when measuring.)

Upright pianos vary quite a bit in height, and very little in width or depth. Like grand pianos, uprights are about sixty inches wide. The height can range from about forty inches from floor to top, to about fifty-two inches. Uprights are usually pushed up against a wall, with the keyboard facing out, making them very space-efficient. Upright pianos are really grand pianos stood on end, with the strings running up and down instead of parallel to the floor. Accordingly, increasing the height of an upright piano affects the sound by providing longer strings, but doesn't have much effect on whether you can fit it into your room (unless your home has surprisingly low ceilings).

Sound Quality

Sure, grand pianos are beautiful pieces of furniture, and sure, they represent an excellently indulgent way to spend a large chunk of money. But is there a musical reason to choose a grand over an upright? Yes, there certainly is. For my money, the musical persuasiveness of grand pianos is their strongest selling point.

There are two essential features of a grand piano, compared to an upright. One is that the strings are longer. The other main difference is that grands have lids that lift up, exposing the full length of the strings to the room. Both these crucial differences have a dynamic result: a much louder instrument.

Of course, the loudness of grand pianos may be a reason *not* to get one, if you live with close neighbors or in a small house or apartment. But there are tonal differences that come into play with the longer strings, too. Grands have greater sonority than uprights, even when played softly. Greater sonority means a richer, fuller, long-lasting tone. The larger the grand, the greater the sonority (generally speaking, though different piano brands have different characteristics), especially in the bass notes.

In a piano store, play an octave toward the left end of the keyboard on a grand, then try a bass octave on an upright. The difference, in most cases, is startling.

Tall uprights have longer strings than short uprights, and are usually correspondingly louder and more sonorous. However, most uprights can only let the sound out through a small lid on the top, limiting the kind of full-throated volume you get by opening the lid of a grand. (Some uprights also let you remove the lower panel beneath the keyboard. Doing so lets out a lot of volume, but exposes the unsightly innards of the piano to the world. For some reason, upright innards are an eyesore, while grand innards are glamorous. Go figure.)

Cost

It should come as no surprise that grand pianos are more expensive than the upright pianos. You may find some very tall, high-end uprights that cost more than very small baby grands, but the two price ranges converge only at the extremes. Cutting right to the chase, here's a rough idea of price ranges from the smallest upright to a large grand.

Grace Notes

A special, very small type of upright is called a **spinet**. Spinets are extremely short, but are technically distinguished by a different type of action—the mechanism that makes a hammer hit the strings when you press a key. Despite the technicalities of action construction, which are far too boring to spell out, most people rightly consider spinets quite simply as very small uprights.

Musical Mouthful

Patient: "Doctor, doctor, will I be able to play the piano after my operation?"

Doctor: "Of course!"

Patient: "That's funny, I never could before!"

—Henny Youngman

Grace Notes

There are certain sizes at which the musical differences between uprights and grands converge. In other words, very tall uprights can produce the volume and tonal richness of very small grands. If considering a large upright and a baby grand, assuming you like the sound of both, the decision should be made on the basis of appearance, interior design, and cost.

Piano price ranges

Piano type	Price
Small upright	$2,000 – 3,500
Medium upright	$2,800 – 4,500
Tall upright	$3,800 – 6,000
Baby grand	$3,500 – 5,500
Medium grand	$4,800 – 10,000
Large grand	$7,500 – 20,000

Please note that the dollar amounts are very general. You should not take that table into a piano store and use it as a negotiating tool! There is a huge divergence in pricing among the various piano builders, not to mention the uneven markups you're liable to see in piano stores. These prices demonstrate, if anything, how difficult it is to estimate the cost of a new piano outside of a store. Although the prices in the table represent extremes, I wouldn't be surprised if you occasionally found prices for the different piano types that fall outside those extremes.

New or Used?

Key Thought
The basic advantage in buying a used piano, as with a used car, is that you can get more for your money as a tradeoff for owning something with some wear and tear built in. The cost savings could result in the opportunity to purchase a used grand for the cost of a new upright.

Key Thought
The technician doesn't need to take the piano anywhere—he or she can give it a once-over right in the store, and there is no piano salesman who should object to this. If you're looking at a private purchase of a piano in someone's home, arrange an appointment to bring a tuner to the piano.

The second big question facing prospective piano shoppers is whether to look at new or used pianos. The considerations are similar to deciding whether to buy a used or new car, except that pianos last much longer than most cars, so your choices represent a greater range of age.

What about damage to a used piano? What happens to pianos as they age, and is it safe to buy an instrument that's five, ten, twenty or more years old? The answers to these questions vary with each individual situation. But generally, shopping for a used piano is worth the effort if you're willing to put in the time and effort to find the right instrument. If a piano is built well, it can last for many decades.

Here are some considerations and tips when shopping for a used piano.

➤ When shopping around, or after having narrowed your choices down to a few pianos, take somebody with you who knows pianos inside and out. It's worth paying a tuner for a few hours of time to check out instruments you're seriously considering. As with buying a used car, it's advisable not to close the deal until the piano is checked by a technician. (Most tuners have a good technical awareness of all aspects of the instrument.)

➤ If buying a used piano from a store, check on the warranty provided by the store. If the piano is younger than about ten years, the original manufacturer's warranty might be transferrable. Older instruments are usually covered by the store in a limited way—a typical store warranty might extend for six months, which is long enough to detect and fix small problems that escaped your notice before buying. Also, try to get a free tuning (or three) worked into the deal.

➤ When looking at used pianos, whether in a store or in a private home, you can do a basic tire-kicking check by yourself. First of all, look at the instrument as a piece of furniture. Spot any scratches in the wood? You probably want to bring them up when discussing price.

Open the piano lid (upright or grand) and look inside. You may not understand the mechanisms, but you can look for rust on the metal parts and strings. Look at the hammers (the felt-tipped things that hit the strings when you play the keys) and see if they are all aligned evenly. Check for any woodworking anomalies like warping or cracks anywhere inside.

➤ Cracked soundboards are a famous drawback of used pianos. But, the truth is, many soundboard cracks don't hurt the instrument or change its sound. However, a crack is a sign that you need to maintain careful control over the climate around the piano in order to protect the soundboard, and other wood parts, from further damage.

➤ Play every note of the keyboard. Playing all the keys is probably the best basic test you can do on a piano, and it's easy enough to tell when a note doesn't work. Common problems with old pianos are notes that don't play at all; keys that stay down after you release them; and keys that play the note twice (the hammer double-strikes the note).

➤ Don't be concerned with used pianos in private homes that are drastically out of tune. The seller is perhaps foolish not to present the piano in its best light by tuning it before showing it, but bad tuning doesn't necessarily indicate any problem with the instrument. However, ask when it was last tuned. If the date is more recent than two months ago, then you know there's a problem.

➤ If you are visiting a store to which you intend to bring a technician at a later date to check some instruments, you might want to ask some questions during the first visit, then check the veracity of the answers when the technician is present. Ask whether the piano still holds its tune well, then have your tuner check the health of the pin block. Ask if the action needs regulation, then have your tuner check that. If the store's answers and reassurances differ too widely from your tuner's verifications, consider shopping elsewhere.

Grace Notes
The presence of dustballs inside an instrument is a sign that the store doesn't have high standards of instrument maintenance, which, though it might not indicate anything wrong with the individual piano, doesn't speak well for the store's general standards. (In a private home, it reflects more on housekeeping habits, and shouldn't be taken as seriously.)

Musical Mouthful
"The Reger Piano Concerto is to our mind a most inflated, pretentious bag of wind, with a very heavily scored and somewhat brutally effective piano part."—Olin Downes, *The New York Times* (1950)

The Asian Connection

Earlier in this century, there were more local piano builders than there are now. Nevertheless, there has been a renaissance of sorts in modern piano building, especially in Asian countries. This brings up the question of what piano brands are worth considering. Although I don't make specific recommendations of piano companies, I can tell you the general differences among some of the most well-known piano builders of our day.

Key Thought

All large-scale piano builders have embraced technology to some degree, but Steinway and other companies of a Euorpean lineage still favor hand-building techniques for some parts of the instrument.

Key Thought

You should never buy a piano on name reputation alone. Although they probably wouldn't admit it, all pianists know that even Steinway has turned out some dreadful instruments from time to time. Any manufacturer can't avoid turning out a clinker now and then.

Asian pianos have proliferated in the United States and other countries, giving consumers a choice of such brands as Yamaha, Kawai, Hyundai, Young Chang, and others. Asian pianos have built a reputation of competitive prices and reliable, assembly-line craftmanship. Some Asian companies have leveraged high-tech automation procedures to create pianos that are essentially built by machines, defying the European tradition of hand-crafting pianos.

No company represents the emergence of Asian piano-building technology more than Yamaha, which is probably the highest-profile piano brand after Steinway. Yamaha concert grands are the choice of some internationally respected pianists, though Steinway still has a more glamorous roster of affiliated artists. Yamaha pianos, on both the concert and home level, have a reputation for consistency, internal precision, and smooth actions. Steinways are renowned for beauty of tone and hand-crafted excellence.

The two major brands have plenty of competition. Baldwin pianos have a long history of quality on the concert stage and in homes, with a reputation for clear, bright tones. Kawai is a Japanese company that has made quite a splash in the United States and elsewhere for reasonably-priced pianos with rich tonal characteristics. Kimball is a company that builds a wide range of piano sizes, and sells them at very tempting prices.

I've spoken with many people who do not consider buying Asian pianos for political reasons. That of course is a personal decision of the same sort that you might make about a car. But there is no reason to discount Asian pianos for musical reasons. Pianos from Japan and other Asian countries are ready for prime time.

The Least You Need to Know

➤ Pianos are less portable than digital keyboards and generally more expensive, but sound and feel far better than electronic instruments.

➤ Upright pianos are less expensive and space-saving compared to grands, but have less sonority. Grand pianos are glorious pieces of furniture.

➤ Take a piano technician with you before deciding to buy a used piano.

➤ There are many fine makers of pianos, including European and Asian brands, from Steinways to Yamahas.

Chapter 25

Piano Maintenance and Repair

In This Chapter

➤ Why maintaining your piano is important

➤ Placing a new piano in the safest place

➤ Finding a good piano tuner

➤ Understanding types of piano regulation

➤ Knowing what the warranty means

Now that you've plunked down a couple thousand dollars on the piano of your dreams, you will want to be able to keep it in A-one, tip-top condition. Small problems—such as placing your new instrument to close to a heater duct—can lead to big headaches, and may even render your instrument useless.

Pianos are a bit finicky, both as musical instruments and pieces of furniture. Their wood cabinetry requires the same care as any other fine furniture, if it is to look its best and endure the ravages of spillage and dust. (Geez, I sound like a commercial for a household cleaning item.) The instrument components within the piano are made of materials that are affected by climate and temperature, so they need frequent attention to keep operating properly.

All in all, the piano is one of the high-maintenance instruments around, thanks to its zillions (approximately) of parts which must fit together perfectly. This chapter will tell you how.

Why Upkeep Is Important

You wouldn't buy a new Mercedes and then park it in a high crime area. Or, you wouldn't take your brand new stereo and leave it outside without any protection in the rain. Yet, many folks spend a life's savings on a new (or used) piano and then fail to keep it up properly.

Musical Mouthful
"If music be the breakfast food of love, kindly do not disturb until lunch time."—James Agee

Here are the main reasons the piano maintenance is so important:

➤ **Health of the instrument.** The piano is really a complex and finely constructed machine, whose interacting parts need adjustment from time to time to continue interacting perfectly. Even the wear and tear of simply playing the piano causes changes in the tight-fitting interconnections of parts. The climate further stresses the many types of wood that go into the delicate construction of the inner mechanism. Maintenance is always required to keep pianos operating at their best.

➤ **Musical satisfaction.** If your instrument isn't healthy, it won't give you the musical satisfaction you bought it for. Some of the unhappy results of a piano going out of adjustment are stuck keys that won't stop playing when you push them down; broken keys that don't play at all; buzzing notes; rattling sounds when you play; and, of course, the ever-popular going out of tune. Believe it or not, none of these problems contributes to the beauty of music.

Key Thought
Pianos generally last a good long time, and good ones can be considered lifetime investments. Keeping a piano well-adjusted is part of protecting your investment.

➤ **Durability.** I'm talking about the piano's durability, not yours. When a piano isn't regulated and adjusted properly, its inner parts don't last as long. When some of the inner parts go bad, they usually affect the life of other inner parts. The ultimate result is that the instrument as a whole may not deliver good performance for as long as you want it to.

➤ **Resale value.** Speaking of protecting your investment, one of the foresightful reasons for maintaining your piano regularly is that if you ever want to sell it, you'll be glad if it's in good shape. In this way pianos are like cars, except they last much longer.

For all these reasons, taking good care of your piano should be a lifestyle habit. Read on to understand your piano's needs and how to service them.

Where Should We Put This Thing?

Amazingly, piano maintenance begins from the moment your bring a new (or used, for that matter) instrument into your home. In fact, it really begins during the shopping process.

Once it reaches your home, you will be faced with a key question: where to place the piano. Of course, interior decorating is part of your concern, especially with grand pianos which are striking pieces of furniture. But whether you are getting an upright or a grand, you want to consider piano-friendly placements in addition to good room decoration.

Pianos are sensitive to climate. Oh, they don't shiver in cold or sweat during heat waves, but they silently undergo changes when the climate takes a sharp turn. You can minimize undesirable alterations inside the piano by placing the piano in a location whose climate can be controlled.

Here are a couple of specific tips:

➤ Don't place the piano near a window that would allow sunlight to strike the piano.

➤ Don't place the piano next to a heating duct. (Imagine how you'd feel if you had hot air blowing in your face!)

Pampering Your Piano

Pianos are more sensitive to humidity changes than temperature changes. Wet air causes the instrument's wood parts to expand, and dry air generally causes contraction. The most obvious way you can tell that a piano is responding to humidity change is when it goes out of tune. The piano's strings are wound around metal tuning pins, and those pins are driven into a block of wood. It is the wood that responds (with expansion or contraction) when the room's humidity changes, which causes the tuning pins to slip, which makes the piano's strings go out of tune.

Slipping out of tune is not a problem for pianos, as long as the tuning is corrected fairly regularly. Two tunings per year is recommended for pianos in most temperate climates. Not only is such maintenance good for your ears, but the piano benefits from keeping the strings at their proper tension.

Some people take piano maintenance seriously enough to install humidifiers in the dry season and dehumidifiers in the wet season, controlling the humidity artificially around the piano. If you go this route you needn't control the climate of your entire home—it is easier and less expensive to focus on the single room that houses the piano. Piano dealers can tempt you with climate-control devices that attach directly to the piano and direct their beneficial influence directly to where it's needed: the inside of the piano. Alternatively, you can make your piano happy simply by using standard humidity control appliances found in department stores.

The All-Important Tuner

Never try to tune a piano yourself! Promise? OK. It's not like tuning a guitar or a fiddle. Pianos have over 150 strings in them, and it takes years of practice and training to manipulate the tuning pins with the delicacy and skill to bring the whole thing into tune. Professional players, especially classical virtuosos, consider piano tuning an art, and some artists have developed lifelong artistic collaborations with favorite tuners.

How do you find your special tuner? I wish there were an easy answer. Fortunately, tuning a home piano is a fairly basic task for a trained tuner, and you're not too likely to go wrong by just picking a name out of the phone book. Still, if you have friends with pianos, ask around for recommendations.

You're looking for someone with the following qualities:

➤ **Not too expensive.** A piano tuning should cost $50 to $65.

➤ **Not too slow.** Tuning a piano can take up to an hour, but shouldn't require much longer than that. If the piano hasn't been tuned for over a year, some additional time to wrestle with the strings may be needed.

Key Thought
Extremes in hot and cold will hurt any musical instrument. Wood expands and contracts, and if it's forced to do so too frequently, it may also crack, warp, and in general deteriorate.

Grace Notes
The effect of humidity on pianos is especially evident in climates that have drastic seasonal humidity changes. In the northeastern United States, for example—the New York, New Jersey, Pennsylvania area—the summers are damp and the winters are dry. Every piano in those three states that doesn't live in a humidity-controlled room goes out of tune in the late spring and late fall, as the air quality changes. It's not a subtle difference, either—it's an ear-wrenching change.

Musical Mouthful
"Can't you listen to chords without knowing their names?"—Claude Debussy (1926)

➤ **Not too incompetent.** I haven't had bad experiences with piano tuners, and I hope you don't either. But if your piano doesn't sound right when the tuner is done, don't call him or her again. If you are a beginning player (most likely if you're reading this book, and if I'm not mistaken you *are* reading this book), have the tuner play some chords and scales up and down the keyboard. Ask the tuner if there are any problems.

➤ **Not too limited.** The best piano tuners are all-purpose piano technicians. They are competent at basic repairs and adjustments beyond simple tuning. Other experts specialize in rebuilding piano actions (the entire internal key mechanism), and sometimes a tuner will recommend someone else to handle a serious repair job. But you want your basic tuner to recognize any problems developing in your instrument, and be able to correct them before they get worse.

Key Thought

When strings are tightened after slipping for more than a year, they don't hold their new positions well at first, and you can usually hear the piano go out of tune again within a month. A second tuning at that point solves the problem and gets you back on the every-six-month track.

➤ **Not too disorganized.** Some piano tuners remind you with a mailed card or phone call when your instrument is due to be tuned—usually about six months after the previous tuning. While they obviously stay in touch for the benefit of their own businesses, it's also a convenience to you not to have to remember the tuning schedule. You are never obligated to receive a tuning—the schedule is always up to you.

If you let your piano go too long without being tuned, and it slips drastically away from its optimal tuning, it may need two or three tunings in quick succession to bring it back "up to pitch." Good piano tuners inform their customers when a single tuning isn't sufficient, but they never insist on multiple tunings. It's always up to you.

Regulating, Adjusting, and Tinkering

Good piano tuners perform a variety of minor adjustments that improve the piano's playability and musicality. Here are some of the symptoms you may notice over time as you break in your piano, and what a tuner can do about them.

Grace Notes

Occasionally, on very old pianos, part of the ivory or plastic covering of the key can break loose and fall off. This makes it very difficult to play and should be fixed as soon as possible.

➤ **Uneven keys.** At some point it may become apparent that some keys are harder to press down than other. Ideally, the keyboard should be completely even up and down its entire length. The tuner can work on the keys or the internal action to correct such discrepencies.

➤ **Double striking.** Occasionally notes play twice when you press a key. The double strike usually isn't obvious, and the second strike isn't usually loud. In many cases, you can only hear the faint second strike when pressing a key very softly—it doesn't happen at all during loud playing. Or if it happens all the time on a certain note, the second strike is very soft. Still, it's annoying, and you shouldn't have to put up with it. In most cases, it's an easy problem for a competent tuner to fix.

➤ **Stuck keys.** Piano keys can be stuck in two ways. First, the key may not return all the way to its natural position when you release it. This is very disconcerting, not least because it makes it hard to play a second time. Another stuck key problem is when a note refuses to stop playing even after you release the key. The two stuck key problems are quite different, but neither is difficult to correct.

➤ **Bad sustain pedal.** A number of problems can plague the sustain pedal, and some of them are strictly a matter of taste. Accomplished piano players are very particular about how the sustain pedal "feels," and the abruptness with which it dampens the strings when the pedal is released. Likewise, it is important that the pedal take effect at just the right point when you depress it—not forcing you to push down too far, nor taking effect too soon. All these conditions can be adjusted by a tuner.

Understanding New and Used Warranties

When you buy a new piano, you receive a warranty for its good repair and flawless operation. You may never use the piano warranty, even though some of them extend for as long as twenty years. (New warranties can also be as short as five years.) The warranty is generally provided by the manufacturer, not the piano store. However, you should get a couple of perks from the store, too. Specifically, the store should warranty a safe delivery of the instrument, and perhaps provide one or two free tunings. (Piano tunings are often thrown out of kilter by moving. Whatever a kilter is.)

New instrument warranties are meant to cover drastic problems like cracked soundboards, broken strings, ineffective pin blocks that are incapable of holding a tune, broken pedal assemblies, and other structural defects. These problems may not mean anything to you, and let's hope they never do. As to other inevitable adjustments that are necessary during the warranty period: when in doubt, ask your tuner.

Warranties for used pianos are a whole other kettle of fish. (Never put fish inside your piano, new or used.) Buying a used piano from a store should involve some kind of warranty, but they vary drastically in length and quality. Furthermore, all used instrument warranties are provided by the store, not the manufacturer.

Generally, store warranties cover the same type of major, or extraordinary, repairs and adjustments that are covered in new warranties. However, the store may specify exactly what is covered depending on the condition of the piano. For example, if the strings are a bit rusty, the store may not replace the strings within the warranty period.

> **Key Thought**
> It's important to understand that tuning is not included in piano warranties, just as normal car maintenance isn't part of an automobile warranty. Normal tuning and regulation is up to you. However, if the piano requires excessive regulation or adjustment when it is brand new, it's a warranty problem. Your tuner can advise you whether to appeal for warranty reimbursement. The store from which you bought the piano can also be helpful.

> **Key Thought**
> Except in situations of absolute calamity—like if the legs crumble (the piano's, not yours) and the instrument crashes onto the floor and explodes—used piano warranties are rarely invoked. They are meant to soothe the worries of the buyer without providing much actual protection.

The Least You Need to Know

➤ Maintaining a piano keeps the instrument more musically satisfying and durable.

➤ If possible, new pianos should be placed away from windows and heating ducts.

➤ Pianos are sensitive to humidity, and go out of tune easily when the air quality changes. Using humidifiers and dehumidifiers helps keep pianos stable and healthy.

➤ In most climates, pianos should be tuned twice a year.

➤ Most piano tuners can make minor repairs and adjustments to the action when needed.

➤ Warranties for new or used pianos generally only cover major defects.

Chapter 26

Buying an Electronic Keyboard

In This Chapter

➤ Exploring the pros and cons of buying a used keyboard

➤ Small and portable or big and unwieldy?

➤ Considerations when shopping for a digital piano

➤ Things to keep in mind before buying a home keyboard

For those who cannot afford to buy a piano, the digital keyboard has become an acceptable alternative. Of course, there are also many folks who are looking for the advantages of sound generation, MIDI, and home recording, and for them there's no choice: the digital keyboard is where it's at. Whatever your situation, there are special circumstances that make buying a digital keyboard a different experience than purchasing a piano.

Choosing a keyboard for your home is complicated by the huge range of choices. The shopping process involves surveying not only a few different *types* of keyboards, but many brands within each type. While it's true that most keyboards within each type have similar characteristics, they each have a distinct sound—they are, after all, despite being digital machines, musical instruments. Furthermore, utilitarian distinctions such as how the buttons and dials are laid out make a big difference in whether the keyboard pleases you in the long run.

This chapter focuses on all the features and distinctions you should consider when shopping for a keyboard.

Where to Shop

Unlike pianos, which are generally only sold at music stores, electronic keyboards are sold at a variety of outlets. Simple home keyboards are available at such consumer palaces as K-Mart, Wal-Mart, and Whatever-Mart. (Don't ask to see my Whatever-Mart credit card!) When buying at one of these places, the most help you can expect from the salesfolks is that they'll point you toward the correct aisle.

On the other hand, professional keyboards and certainly electronic pianos are generally available at larger music retailers or specialty dealers that specialize in musical merchandise. This means (hopefully) you will be given the same attention and help that you'd expect from a reputable piano dealer.

There are also mail-order and Web-based specialty dealers who offer a wide variety of equipment, sometimes at discounted prices. However, unlike a walk-in store, you won't be able to "try before you buy," and the information provided by phone clerks will probably be fairly minimal.

New or Used?

Key Thought
If you are fairly knowledgable about what you want, buying mail order or from discount dealers is not a bad thing. You'll save money and probably don't need the TLC that a music store can provide. If you don't know the first thing about what you want or need, then spending the extra bucks in return for some knowledgable advice may be the route to take.

Key Thought
Essentially, a music digital music instrument consists of a keyboard attached to a circuit board, controlled by dials and buttons. Keyboards can be damaged if they are dropped, but if you find a used instrument that has been treated well, and is in good working order, it is probably almost as good as new.

It's not surprising that a large and dynamic used marketplace has developed for keyboards. Consider how popular music keyboard have become since the late 1970s, and how hobbyists and professionals alike tend to shed last year's model for the newest high-tech instrument, and it's obvious that all those older keyboards must exist somewhere. That "somewhere" is classified ads in newspapers all over the world, as well as music stores that stock preowned instruments.

Is it safe to buy a used keyboard? As preowned purchases go, music keyboards are one of the safest items. Whenever you're buying used electronic equipment, the main risk lies with devices that have delicate moving parts. Accordingly, tape recorders are more risky, say, than computer monitors, because tape recorders have motors with moving parts and delicate recording heads. Just about the only moving parts in a music keyboard are the keys themselves, and they are hardly delicate. You could hit most keyboards with a hammer and the keys would still work fine. (I'm not recommending that your treat your instrument in such a brutal fashion, mind you. Keyboards have feelings, too.)

If you are dabbling with the idea of buying a used keyboard, here are some important considerations to keep in mind:

➤ **The warranty, or lack thereof.** Although used keyboards are relatively safe purchases, things can definitely go wrong with keyboards sometimes. These instruments are reliably built, but when one stops working, you may want to have warranty protection.

Buying a used keyboard from a store generally gives you some kind of limited warranty, with an accent on the word *limited*. In most cases you can count on (and should request) a warranty period within which the store makes good on defects with either store credit or returned cash. The warranty period on a used keyboard may be between one and six months (usually quite a bit closer to one month).

Buying a used keyboard privately, from someone's home, guarantees the lack of any guarantee. By contrast, purchasing a new instrument from a major manufacturer, through a reputable store, makes it easy to get a replacement instrument if your original is a lemon.

➤ **The shininess, or lack thereof.** You don't have to be a compulsive consumer to appreciate the new-product shine on a factory-fresh keyboard. Used instruments sometimes show sign of wear on the keys and dials.

➤ **The newness, or lack thereof.** Music keyboard technology is constantly evolving. So are the designs in which that technology is packaged. Buying a model that's one, two, or three years old may save you some bucks, but it deprives you of whatever new features have become standard in the interim.

Portable or Not-So-Portable

Another shopping consideration, whether you are buying a new or used keyboard, is how big and heavy you want your instrument to be. One of the great advantages to electronic keyboards compared to real pianos is that you can tuck one under your arm and go to another room. Or put one in a carrying case, sling it over your shoulder, and haul it to a friend's house. (Slinging a grand piano over your shoulder is likely to result in a slight strain of the tricep muscle, plus a wrinkled shirt.)

The most significant factors in determining the weight and portability of a keyboard are the keys themselves. Take these two aspects into consideration:

➤ **The size of the keyboard.** Most home keyboards have a five-octave range (sixty keys), but some professional keyboards, like synthesizers and keyboard workstations, have an extra octave and a half (seventy-six keys in all). The larger range makes for a more heavy instrument. Naturally, a piano-sized keyboard of eighty-eight keys weighs even more.

➤ **The weight of the keys.** It's not necessary to get out a scale or otherwise try to weigh the keys. Simply find out if the keyboard is weighted or unweighted. Weighted keyboards are heavier—you don't say!—than unweighted keyboards.

Of course, the true test of a keyboard's portability is to simply lift the darn thing up, and listen for ominous crackling sounds emanating from your vertabrae. The more cracks, the less portable.

Shopping for a Digital Piano

If you want the closest thing to a real piano that the electronic realm offers, a digital piano is the instrument for you. A good digital piano approximates the sound and feel of the real item at a fraction of the cost, with greater convenience.

There is considerable variety in the features of different digital piano models. Here's a summary of what you can expect to find as you shop:

➤ **Keyboard.** It goes without saying that every digital piano is equipped with a keyboard, but I feel like saying it anyway. Every digital piano is equipped with a keyboard. You almost never see a digital piano with only a five-octave keyboard range, which is a typically small keyboard on home

Key Thought
Let's be honest. What are these new features worth? The truth is, there haven't been many ground-breaking advances in home keyboards in the last few years. For one thing, a keyboard is still a keyboard, with the same arrangement of black and white keys that has held forth for centuries. If your goal is to learn basic keyboard technique, it really doesn't matter what fancy gizmos surround the basic keyboard.

Grace Notes
Not all electronic keyboards are equally portable. Home keyboards that have five-octave, unweighted keyboards are a breeze for most people to pick up. Professional synthesizers tend to be heavier, thanks to the additional circuitry, larger control panel, and heavier materials. Digital pianos are the weightiest members of the electronic keyboard family, and usually require two people to move from one room to another.

Grace Notes
Portability doesn't mean that you can treat your electronic keyboard like a paperback book that you sling carelessly into your backpack. Getting your keyboard wet, cold, or otherwise exposing it to the elements; spilling drinks on it; leaving it out all night for the squirrels, bears, and beasts to trample; all are likely to damage your instrument.

keyboards. Five octaves (sixty keys) really isn't enough to play intermediate or advanced piano pieces, and since digital pianos are piano alternatives, they usually forego the small keyboards for larger, seventy-six-key or eighty-eight-key arrangements.

Furthermore, in a continuing effort to mimic real pianos, most digital instruments weight the keys to some degree. Shop around enough, and you will end up playing a range of weights, from keys that are barely heavier than home keyboards to key actions that feel as meaty as concert grand pianos.

Key Thought

How much weight is enough weight? Well, if you're used to a real piano, a truly weighted keyboard will be extremely important. But, just like power steering on cars, you'll want to try a number of models to find one that fits your own particular playing needs.

➤ **Sounds.** Every digital piano has at least one sound built in: that of a piano, of course. Most digital pianos feature multiple piano sounds for variety. Related instruments—like electric piano, organs, and vibraphones—may be built into the instrument's memory, available by pushing buttons. In some cases a whole range of orchestral instruments is represented on the button panel, but only in the most expensive models.

➤ **Miscellaneous features.** The playing experience of some digital pianos is enhanced through sound-altering features like reverb. Reverb adds an echoing quality to the notes, as if you were playing in an auditorium or concert hall. Other tone controls may be at your disposal, such as an equalizer, or treble and bass sliders. Advanced features such as MIDI recording and disk drive storage polish off fancy digital pianos.

Surveying the range of digital piano products, it's useful to separate all the instruments into three general categories:

➤ **Entry-level digital pianos.** The smallest, lightest, least-expensive digital pianos offer a good basic piano sound or two, a decent keyboard, and little else. A scant choice of other instrument sounds may be available. The keyboard may be slightly weighted, but probably has a less substantial feel than most pianos. The price range of entry-level digital pianos is about $1,200–2,500.

Key Thought

Before being overly enticed by all the bells and whistles available on high-end digital keyboards, ask yourself (realistically) how many of these features do you really need? If you just plan to play "Chopsticks" with your friends, you probably don't need fancy built-in recording capabilities!

➤ **Middle-of-the-road digital pianos.** The vast middle ground in the digital piano kingdom contains midpriced instruments with an assortment of features. Keyboards are either seventy-six-key or eighty-eight-key models, and are weighted to appeal to pianists and professional keyboardists. A good instrument selection is sure to include at least a few different pianos, electric pianos, organs, and a smattering of others—you can expect to find eight to twenty instrument settings, enhanced by reverb. Some mid-priced models include a rudimentary sequencer and a disk drive for storing recordings. Instruments in this category range in price from $2,000-3,500.

➤ **Advanced digital pianos.** When manufacturers pull out the stops, the result is an impressive modern instrument that sounds and feels great, and is bristling with miscellaneous features. Some of these digital wonders sport a hundred instrument settings, and extensive tone controls and reverb settings. On-board sequencers let you record your own playing, and disk drives both record your performances and play back prerecorded pieces from an available library of disks. Advanced digital pianos are almost like computer workstations, and are rewarding instruments for technically inclined players. The price range for such sophisticated digital pianos is $3,000–6,000.

As you shop for the right digital piano, there are several questions to keep in your mind. Here are the crucial considerations:

➤ **Does it sound right?** Regardless of your playing expertise or level of experience, you must be pleased with the sound of the instrument you buy. Contrary to what you might think, digital pianos do not all sound alike. In fact, there is almost as much variety in the sonority of digital pianos as there is among acoustic pianos. Each model features digital samples of different grand pianos, so they sound almost as different from each other as the original grand pianos would.

➤ **Does it feel right?** If you are upgrading from a home keyboard, digital pianos will universally feel stiff to the touch, and perhaps hard to play. The difference in touch is due to the weighted actions of digital pianos compared to the unweighted feel of home keyboards. If you prefer the light action, select a digital piano with a slightly weighted keyboard, as opposed to the heavier actions of digital instrument that emulate real pianos. If, on the other hand, your playing background includes real pianos, and you prefer a more substantial feeling to the keyboard, find a digital piano with the heaviest action possible.

➤ **Does it look right?** In this category, you don't have much choice. Most digital pianos look pretty much the same. Still, you may prefer a clean button panel that doesn't have lots of dials and flashing lights—or you may go for the high-tech look.

➤ **Does it cost the right amount?** This consideration goes without saying, perhaps. You need to find the instrument that meets your personal needs in the best way, while sticking to your budget. Refer to the earlier paragraphs in this section for general price guidelines.

Key Thought
Most digital pianos offer a choice of pianos sounds, so look (and listen) for the model that gives you the best choices, or even just one choice that you can really fall in love with.

Grace Notes
Some manufacturers offer digital pianos housed in wood, which look very much like regular upright pianos. Such instruments are for people who want the appearance of a piano without the maintenance headaches or the high cost.

Shopping for a Home Keyboard

Home keyboards are popular because of their potent combination of features and cost-efficiency. Simply put, you get a lot of bang for your buck. The "bang" consists of a five-octave keyboard, which is large enough to learn on and to play simple keyboard arrangements; several sound selections; auto-accompaniment features that make the keyboard sound like a one-person band; built-in speakers and battery power; and a light, portable package that you can pick up and carry into the next room or put in an airplane luggage compartment. All these basic features come to you at a price that shames most digital pianos, and doesn't even appear on the radar screen of somebody shopping for a real piano. The downside to the home keyboard marketplace is

Musical Mouthful
"All the sounds of the earth are like music."—Oscar Hammerstein II

sound quality: home keyboards just don't sound as rich or sonorous as professional keyboards or digital pianos. Still, they are good enough to learn on, and you can always upgrade later if you (or your kids) get serious about playing.

The main problem when shopping for a home keyboard is that there are so darn many of them. Each manufacturer has several new models at all times, and there is a bustling used-instrument marketplace at the same time. The following sections outline the main considerations to keep in mind as you browse.

Making Sense of the Bells and Whistles

First and foremost when shopping for a home keyboard, you must feel comfortable with the controls. If you're new to electronic keyboards, viewing all the buttons and dials coherently may seem like too much to ask for. Here's how to handle the techno-intimidation:

➤ The first key is to *take your time* when shopping. Don't be rushed into any purchase.

➤ Find salespeople who can explain what all the buttons do.

➤ Ask the salesperson to get the owner's manual for the display unit, so you can simulate the learning experience you'll have at home if you buy that instrument.

> **Grace Notes**
>
> Some manufacturers offer big, well-marked controls, with each button, joystick, or knob performing a single function. Others offer little, chicklet-sized buttons, row upon row, with no clear indication of their functions. (Yes, a single button can be used to control multiple functions.) What you choose will depend on how comfortable you are with the controls.

By spending some time with a possible purchase in the store, you can get familiar (and possibly comfortable) enough with all the controls to determine if the keyboard is configured in a friendly fashion. Here are some questions to ask yourself as you fiddle with any home keyboard in a store:

➤ Is the keyboard *touch sensitive*? Touch sensitivity means that if you play a key softly, it makes a soft note, and striking a key hard results in a loud note. Keyboards that lack touch sensitivity make the same volume no matter how you play the keyboard, though even they are equipped with a volume control that affects all the notes equally. You can learn the basics of music and music notation on a non-sensitive keyboard, but it's impossible to play musically when the notes don't get louder and softer according to your playing touch.

➤ Is the screen easy to read, and large enough to spell out clearly what functions you're accessing? Small screens often use cryptic abbreviations for various functions and features—if you can decipher them, you earn an honored place in the Secret Service's cryptography division. The larger screens inform you clearly what sound you're playing, what auto-accompaniment style is currently in use, and which sequencer track is recording or playing.

> **Music Speak**
>
> **Touch sensitivity** is a term applied to electronic keyboards whose loudness is responsive to the force with which the keys are played. Almost all modern digital keyboards are touch sensitive, and play louder when you play the keys harder. However, some inexpensive home keyboards can be found with non-sensitive keys that play at the same volume all the time.

➤ Do you like the keyboard's sounds? In most cases, you have plenty of sounds to choose from—possibly a hundred or more. Don't expect the quality of a symphony orchestra, but you should at least feel that the keyboard's basic tonal quality won't drive you crazy during extended use.

Also, check out the auto-accompaniment styles for an indication of the on-board sounds. The single sound that probably gets the most use is the built-in piano sound, which may not sound the slightest bit like a piano.

➤ Does the auto-accompaniment provide the kinds of styles you like? If you're a rock 'n' roll type, and the on-board styles feature waltzes and military marches, you're likely to suffer a pang or two of disappointment. Most keyboards have a broad range of styles, aiming to please everyone a little bit. Pick out the styles you figure using most heavily, and see if you like the way they sound.

➤ Does the auto-accompaniment provide enough flexibility? One specific question you should ask about the auto-accompaniment is whether you can change the tempo easily. Making the styles faster and slower is crucial to their usefulness. Then, find out whether you can change the key of the style. Check out whether you can add and subtract instruments from the style while it's playing—it's handy and fun to reduce the style to drums alone while it's playing, then add bass, chords, and other musical elements as the style continues playing.

Finally, make sure there are left-hand style controls. The left-hand is used to determine the chords played by the style arrangement, and better keyboards give you three ways of doing so: full-chord playing; two-finger chords; and one-finger bass lines. Full-chord playing is for people who know chords well and can play them on the fly. Two-finger playing is a kind of chord shorthand that's easier to play, but still requires a knowledge of chords. One-finger playing reduces the auto-accompaniment to either a bass line or all major chords, and is the least useful way of controlling a style's harmony.

Many home keyboards feature built-in demonstration songs that salespeople use to show off the instrument in its best light. In addition to the demos, other songs may be included for playing at your leisure. These songs are different from the auto-accompaniment styles, which are meant to be used as an accompaniment to your playing.

The Least You Need to Know

➤ Used keyboard are relatively safe, as used purchases go, because of their lack of delicate moving parts.

➤ Digital pianos are heavier and harder to move than home keyboards, but have better sound quality. They cost between $1,200 and $6,000.

➤ When shopping for home keyboards, check out the function of all the buttons and dials, and try to see an owner's manual of the model you're considering. The keyboard must sound pleasing, too.

Grace Notes

Not all home keyboards have such screens at all. Less-expensive models indicate sound and style selections with simple lights illuminating the selection buttons, which works fine. My point is, if you're going for a model with a screen, make it a good screen.

Key Thought

One good way to test the keyboard's overall sound is to play any demo songs that are built in. The songs use keyboard sounds in a more complex manner than the keyboard may allow you to, but you can get an idea of the instrument's capability nonetheless.

Musical Mouthful

"It's only rock 'n' roll (but I like it)."—Mick Jagger

Key Thought

What purpose do the built-in songs have? Very, very little. It's important not to be too impressed by demo and built-in songs, or to—heaven forbid!—buy a keyboard on the basis of them. Have fun with the demos, be briefly impressed by them if you must, then move on to the business of getting to know the useful features of the keyboard.

Glossary

Accidentals   Another name for the notation symbols that indicate sharps and flats in sheet music. Nobody knows how accidentals got their name, so it should just be considered, well, an accident.

Accompaniment   The musical part (or parts) that is played underneath, and supports, the main melody. In piano music, the left hand usually plays the accompaniment, though in classical music the accompaniment switches between the two hands.

Acoustic instruments   A fancy way of referring to musical instruments that don't get plugged in. Every instrument in the orchestra is an acoustic instrument. Electronic guitars and keyboards, by contrast, require electrical power to make a sound.

Action   The action of a piano is the entire mechanism that starts with pressing a **key** and ends with a hammer hitting the strings. Included in the piano action are many finely crafted wood, plastic, metal, and leather parts that work together, giving the piano its characteristic "feel" and sound. Piano technicians can remove the entire action from the piano case to adjust its parts.

Arpeggios   Chords played by rippling the notes quickly from bottom to top.

Auto-accompaniment   A feature of home keyboards that provides continuous rhythms and harmonies in preset musical styles. You can play the keyboard while the auto-accompaniment is pounding out a rock 'n' roll groove, or swinging to a jazz beat. Most auto-accompaniments let you determine the harmonies with your left hand while playing a melody with your right hand.

Bar lines   Divide the music staff into **measures**, and every measure of a piece contains the same number of beats. All the note values in any measure add up to the same number of beats.

Baroque   A period of music that ran through the seventeenth and early eighteenth centuries, and featured complex, ornate music. Typically, composers fashioned multiple melodies to play at the same time, fitting them together with mathematical accuracy in pleasing harmonies. Bach is the most famous Baroque composer.

Broken chord   Chords whose notes are played one at a time. A left-hand accompaniment style popular in classical music from the eighteenth and nineteenth centuries, Mozart and Beethoven used broken chords extensively.

Chart   Also called **lead sheets**, a chart notates the melody of a song, with chord symbols above the notes to indicate the accompaniment harmonies for the left hand. Charts (lead sheets) are compiled in **fake books**.

Chord   Clusters of notes played simultaneously. Most chords create a pleasing harmonic effect, but strictly speaking, a chord can be any group of notes, regardless of how awful it sounds.

Clef   Signs used at the beginning of staffs to indicate which hand should play that staff. The **treble clef** is for the right hand, and the **bass clef** is for the left hand. Actually, in intermediate and advanced piano music, the right hand sometimes plays bass clef notes, and the left hand sometimes strays into treble clef territory. But mostly, each hand stays in its own clef.

Counterpoint   **Contrapuntal** music features separate melodies that sound good when played against each other. (Contra means against.) One of the most mathematical styles of music composition, it has many rules that the composer must follow. (Otherwise the contrapuntal police get you.) Bach was a master of counterpoint music.

Digital keyboard   Throughout this book, I refer to both **digital keyboards** and **electronic keyboards**. Practically speaking, they are the same thing, since all electronic keyboards these days are digital. Being digital means that the keyboard uses computer-type circuitry to store and play sounds, unlike the older electronic keyboards of the 1970s.

Digital piano   Computer-age alternatives to real pianos. By storing sampled (recorded) notes from acoustic pianos in their memory chips, digital pianos can sound reasonably like concert grand pianos. The verisimilitude only goes so far, though, and experienced pianists agree that digital pianos are no replacement for the real thing.

Dotted notes   The dot extends the time value of the note by one half its original value. For example, a dotted half note equals three beats, and a dotted quarter note equals one and a half beats.

Drum machines   Electronic instruments that provide drum sounds for people using the MIDI capabilities of digital keyboards. You can hook up a drum machine to a keyboard, and automatically have access to many realistic drum and percussion sounds.

Dynamics   The loudness of sound and music. Pianists talk about the dynamics of a piece, meaning that some passages are played loudly, and others softly. **Dynamic range** indicates the limits of loudness and softness contained in a piece, or capable of being played by an instrument. The piano has one of the largest dynamic ranges of any instrument.

Electronic keyboard   Throughout this book, I refer to both **digital keyboards** and **electronic keyboards**. Practically speaking, they are the same thing, since all electronic keyboards these days are digital. Being digital means that the keyboard uses computer-type circuitry to store and play sounds, unlike the older electronic keyboards of the 1970s.

Fake book   Each song in a fake book consists of the melody, written in music notation, and chord symbols above the notes. Taking cues from the chord symbols, the player must improvise (fake) an arrangement for the song.

Fingerings   Music notation sometimes labels notes with numbers that indicate which finger should play which note.

Flat   Accidentals that lower any note by one half step.

Hammers Piano hammers are the last parts of the piano action, and perform the impactful assignment of striking the strings. When a hammer hits the piano strings, it immediately and automatically rebounds, letting the strings vibrate, which causes the piano to sound. Hammers are covered with felt—the perfect material for producing the sound of piano notes.

Harmony The musical underpinning of a piece. Harmony is usually created by clusters of notes played together, called chords, that provide a context for the melody. You may not notice the harmony when you hear a song, or sing it in your mind. But without the tune's harmony, the melody would be harder to learn and remember.

Harpsichord One of the predecessors of the piano. Harpsichords had a metallic, unvarying sound. They could not be played loudly and softly as a piano can, and their strings were plucked by mechanical quills, not struck with small felt hammers as a piano's strings are.

Home keyboards Small, relatively inexpensive digital instruments with built-in speakers for hearing their sounds.

Improvisation Creating the music as you play. It is an essential skill in playing jazz piano.

Intervals The distances between notes on a keyboard. Play any two notes, and you're playing an interval. Intervals are named with ordinal numeral: thirds, sevenths, twelfths, fifteenths, and so on. The size of the interval is determined by how many keys lie between the two notes.

Inversions Different varieties of the same chord, with the notes stacked in different orders.

Key signature A symbol showing the key of a piece by indicating which sharps of flats are necessary to play a scale in that key. Key signatures make their appearance at the beginning of every staff in a piece, and look like a cluster of sharp or flat symbols.

Keyboard Refers to a traditional arrangement of black and white keys that play musical notes. The keyboard may be attached to an acoustic piano or an electronic instrument. Electronic keyboard instruments are usually referred to simply as "keyboards," confusing things somewhat. A keyboard (an electronic keyboard instrument) contains a keyboard (an arrangement of keys), just as a piano does.

Key In music, the key indicates the main note of the piece, and which sharps or flats are needed to play the piece around that central note. Every key has a scale, which is a sequence of notes starting with the main key note.

Lead sheet Music *charts*, also called lead sheets, notate the melody of a song, with chord symbols above the notes to indicate the accompaniment harmonies for the left hand. Charts (lead sheets) are compiled in fake books.

Legato Means smooth playing, without undue breaks between notes.

Leger lines Lines used to extend the five-line staff upwards and downwards. Leger lines (and the spaces between them) are used to hold notes that are above or below the notes of the five-line staff.

Measure One measure is the space between two bar lines, and the notes in that space. Each measure of a piece contains notes that add up to the same number of beats.

Melody A sequence of notes strung together into a tune. Melodies are often the most important part of a musical piece, certainly in popular music.

Metronome A mechanical instrument that keeps you "on tempo" by clicking audible beats while you play a piece. By setting the metronome to a faster or slower tempo, you can keep up the pace or stop yourself from rushing the pace. Metronomes come in mechanical and electronic models.

MIDI   An acronym for Musical Instrument Digital Interface—a fancy way of saying that MIDI connects keyboards to other keyboards, and keyboards to computers. There are other types of MIDI devices as well, including drum machines, tone modules, and sequencers.

Modes   Scales based on ancient music systems, which can be played on the white keys of the piano, beginning on any note. They have seven notes, just like major and minor scales.

Music notation   The written form of music. Notation is what music looks like on the printed page, in sheet music and music books. For the most part, notation consists of round notes placed on the lines and spaces of a music staff, but even guitar chord symbols are music notation. In short, notation is anything written down that tells you what to play on an instrument.

Natural   A sign that neutralizes previously established sharps and flats. The natural sign is an accidental just like a sharp sign or flat sign. Naturals lower sharped notes by a half step, and raise flatted notes by a half step.

Octave   The keyboard distance between any note and the next (higher or lower) same note. The two notes that form an octave are said to be an octave apart from each other.

Patch   The instrument sounds that are built into digital keyboards are alternately called *patches*, *sounds*, and *sound programs*. Professional keyboards (and musicians) usually refer to sounds as patches. Home keyboards generally call them just sounds.

Pianoforte   The first pianos were called *pianofortes*, which in Italian means "softloud." Pianofortes were the first keyboard instrument whose volume (loudness) could be altered by playing the keys more or less forcefully.

Pins   Metal pins hold the piano strings at one end of their length. Piano tuners turn the pins with a special tool when tuning the strings. Pins are driven into a block of wood called the **pin block**.

Pitch   Refers to the highness or lowness of a note. Women can sing higher pitches than men. (Except for men who don't mind sounding ridiculous.) **Pitch range** is defined by the highest and lowest possible note of an instrument, a human voice, or a piece of music. Tubas have a lower pitch range than piccolos. Pianos have a larger pitch range than any non-keyboard instrument.

Ragtime   One of the first forms of jazz piano, developed early in the century in southern urban centers like New Orleans. Featuring a *stride* left hand, bouncing back and forth between bass notes and mid-range chords, set against jaunty melodies in the right hand, ragtime is joyful and playful music.

Relative major and minor   Keys that share the same key signature. The major key with a key signature of two sharps (D major) is the relative major of the minor key with a key signature of two sharps (B minor). By the same token, B minor is called the relative minor of D major.

Repeat sign   Symbols that bracket portions of a piece to indicate that it should be repeated. Repeat signs make music notation more compact, especially in pop music, since the repeated portion doesn't have to be written out a second or third time.

Repertoire   The collected works for any instrument. The piano repertoire includes great music from most of the composers in classical and jazz traditions, as well as the work of modern composers who are not so easily categorized.

Rests   Symbols that indicate when you should not play. Rests are the opposite of notes, which tell you when to play. Rests have the same time value as notes, and they make measures add up to the right amount of beats when there aren't enough notes.

Rhythm   A term that refers to the beat of music, and its movement through time. Quick rhythms create music that makes you tap your foot quickly, and slow rhythms are more langorous, used in ballads and torch songs.

Sampler   The most acoustically realistic of all digital instruments, samplers reproduce actual recordings of real instruments when you play the keyboard. With enough real instrument recordings stored in its memory chips, a sampler can sound just like a piano one minute, and a flute the next. Furthermore, you can record any sound into a sampler, and suddenly the keyboard mimics that sound perfectly.

Scale   A sequence of notes starting with the tonic note of a key, and going up or down to the next tonic note. Every key has its own scale.

Sequencer   A recording device that keeps track of keystrokes on a music keyboard, then plays them back exactly as originally performed. Recording in this manner is called **sequencing**. Sequencers are built into many digital keyboards, enabling the player to quickly and easily record his or her playing.

Sharp   Alterations to music notes that raise any individual note upward by one half step.

Slur   Phrase marks, or slurs, indicate when groups of notes should be played without any breaks between the notes. The effect of a slurred phrase is smooth and seamless.

Soft pedal   The left-most pedal of the piano, the soft pedal makes the whole instrument softer by affecting how the hammers hit the strings.

Sonata   A piano piece written in three connected parts. Each part is called a *movement*. The movements may sound like entirely separate pieces, and in a sense they are. Ideally, the entire sonata hangs together as a satisfying musical experience. Handel, Haydn, Mozart, and Beethoven wrote famous sonatas.

Sostenuto pedal   The least-used of the piano's three pedals, it sustains any notes being played as the pedal is being pushed down. While holding down the sostenuto pedal, other notes are *not* sustained after being played. On some smaller pianos, the sostenuto pedal is missing.

Soundboard   A large piece of wood placed just a couple of inches away from the strings inside a piano. When the strings are struck by hammers and caused to vibrate, the soundboard picks up the vibration and amplifies it to a volume that is easily heard.

Spinet   A special, very small type of upright. Spinets are extremely short, but are technically distinguished by a different type of action — the mechanism that makes a hammer hit the strings when you press a key. Despite the technicalities of action construction, which are far too boring to spell out, most people rightly consider spinets quite simply as very small uprights.

Staccato   Sharp, detached playing, with breaks between the notes.

Staff   A group of five parallel lines stretching across the width of a page. Notes representing the keys of the keyboard are placed on the lines and the spaces between lines, indicating which keys to play. In piano music, each hand gets its own staff.

Stem   The stick-like line that extends upward or downward from the circle of the note. Whole notes are the only type of note that doesn't have a stem.

Stride   A style of piano playing in which the left hand bounces between bass notes and chords. Stride is used in various types of jazz playing, but was made popular by ragtime.

Strings   Piano strings are thin metal cords stretched tautly around a frame called a harp. When struck by piano hammers, the strings vibrate, and it is the vibrating strings that create a piano's sound.

Sustain pedal   The right-most pedal of the piano, and the pedal used most. The sustain pedal holds notes even after you release the keys.

Synthesizer   A specialized type of digital keyboard, able to mimic acoustic instruments as well as produce unearthly sounds that don't sound like any known instrument.

Tempo   The speed of music. It's mostly classical music that refers to fast tempos and slow tempos, but it's also a general term for all kinds of music, and the speed with which it's played.

Ties   Tied notes are connected by a curved line, indicating that the time value of the two notes is added together. You only play the first note, but hold it for the duration of both notes.

Time signature   A symbol placed at the beginning (far left end) of the music staff that tells you how many beats are in every measure, and what note value is assigned one beat. For example, 4/4 time has 4 beats per measure, and a quarter note receives one beat.

Tone module   The brain of the electronic keyboard, including all the sounds the keyboard can make. Tone modules are used in MIDI studios with one master keyboard that controls various tone modules and drum machines.

Touch sensitive   Touch sensitivity is a term applied to electronic keyboards whose loudness is responsive to the force with which the keys are played. Almost all modern digital keyboards are touch sensitive, and play louder when you play the keys harder. However, some inexpensive home keyboards can be found with non-sensitive keys that play at the same volume all the time.

Transpose   Changing a piece from one key to another is called *transposing* the piece. Transposing a piece from C to D, for example, moves it up one whole step. Transposing a piece from G to F moves it down one whole step. You can transpose any piece to any key, and the process moves every note of the piece up or down the same number of whole or half steps.

Triplet   A triplet is a group of three notes grouped into a certain rhythm. Quarter-note triplets are played in the time value of a single half note, and eighth-note triplets are played in the same number of beats as a quarter note.

Tuning hammer   The primary tool of piano tuners, the tuning hammer fits around the pins, letting the tuner turn them to adjust the tension of the strings, changing their pitch.

Una corda   In classical piano music, very occasionally, you see a notation marking indicating use of the soft pedal. That marking is the phrase *una corda* written into the music. By and large, though, players use the soft pedal whenever they desire the softest touch possible in a delicate musical passage.

Unison   When two parts are playing the exact same note, that also is considered an interval, even though there is *no* distance whatsoever between the two notes. The interval is called unison, and when two singers or two instrumentalists are singing or playing the same notes, they are said to be singing or playing *in unison*.

Resources for the Beginning Pianist

Unfathomable though it may seem, there are other books about how to play the piano. Needless to say, none of them combine such depth of information with poetry of expression as this one does. Nor do they have such modest authors. Nonetheless, you may want to broaden your learning approach by checking some of these out.

I've included three categories of resources in this appendix. First, a large number of so-called method books. Some of the method books are general, and others concentrate on a type of playing, like jazz or blues. Second, I've listed a few books by great pianists of the past—in some cases, the long-ago past. These are for interest more than useful instruction, as they deal with learning how to play older versions of the piano, or pianoforte. The third and final section of this appendix points you toward instructional videos that might be helpful.

Not all the books may be easy to find. I've included the ISBN number in all cases, so you can order any book that strikes your interest. If you have access to the Internet, you may search for any of these titles at the Amazon bookstore, located at the following URL: http://www.amazon.com.

Modern Method Books

How to Play Piano
Roger Evans
St. Martin's Press
ISBN: 0312396015

How to Play Popular Piano in 10 Easy Lessons
Norman Monath
Simon & Schuster
ISBN: 0671530674

Instant Keyboard: Quick and Easy Instruction for the Impatient Student
Gary Meisner
Hal Leonard Publishing
ISBN: 0881886246

Mastering Piano Technique : A Guide for Students, Teachers, and Performers
Seymour Fink
Amadeus Press
ISBN: 0931340462

The Piano
King Palmer
Teach Yourself Books
ISBN: 0844239364

Piano Technique: Tone, Touch, Phrasing, and Dynamics
Lilly H. Philipp
Dover Publications
ISBN: 0486242722

The Osborne Piano Course
Katie Elliot
EDC Publications
ISBN: 0746020007

You Can Play Piano
Amy Appleby
Music Sales Corp.
ISBN: 082561516X

12-Bar Blues Bible for Piano/Keyboards (book and CD)
Andrew D. Gordon
A.D.G. Productions
ISBN: 1882146581

24 Karat Piano Skills
Billie Ray Erlings
Kendall/Hunt Publishing
ISBN: 0787234680

60 of the Funkiest Keyboard Riffs Known to Mankind
Andrew D. Gordon
A.D.G Productions
ISBN: 1882146484

Encyclopedia of Picture Chords for All Keyboards
Leonard Vogler
Music Sales Corp.
ISBN: 0825615038

Contemporary Keyboard Styles for the Absolute Beginner (book and cassette)
Andrew D. Gordon
A.D.G. Productions
ISBN: 1882146166

David Bennett Cohen Teaches Blues Piano: A Hands-On Course in Traditional Blues Piano
David Cohen
Hal Leonard Publishing
ISBN: 0793562570

The John Brimhall Piano Method
John Brimhall
Hansen House
ISBN: 0849427681

Precious Lord! How to Play Black Gospel
Robert L. Jefferson
Pensacola Publications
ISBN: 1880549042

A Whole Approach to Jazz
Marc Sabatella
A.D.G. Productions
ISBN: 1882146557

Great Pianists as Teachers

Basic Principles of Pianoforte Playing
Joseph Lhevinne
Dover Publications
ISBN: 0486228207

Essay on the True Art of Playing Keyboard Instruments
C.P.E. Bach (translated by William J. Mitchell)
W.W. Norton & Co.
ISBN: 0393097161

On Piano Playing: Motion, Sound and Expression
Gyorgy Sandor
Schirmer Books
ISBN: 0028722809

Piano Playing With Piano Questions Answered
Josef Hofmann
Dover Publications
ISBN: 0486233626

Letter to a Young Lady: On the Art of Playing the Pianoforte
Carl Czerny
Da Capo Press
ISBN: 0306761238

Video Instruction

Learn the Essentials of Piano (4 graded tapes, available separately)
Talc Tolchin
Kaleidospace
http://kspace.com/tolchin

Piano-by-Ear (adult and kid video courses)
David Wayne Lawrence
1-800-44-BY-EAR
http://www.piano-by-ear.com/

Easy Piano; Country & Rock Piano; Blues Piano; Jazz Piano (4 separate video courses)
Homespun Tapes
1-800-338-2737
http://www.homespuntapes.com/

Index

Other Best-Selling Titles in the *Complete Idiot's Guide*® Series:

Business

Personal Finance

The Complete Idiot's Guide to Buying Insurance and Annuities
ISBN: 0-02-861113-6
$16.95

The Complete Idiot's Guide to Managing Your Money
ISBN: 1-56761-530-9
$16.95

The Complete Idiot's Guide to Making Money with Mutual Funds
ISBN: 1-56761-637-2
$16.95

The Complete Idiot's Guide to Getting Rich
ISBN: 1-56761-509-0
$16.95

The Complete Idiot's Guide to Finance and Accounting
ISBN: 0-02-861752-5
$16.95

The Complete Idiot's Guide to Investing Like a Pro
ISBN:0-02-862044-5
$16.95

The Complete Idiot's Guide to Making Money After You Retire
ISBN:0-02-862410-6
$16.95

The Complete Idiot's Guide to Making Money on Wall Street
ISBN:0-02-861958-7
$16.95

The Complete Idiot's Guide to Personal Finance in Your 20s and 30s
ISBN:0-02-862415-7
$16.95

The Complete Idiot's Guide to Wills and Estates
ISBN: 0-02-861747-9
$16.95

The Complete Idiot's Guide to 401(k) Plans
ISBN: 0-02-861948-X
$16.95

Careers

The Complete Idiot's Guide to Changing Careers
ISBN: 0-02-861977-3
$17.95

The Complete Idiot's Guide to Freelancing
ISBN: 0-02-862119-0
$16.95

The Complete Idiot's Guide to Getting the Job You Want
ISBN: 1-56761-608-9
$24.95

The Complete Idiot's Guide to the Perfect Cover Letter
ISBN: 0-02-861960-9
$14.95

The Complete Idiot's Guide to the Perfect Interview
ISBN: 0-02-861945-5
$14.95

Education

The Complete Idiot's Guide to American History
ISBN: 0-02-861275-2
$16.95

The Complete Idiot's Guide to British Royalty
ISBN: 0-02-862346-0
$18.95

The Complete Idiot's Guide to Civil War
ISBN: 0-02-862122-0
$16.95

The Complete Idiot's Guide to Classical Mythology
ISBN: 0-02-862385-1
$16.95

The Complete Idiot's Guide to Creative Writing
ISBN: 0-02-861734-7
$16.95

The Complete Idiot's Guide to Dinosaurs
ISBN: 0-02-862390-8
$17.95

The Complete Idiot's Guide to Genealogy
ISBN: 0-02-861947-1
$16.95

The Complete Idiot's Guide to Geography
ISBN: 0-02-861955-2
$16.95

The Complete Idiot's Guide to Getting Published
ISBN: 0-02-862392-4
$16.95

The Complete Idiot's Guide to Grammar & Style
ISBN: 0-02-861956-0
$16.95

The Complete Idiot's Guide to an MBA
ISBN: 0-02-862164-4
$17.95

The Complete Idiot's Guide to Philosophy
ISBN:0-02-861981-1
$16.95

The Complete Idiot's Guide to Learning Spanish On Your Own
ISBN: 0-02-861040-7
$16.95

The Complete Idiot's Guide to Learning French on Your Own
ISBN: 0-02-861043-1
$16.95

The Complete Idiot's Guide to Learning German on Your Own
ISBN: 0-02-861962-5
$16.95

The Complete Idiot's Guide to Learning Italian on Your Own
ISBN: 0-02-862125-5
$16.95

The Complete Idiot's Guide to Learning Sign Language
ISBN: 0-02-862388-6
$16.95

Food/Beverage/Entertaining

The Complete Idiot's Guide to Baking
ISBN: 0-02-861954-4
$16.95

The Complete Idiot's Guide to Beer
ISBN: 0-02-861717-7
$16.95

The Complete Idiot's Guide to Cooking Basics
ISBN: 0-02-861974-9
$18.95

The Complete Idiot's Guide to Entertaining
ISBN: 0-02-861095-4
$16.95

The Complete Idiot's Guide to Etiquette
ISBN0-02-861094-6
$16.95

The Complete Idiot's Guide to Mixing Drinks
ISBN: 0-02-861941-2
$16.95

The Complete Idiot's Guide to Wine
ISBN: 0-02-861273-6
$16.95

Health and Fitness

The Complete Idiot's Guide to Beautiful Skin
ISBN: 0-02-862408-4
$16.95

The Complete Idiot's Guide to Breaking Bad Habits
ISBN: 0-02-862110-7
$16.95

The Complete Idiot's Guide to Eating Smart
ISBN: 0-02-861276-0
$16.95

The Complete Idiot's Guide to First Aid Basics
ISBN: 0-02-861099-7
$16.95

The Complete Idiot's Guide to Getting and Keeping Your Perfect Body
ISBN: 0-02-861276-0
$16.95

The Complete Idiot's Guide to Getting a Good Night's Sleep
ISBN: 0-02-862394-0
$16.95

The Complete Idiot's Guide to a Happy, Healthy Heart
ISBN: 0-02-862393-2
$16.95

The Complete Idiot's Guide to Healthy Stretching
ISBN: 0-02-862127-1
$16.95

The Complete Idiot's Guide to Jogging and Running
ISBN: 0-02-862386-X
$17.95

The Complete Idiot's Guide to Losing Weight
ISBN: 0-02-862113-1
$17.95

The Complete Idiot's Guide to Managed Health Care
ISBN: 0-02-862165-4
$17.95

The Complete Idiot's Guide to Stress
ISBN: 0-02-861086-5
$16.95

The Complete Idiot's Guide to Vitamins and Minerals
ISBN: 0-02-862116-6
$16.95

Home and Automotive

The Complete Idiot's Guide to Buying or Leasing a Car
ISBN: 0-02-861274-4
$16.95

The Complete Idiot's Guide to Buying and Selling a Home
ISBN: 0-02-861959-5
$16.95

The Complete Idiot's Guide to Decorating Your Home
ISBN: 0-02-861088-1
$16.95

The Complete Idiot's Guide to Gardening
ISBN: 0-02-861-096-2
$16.95

The Complete Idiot's Guide to Motorcycles
ISBN: 0-02-862416-5
$16.95

The Complete Idiot's Guide to Smart Moving
ISBN: 0-02-862126-3
$16.95

The Complete Idiot's Guide to Trouble-Free Car Care
ISBN: 0-02-861041-5
$16.95

The Complete Idiot's Guide to Trouble-Free Home Repair
ISBN: 0-02-861042-3
$16.95

Leisure/Hobbies

The Complete Idiot's Guide to Antiques and Collectibles
ISBN: 0-02-861595-6
$16.95

The Complete Idiot's Guide to Astrology
ISBN: 0-02-861951-X
$16.95

The Complete Idiot's Guide to the Beatles
ISBN: 0-02-862130-1
$18.95

The Complete Idiot's Guide to Boating and Sailing
ISBN: 0-02-862124-7
$18.95

The Complete Idiot's Guide to Bridge
ISBN: 0-02-861735-5
$16.95

The Complete Idiot's Guide to Chess
ISBN: 0-02-861736-3
$16.95

The Complete Idiot's Guide to Cigars
ISBN: 0-02-861975-7
$17.95

The Complete Idiot's Guide to Crafts with Kids
ISBN: 0-02-862406-8
$16.95

The Complete Idiot's Guide to Elvis
ISBN: 0-02-861873-4
$18.95

The Complete Idiot's Guide to Extra-Terrestrial Intelligence
ISBN: 0-02-862387-8
$16.95

The Complete Idiot's Guide to Fishing Basics
ISBN: 0-02-861598-0
$16.95

The Complete Idiot's Guide to Gambling Like a Pro
ISBN: 0-02-861102-0
$16.95

The Complete Idiot's Guide to a Great Retirement
ISBN: 0-02-861036-9
$16.95

The Complete Idiot's Guide to Hiking and Camping
ISBN: 0-02-861100-4
$16.95

The Complete Idiot's Guide to Needlecrafts
ISBN: 0-02-862123-9
$16.95

The Complete Idiot's Guide to Organizing Your Life
ISBN: 0-02-861090-3
$16.95

The Complete Idiot's Guide to Photography
ISBN: 0-02-861092-X
$16.95

The Complete Idiot's Guide to Reaching Your Goals
ISBN: 0-02-862114-X
$16.95

The Complete Idiot's Guide to the World's Religions
ISBN: 0-02-861730-4
$16.95

Music

The Complete Idiot's Guide to Classical Music
ISBN: 0-02-8611634-0
$16.95

The Complete Idiot's Guide to Playing the Guitar
0-02-864924-9
$17.95

The Complete Idiot's Guide to Playing the Piano and Electric Keyboards
0-02-864925-7
$17.95

Parenting

The Complete Idiot's Guide to Adoption
ISBN: 0-02-862108-5
$18.95

The Complete Idiot's Guide to Bringing Up Baby
ISBN: 0-02-861957-9
$16.95

The Complete Idiot's Guide to Grandparenting
ISBN: 0-02-861976-5
$16.95

The Complete Idiot's Guide to Parenting a Preschooler and Toddler
ISBN: 0-02-861733-9
$16.95

The Complete Idiot's Guide to Raising a Teenager
ISBN: 0-02-861277-9
$16.95

The Complete Idiot's Guide to Single Parenting
ISBN: 0-02-862409-2
$16.95

The Complete Idiot's Guide to Stepparenting
ISBN: 0-02-862407-6
$16.95

Pets

The Complete Idiot's Guide to Choosing, Training, and Raising a Dog
ISBN: 0-02-861098-9
$16.95

The Complete Idiot's Guide to Fun and Tricks with Your Dog
ISBN: 0-87605-083-6
$14.95

The Complete Idiot's Guide to Living with a Cat
ISBN: 0-02-861278-7
$16.95

The Complete Idiot's Guide to Turtles and Tortoises
ISBN: 0-87605-143-3
$16.95

Relationships

The Complete Idiot's Guide to Dating
ISBN: 0-02-861052-0
$14.95

The Complete Idiot's Guide to Dealing with In-Laws
ISBN: 0-02-862107-7
$16.95

The Complete Idiot's Guide to a Healthy Relationship
ISBN: 0-02-861087-3
$17.95

The Complete Idiot's Guide to a Perfect Marriage
ISBN: 0-02-861729-0
$16.95

The Complete Idiot's Guide to the Perfect Wedding
ISBN: 0-02-861963-3
$16.95

The Complete Idiot's Guide to Surviving Divorce
ISBN: 0-02-861101-3
$16.95

Sports

The Complete Idiot's Guide to Golf
ISBN: 0-02-861760-6
$16.95

The Complete Idiot's Guide to Pro Wrestling
ISBN: 0-02-862395-9
$17.95

The Complete Idiot's Guide to Skiing
ISBN: 0-02-861965-X
$16.95

The Complete Idiot's Guide to Tae Kwon Do
ISBN: 0-02-862389-4
$17.95

The Complete Idiot's Guide to Understanding Football Like a Pro
ISBN:0-02-861743-6
$16.95

The Complete Idiot's Guide to Yoga
ISBN: 0-02-861949-8
$16.95

Look for the Complete Idiot's Guides at your local bookseller, or call 1-800-428-5331 for more information.